BEHIND *BAKKE*
Affirmative Action and the Supreme Court

BEHIND *BAKKE*

Affirmative Action and
the Supreme Court

Bernard Schwartz

NEW YORK UNIVERSITY PRESS
New York and London

Library of Congress Cataloging-in-Publication Data
Schwartz, Bernard, 1923–
    Behind Bakke : affirmative action and the Supreme Court / Bernard
Schwartz.
    p. cm.
    Bibliography: p.
    Includes index.
    ISBN 0-8147-7878-X
    1. Bakke, Allan Paul—Trials, litigation, etc. 2. University of
California, Berkeley—Trials, litigation, etc. 3. Discrimination in
medical education—Law and legislation—California. 4. Medical
colleges—California—Admission. 5. Affirmative action programs—
Law and legislation—United States. I. Title.
KF228.B34S39   1988
347.73'0798—dc19
[347.304798]   87-28086
                                                    CIP

c 10 9 8 7 6 5 4 3 2

Clothbound editions of New York University Press books are Smyth-
sewn and printed on permanent and durable acid-free paper.

Book design by Ken Venezio

Carissimae uxori suae

Contents

Preface

I HAVE not told what happened behind the scenes in the *Bakke* case with the intent to produce a mini-*Brethren*. My purpose is to give students of the Supreme Court further insight into the Court's largely unrevealed decision process. Even Court specialists, who have never been privy to the Court's internal workings, do not fully realize that Court decisions are basically collaborative efforts in which nine individuals must cooperate to achieve the desired result. Before the final opinions are issued, there may be politicking, vote switches, and horsetrading to secure them; and ultimately compromises are needed to obtain the necessary working majority. In the process, the quondam opinion of the Court may become the ultimate dissent, and vice versa; or the potential constitutional landmark may become a minor footnote in Supreme Court history. It is my hope here, as in my other books on the Court, that the actual operation of the Court will be made clearer by this account of the decision process in an important case.

The book is based upon both oral and documentary sources. The oral sources were personal interviews with members of the Supreme Court, former law clerks, and others familiar with the Court and the *Bakke* case. Every statement not otherwise identified was either made to me personally or I was given information about it by an unimpeachable source. I have tried to identify the statements made to me by different people, except where they were made upon a confidential basis. In the latter case, I have given the position of the person involved, but not his name. This book could never have been written without the cooperation of those who shared their time and experience so generously with me.

The documentary sources are conference notes, docket books, correspondence, notes, memoranda, and draft opinions of Justices. The documents used and their location are identified, except where they were made available upon a confidential basis. In the latter case, I have tried to identify the documents, usually by title and date, in the text. I have personally examined every document to which reference is made. Almost all of them have never before been published.

I have been afforded generous access to the papers of the Justices and gratefully acknowledge the help given by the Manuscript Division, Library of Congress. I also wish to acknowledge the generous support of Dean Norman Redlich and the New York University School of Law, as well as the work of my tireless secretary, Mrs. Barbara Ortiz. Mere words cannot express my obligations and gratitude to her to whom all my work is dedicated.

ONE

"White/Caucasian and Rejected"

On his retirement from the Supreme Court, Justice Lewis F. Powell, Jr., was asked which of his opinions he considered most important. That in the *Bakke* case,[1] he replied without hesitation.[2] The *Bakke* case itself, recalls a Supreme Court Justice, "aroused more interest in the Nation, the press, and the Bar than any I have seen in my—terms on the Court. Some 63 amicus briefs were filed in this Court; the case—and in the end the disposition—was the subject of countless newspaper and magazine articles and television and radio broadcasts, and I received a nearly unprecedented number of letters from private persons."

Bakke[3] was a *cause célèbre* as soon as it started. By the time it reached the high tribunal, it had all the markings of a legal landmark—the culmination of the developing law on racial equality that had started a quarter century earlier in the *Brown* school segregation case.[4] Like all cases, however, *Bakke* began as an action brought by an individual plaintiff against an individual defendant. *Bakke*, like the previous cases alleging racial discrimination, was based upon the Fourteenth Amendment's guaranty of equal protection. Yet there was a fundamental difference between the *Bakke* plaintiff and those in the prior cases. This time the plaintiff was not a black or representative of some other racial minority. Instead, he was, in the characterization of a *New York Times* article, "White/Caucasian and Rejected."[5]

A REPRESENTATIVE WHITE MALE

He had blond hair, was broad-shouldered, and stood just under six feet. His fjord-blue eyes and fair complexion were signs of his Norwegian ancestry. As the first faculty member to interview Bakke at the Davis Medical School put it, "He is a pleasant, mature person, tall and strong and Teutonic in appearance." He was, in short, the casting director's ideal of the representative white male—anything but in the mold of the usual plaintiff in important civil-rights litigation. Yet it was Allan Bakke who brought what became the most significant racial equality action since the *Brown* case itself.

Bakke's precase career has been described by a federal judge as "a storybook life of middle-class virtue."[6] He was born in Minnesota in 1940—the son of a mailman and a teacher. He majored in engineering at the University of Minnesota, where he earned close to a straight A average. To help pay for college, he joined the Naval Reserve Officers Training Corps, then served in combat as a Marine officer in Vietnam. He ended his service as a captain and then "enlisted in the nation's race to the moon."[7] In 1967 he became a research engineer at the NASA Ames Research Center, near Palo Alto, California. He earned $28,000 a year designing equipment used in NASA research programs. He also earned an M.S. degree in mechanical engineering from Stanford. Living in a comfortable house in a well-to-do suburb with his wife and three children, he appeared set for life.

But Bakke's Teutonic stolidity masked a growing inner obsession to become a doctor, which had started during his military service. When he was in Vietnam, he said later, he had become fascinated with the work of doctors and decided that he wanted to become a physician. He grew increasingly interested in medicine as he studied the effects of space flight upon the human body. Hence, as he wrote to a friend while waiting for the Supreme Court decision in his case, "If . . . we prevail, I may be the first person to retire from engineering to study medicine."

No one who dealt with him doubted his sincerity; he had what one of his friends called "an almost religious zeal" to become a doctor. "Bakke was a man who felt as strongly as anyone I've ever known about his potential as a healer of the sick and as a benefactor of his community," recalled an admissions officer at Davis during Bakke's fight to enter the medical school there.

Bakke himself explained his passion in his second application to the Davis Medical School in 1973: "I have an excellent job in engineering and am well-paid. I don't wish to change careers for financial gain, but because I truly believe my contribution to society can be much greater as a physician-engineer than in my present field. I'm not afraid of hard work, I enjoy and have been successful at working with others, and know my motivation is as strong and honest toward a career of service in medicine as that of any applicant. More than anything else in the world, *I want to study medicine.*"[8]

Bakke did not have all the prerequisites for medical school. So, he later wrote, while continuing his full-time work for NASA, "I undertook a near full-time course load of medical prerequisites—biology and chemistry. To make up class and commuting hours, I worked early mornings and also evenings at my job." He also became a hospital volunteer, an incongruous male figure among the "pink ladies" who normally did such volunteer work. As a reporter described it, "He took tough assignments, often working late with battered victims of car accidents or fights."[9]

By now Bakke was a husky, balding 32-year old. He knew that his age was a big mark against him. He began the personal statement part of his application to the University of California at Davis Medical School by directly addressing the age issue: "Although I am 32 years old, the usual factors which detract from an older applicant do not apply in my case." He stressed the medical prerequisite courses he had taken, which "removes the question of current academic inclinations and aptitudes." Above all the statement stressed, "I am in excellent health. Actuarially it may be predicted that I might not serve as a physician as long as a younger applicant. But I believe my high general level of health, good health maintenance habits, and balanced outlook offset these cold statistics."

Bakke sent in his first application to Davis, as well as ten other medical schools, in the fall of 1972. As he filled out the Davis application, he came to Line 22: "Applicants from economically and educationally disadvantaged backgrounds are evaluated by a special subcommittee of the admissions committee. If you wish your application to be considered by this group, check this space." Bakke typed an "X" in the "No" box.

Line 13 of the application had asked, "How do you describe yourself?" and had listed nine racial categories, ranging from "1. Black/Afro American" to "9. Other." Bakke had typed his "X" next to "3. White/Caucasian."

DAVIS ADMISSIONS PROCESS

Halfway between San Francisco and the High Sierras, on the dusty floor of the Sacramento Valley, the campus of the University of California at Davis seemed an unlikely place for the birth of a legal landmark. Yet the delivery to that rural outpost on November 26, 1972, of the small envelope containing Allan Bakke's application for admission to the Davis Medical School set in motion the events that were to culminate in the Supreme Court's *Bakke* decision.

In the beginning, however, the *Bakke* case was controlled by the administrative routine of the Davis admissions process. After Bakke's application arrived at Davis, a manila folder was pulled out of a drawer. Into it would soon go grades, transcripts, letters of recommendation, and other supporting data. And it would be placed in a cabinet with most of the other applications. On the other hand, if Bakke had typed an "X" in the "Yes" box on Line 22, a clerk with a pen would have marked "Task Force" on the folder. It would have been placed in a different cabinet and faced a different course through the admissions process.[10]

It was this simple action—the segregation of application folders—that laid the foundation for the *Bakke* case. For Davis had set up a special admissions program for disadvantaged medical applicants, from which Bakke was automatically excluded.

The Davis Medical School itself had opened only in 1968. The first class had contained no black students. The faculty, concerned about this, had voted to set up a special admissions program "to compensate victims of unjust societal discrimination." The program was designed, according to the school's catalogue, for the "economically or educationally disadvantaged." The application forms for admission, as seen, contained questions on whether the applicant wished to be considered as "disadvantaged" and on his race. The record indicated that, while 272 whites applied as "disadvantaged" from 1971 to 1974, not one had been accepted under the special admissions program. During the same period, 26 blacks, 30 Mexican-Americans, and 12 Asians were admitted through the special program.[11] When Bakke applied, the size of the entering class was fixed at 100; of these 16 places were reserved for applicants under the special admissions program.

The regular and special admissions programs were separate and distinct processes. Applicants under the regular program with a grade average of less than 2.5 were dropped summarily, and the others were rated on a 500-point scale according to grades, test scores, recommendations and interviews.

On the other hand, students who marked "yes" to the question on Line

22—those who wanted to be considered "disadvantaged"—were screened by a separate student-faculty committee, consisting mostly of minority group members, called the "task force."

The task force used different criteria: a 2.5 grade average did not disqualify applicants automatically, and test scores substantially lower than the minimum for regular applicants were considered acceptable. In 1973, when Bakke's application was considered, the 16 applicants selected under the special program had undergraduate grade averages of only 2.88, compared with 3.49 for students admitted in the regular channels; their scores on the medical school admissions tests were considerably lower.

BAKKE REJECTED

Bakke's application was, of course, considered by Davis under its regular admissions program. Despite his age, Bakke made an impressive applicant. Not only were his undergraduate grades far higher than those of the applicants admitted under the special program, he also was outstanding in other respects—with laudatory recommendation letters, proven motivation and professional background, and medical school admissions test scores substantially higher than those of the average medical student admitted to Davis that year. Indeed, had Bakke been able to complete his application in the fall of 1972, he probably would have been admitted as a regular student. But his mother-in-law became critically ill and, preoccupied with looking after her, Bakke was unable to complete his application for final consideration until January 9, 1973. By that time, the earliest interview that could be set on the application had to be scheduled for March 21.

This meant that the Bakke application now labored under a substantial handicap. By the time Bakke's interview took place, seats in the freshman class were growing scarce, since over three quarters of the admission acceptances had already been sent. Probably unaware of this, Bakke appeared for his March 21 interview by a faculty member, who made a most favorable report to the regular admissions committee. Its conclusion read, "On the grounds of motivation, academic record, potential promise, endorsement by persons capable of reasonable judgments, personal appearance and demeanor, maturity and probable contribution to balance in the class I believe that Mr. Bakke must be considered as a very desirable applicant to this medical school and I shall so recommend him."

The interviewer, however, cast only one vote on the five-member admissions committee. Their combined evaluations gave Bakke a total rating of 468 out of a possible 500. By that late date in the admissions process, this score fell just short; at least a 470 score was required for the few remaining places. On May 14, 1973, Bakke received a formal letter notifying him that he had been rejected.

Two weeks later, Bakke wrote to Dr. George Lowrey, chairman of the admissions committee, appealing for reconsideration, stressing, "I want to study medicine more than anything else in the world."

There was no answer from Lowrey and Bakke wrote again on July 1. This time the letter had a different tone. It protested against the Davis special admissions program. Bakke wrote that the program provided for "quotas, open or covert, for racial minorities." He realized, the letter went on, "that the rationale for these quotas is that they attempt to atone for past racial discrimination. But instituting a new racial bias, in favor of minorities is not a just solution."

Bakke concluded his letter by declaring, "I believe that admissions quotas based on race are illegal," and informing Lowrey, "I am inquiring of friends . . . about the possibility of formally challenging these quotas through the courts."

Dr. Lowrey asked one of his assistants, Peter Storandt, to reply to Bakke. There then began a correspondence and ultimately a meeting between the two that played a part in inducing Bakke to begin his lawsuit. Storandt, a little younger than Bakke and new to Davis, had himself been troubled by the minority admissions program because, as he later commented, though it had "a supportable aim, . . . it had the effect of bringing hardships on other kinds of candidates. I couldn't be fully comfortable with that arrangement."

Storandt, in effect, became Bakke's "mentor—his coach in filing suit against Storandt's own employer."[12] (Because of this, Storandt himself was eventually fired.) There is no doubt that Storandt was strongly impressed by Bakke, particularly after he had met him personally. "He struck me," Storandt later recalled, "as a character out of a Bergman film—somewhat humorless, perfectly straightforward, zealous in his approach; it was really striking; he was an extremely impressive man."

In his reply letter, Storandt informed Bakke that he had come very close to being admitted and urged him to reapply for 1974 early admission. He also encouraged Bakke "to pursue your research into admissions policies based on quota-oriented minority recruiting." Concerning Davis's special admissions program, he observed, "I don't know whether you would consider our procedure to have the overtones of a quota or not; certainly its design has been to avoid any such designation, but the fact remains that most applicants . . . are members of ethnic minority groups." Storandt then called Bakke's attention to the *DeFunis* case,[13] at that time on its way to the Supreme Court, and gave him the names of two university legal specialists on the issue of racially motivated admission policies.

After the two had met, Bakke wrote Storandt that he intended to follow two approaches: (1) "my first concern is to be allowed to study medicine" and hence he would reapply to Davis; (2) "challenging the concept of racial quotas," which might require litigation. In other letters, Storandt encouraged Bakke to follow both approaches, going so far as to urge that "you press the suit—even if admitted—at the institution of your choice." (Without legal training, Storandt apparently did not realize that, as an accepted applicant, Bakke would lack standing to sue in such a case.)

Looking back a few years later, Storandt commented, "My main view is that I didn't actually encourage the suit—I suggested that it could be pursued." In practice, however, Storandt's supportive posture definitely helped to induce Bakke to undertake the litigation. Perhaps Storandt's words were only, as he says, a "suggestion." But the person making the suggestion happened to be an admissions official of the school to be sued.[14]

SECOND REJECTION

Whether Bakke would have to sue would depend on the outcome of his second application to Davis. Bakke was interviewed on that application in August 1973, both by the student member who had been added to the admissions committee (who recommended in Bakke's favor) and Dr. Lowrey. The evaluation of Lowrey, unfavorably impressed by Bakke, played a decisive part in lowering the applicant's evaluation scores below that required for acceptance. It is undisputed that the interview discussion with Lowrey turned in large part upon Bakke's opposition to the special admissions program, which had already been made clear in his July 1 letter to Lowrey.

Lowrey's report stressed that Bakke "had very definite opinions which were based more on his personal viewpoints than upon a study of the whole problem. His opinion of the special selection of minority students is stated in one of his letters. He was very unsympathetic to the concept of recruiting minority students so that they hopefully would go back to practice in . . . presently neglected areas. . . . One of his main reasons . . . was that this decreased his own chances of getting into medical school. He did not have any alternative." Because of this, Lowrey concluded, Bakke was "a rigidly oriented young man who has a tendency to arrive at conclusions based more upon his personal impressions than upon thoughtful processes using available sources of information."

In the California courts, Bakke asserted that, from the foregoing, "It becomes evident not only that Dr. Lowrey disagreed with plaintiff's position regarding special admissions, but also that the dispute over the program caused Dr. Lowrey to downgrade plaintiff during the interview. Dr. Lowrey in effect penalized plaintiff for challenging the University's Special Admissions Program."[15]

There was also the following exchange on the matter when counsel for the University of California was arguing in the state supreme court:

Justice Mosk: ". . . for some strange reason, in reviewing Dr. Lowrey's evaluation of Bakke, more than half of the discussion is about Bakke's views on minority admissions. What does that have to do with Mr. Bakke's potential ability to someday remove my appendix?"

Mr. Reidhaar: ". . . The point of Dr. Lowrey's remarks is not that Mr. Bakke would be disadvantaged because of his views on the minority admissions program, but rather, Dr. Lowrey found that Mr. Bakke's approach to this particular question seemed to involve more assertion and preconception rather than a careful analysis."[16]

Be that as it may, there is little doubt that Dr. Lowrey played a crucial role in the rejection of Bakke's second application. Once again the members of the admissions committee evaluated Bakke. The other five gave him high scores; but Lowrey's evaluation was so low that Bakke's combined evaluation was only 549 out of the 600 points used on the new scale that year—actually lower than the score on his first application. Bakke was notified in late September that Davis would not admit him under its early admission plan. Then on April 1, 1974, he was sent a form letter of rejection similar to the one that had disposed of his first application.

BAKKE UNDER WAY

An internal memo in the Davis admissions office, dated "4/22/74" and headed "BAKKE, Allan," reads: "initiating legal action for admittance into medical school. Similar to DeLunis [sic] case suing [sic] the University of Washington Law School. Below, there was written, "Dr. Levitt [associate dean, academic affairs] asked that we [have?] the info ready when counsel asks for it."[17]

When it turned down Bakke's second application, Davis was well aware that the result might be a lawsuit—something Bakke had begun to consider as soon as his May 30 letter to Dr. Lowrey. The matter had also been discussed in the Bakke–Storandt correspondence. Soon after his second rejection, Bakke filed a complaint with the San Francisco office of the Department of Health, Education and Welfare charging Davis with "racial discrimination" because it had adopted "a 16% racial quota." Nothing much came of this complaint.

Bakke now began to look seriously at the possibility of litigation. He inquired about appropriate attorneys. One name that was mentioned was that of Reynold H. Colvin, who had been a member of the Bar since 1941 and was senior partner in a small general-practice firm located in a marble medium-rise building in the San Francisco financial district. Colvin, a heavyset jowly man, who was then 57, had been on the city's board of education and had brought a successful federal suit challenging a local program which the court interpreted as providing for hiring and promotion of only minority school administrators. The court stated, "Preferential treatment under the guise of 'affirmative action' is the imposition of one form of racial discrimination in place of another."[18] In an interview in 1976, Colvin indicated that he shared that view; he was particularly concerned that preferential treatment of minorities might result in substituting group rights for individual rights.

Colvin told Bakke that he should wait for the Supreme Court's *DeFunis* decision before taking any further action, since that decision might settle the question of whether the Davis program was legal. After the Court avoided decision on the merits in *DeFunis*, Colvin agreed to represent Bakke. He first tried to persuade Davis to reconsider Bakke's application and admit him. When Davis refused to do so, Colvin instituted a lawsuit. On June 20, 1974, he filed a complaint in the California Superior Court against the University of California to compel Bakke's admission to Davis Medical School.

NOTES

1. Regents of the University of California v. Bakke, 438 U.S. 265 (1978).
2. N.Y. Times, June 27, 1987, p. 32.
3. Supra note 1.

4. Brown v. Board of Education, 347 U.S. 483 (1954).
5. Lindsey, "White/Caucasian—and Rejected," *N.Y. Times Magazine*, April 3, 1977, p. 42. The facts stated in this chapter are derived from ibid.; Sindler, *Bakke, DeFunis, and Minority Admissions* (1978); O'Neill, *Bakke and the Politics of Equality* (1985); 1 Allan Bakke versus Regents of the University of California (Slocum ed. 1978); and the Bakke trial record.
6. Wilkinson, *From* Brown *to* Bakke 254 (1979).
7. Lindsey, supra note 5, at 43.
8. Emphasis in original.
9. Lindsey, supra note 5, at 43.
10. Ibid.
11. Bakke, 438 U.S. at 274. O'Neill, supra note 5, has slightly different figures.
12. Lindsey, supra note 5, at 45.
13. DeFunis v. Odegaard, 416 U.S. 312 (1974), infra p. 32.
14. Compare Sindler, supra note 5, at 73.
15. Slocum, supra note 5, at 132.
16. 2 id. at 23–25.
17. Sindler, supra note 5, at 63.
18. Anderson v. San Francisco School District, 357 F. Supp. 248, 249 (N.D. Cal. 1972).

TWO

In the California Courts

LANDMARK cases are associated in the public mind with the Supreme Court. But, of course, they do not begin in the Marble Palace. Instead, they must be started in a trial court—often a little-noticed tribunal in some remote part of the country. The *Bakke* case began in just such an obscure tribunal. In the Yolo County Courthouse in Woodland, a rural community northwest of Sacramento noted till then primarily for the growing of tomatoes, Bakke filed his complaint and began the case that was to dominate the Supreme Court's docket for the 1977 term.

AFFIRMATIVE ACTION OR REVERSE DISCRIMINATION?

Bakke's complaint alleged that under the Davis program, "a quota of 16%, or 16 out of 100 first-year-class members, was selected; that in fact, all applicants submitted to said Medical School as members of this group were members of racial minorities; [and] that the use of such separate standards resulted in the admission of minority applicants less qualified than plaintiff and other non-minority applicants who were therefore rejected." Because of defendants' action "in excluding plaintiff from the first-year Medical School class under defendants' minority preference admission program plaintiff has been invidiously discriminated against on account of his race in violation of the Equal Protection Clause of the Fourteenth Amendment to the United States Constitution."[1] The complaint sought a judgment ordering Bakke's admission to Davis.

11

The issue posed by Bakke's complaint had become the critical one in American constitutional law. The starting point for the legal development in this area had been the 1954 *Brown* decision[2] striking down school segregation. But *Brown* had involved a relatively simple choice for the Court, once the Justices had become convinced that the correct view was that stated by Chief Justice Warren at his first *Brown* conference: "I don't see how in this day and age we can set any group apart from the rest and say that they are not entitled to exactly the same treatment as all others. To do so would be contrary to the Thirteenth, Fourteenth, and Fifteenth Amendments. They were intended to make the slaves equal with all others. Personally, I can't see how today we can justify segregation based solely on race."[3]

Justices who agreed with Warren had no alternative but to rule school segregation invalid. More difficulty was to be encountered in determining how to enforce the *Brown* principle. To comply with *Brown*, was it enough for education authorities to cease *governmental* action legally excluding black children from "white" public schools? Or was there a further duty to end existing dual school systems, even if they were no longer compelled by state law? As a federal judge points out, the distinction between "Thou Shall Not Segregate" and "Thou Shall Integrate" became of crucial importance.[4]

As I have shown elsewhere,[5] in the years following *Brown*, the Supreme Court moved from the simple *Brown* prohibition of segregation to an "affirmative duty to take whatever steps might be necessary to convert to a unitary system."[6] If necessary, the courts might order extensive desegregation plans, including busing between white and black areas, if they were needed to ensure meaningfully integrated schools.[7]

But even such far-reaching measures proved inadequate to eliminate racial discrimination in this country. To achieve that result, a wholly new approach to the problem was urged. Previous attempts to resolve the problem had focused upon the formal equality before the law established by the Equal Protection Clause. Now the concept of legal equality, presented in traditional negative terms, was said to be inadequate to deal with the factual inequalities caused by racial discrimination. Instead, ensuring equality to white and black alike may require more than adherence to formal equality in the application of legal precepts and doctrine. The existence of true equality between the races may depend, not only on the absence of disabilities, but also on the presence of abilities.[8]

The result has been the claim that there is a social duty to make "compensation" for the inequalities under which racial minorities have had to live. The *Bakke* case arose because the society had begun to recognize this claim. Racially neutral programs of nondiscrimination were giving way to programs that gave a preference to members of minority groups which had been the victims of racial discrimination.

The new programs owed their genesis to Presidential orders which not only established them upon a broad basis but also gave the name usually used by their proponents. In a 1961 Executive Order President Kennedy issued a call for "affirmative action" by government contractors to recruit minorities and encourage their promotion.[9] Later Presidents, as well as the Civil Rights Act of 1964, strengthened these programs, so that by the time of *Bakke* they were an essential part of federal administration. Kennedy's successor explained the rationale for these programs in an oft-quoted 1965 address: "you do not take a person who, for years, has been hobbled by chains and liberate him, bring him up to the starting line of a race and then say, 'You are free to compete with all the others,' and still justly believe that you have been completely fair." The nation needed to move beyond equality "as a right and a theory" to "equality as a fact and equality as a result."[10]

However, this approach posed a basic dilemma that had not been present in prior efforts to enforce the *Brown* principle. In *Brown* and the later desegregation cases, the courts were confronted with school systems which violated the right guaranteed by the Equal Protection Clause. Judicial enforcement of that right did not deprive anyone else of the right to an equal education or any other legal right. In the words of one judge explaining the *Brown*-type case, "providing one child with a better, i.e., integrated, education did not operate to deprive another of an equal, integrated education. Benefit to one would not be at the expense of another."[11] Yet such a result was precisely what the decision in a case like *Bakke* would have to reach. As Justice Marshall was to express it in an April 13, 1978, memorandum (infra p. 127), "the decision in this case depends on whether you consider the action of the Regents as *admitting* certain students or as *excluding* certain other students."

The real problem was that the Davis special admissions program did provide both for admitting the specified number of minority students and for excluding those who might otherwise have filled their places. During the oral argument, Justice Marshall was to put his finger on the case's dilemma in this respect, when he told Bakke's counsel, "You are arguing about keeping somebody out and the other side is arguing about getting somebody in."[12] A decision for Davis would keep Bakke and others like him out of medical school; a decision for Bakke would keep out the minority applicants who otherwise would be getting in under the special program.

In his referred-to April 13, 1978, memo, Justice Marshall was also to note that the Davis program would be labeled according to whether the "getting in" or the "keeping out" was emphasized: "If you view the program as admitting qualified students who, because of this Nation's sorry history of racial discrimination, have academic records that prevent them from effectively competing for medical school, then this is affirmative action to remove the vestiges of slavery and state imposed segregation by root and branch. If you view the program as excluding students, it is a program of quotas which violates the principle that the Constitution is color-blind."

To those who favored the Davis program, it was *affirmative action* designed to correct centuries of racial discrimination by positive measures aimed at moving minorities into the mainstream of the society. To opponents it was *reverse discrimination*, which, however benign its intentions, was replacing discrimination against minorities with discrimination against whites such as Bakke, who were themselves wholly innocent in the matter. A year before *Bakke* was decided by the Supreme Court, Justice Brennan had attempted to soften the discriminatory connotation by calling the Davis program *benign discrimination*.[13] Semantics alone could not, however, disguise the impact of the special admissions program upon people such as Bakke. In the *DeFunis* case (infra p. 32), the state court dealt with the claim that "because the persons normally stigmatized by racial classifications are being benefited, the action complained of should be considered 'benign.'" According to the Washington court, "However, the minority admissions policy is certainly not benign with respect to non-minority students who are displaced by it."[14]

A JUDGE "DONE IN"

The University of California at Davis is located in Yolo County, an agricultural county in the north central core of California's farm belt. It was in the courthouse in Woodland, the county seat, that in late June 1974, Bakke's lawyer, Reynold Colvin, filed suit challenging the Davis program. Colvin brought the action there in order to secure a quicker trial schedule. He also hoped that a "country judge" would be more willing than a "big-city judge" to grant the injunctive relief Bakke sought.[15]

The Yolo County Courthouse, built in 1917, is still a good example of early-twentieth-century courthouse style. Its entrance is dominated by a large staircase and four massive Ionic columns. The interior halls are covered in speckled marble, including the corridor leading to the third-floor courtroom where the *Bakke* case was tried. Painted beige, with all its furniture and trim in blond oak, the courtroom itself was somewhat more elegant than those in most American courts. At the end of the chamber was the bench; behind it the judge's black-leather contour chair and, at one side the flag of the United States, on the other, the flag of California. In front of the bench were the clerk's desk, a table for the court reporter, and, before them, tables for the opposing counsel. To the bench's right was the vacant jury box, and there were five rows of seats for the audience. They would remain far from full while the case was tried, since the public was as yet unaware of the case's significance.

There were only two Superior Court judges assigned to Yolo County. One was too busy with other cases at the time and the other disqualified himself because of some unspecified relationship with the university. The case was therefore heard by a retired judge from Santa Rosa county, F. Leslie Manker, who was called up just to try the *Bakke* case. A graduate of the University of California Law School at Berkeley, Judge Manker had been appointed to the Superior Court by Governor Edmund G. (Pat) Brown in 1964.

Judge Manker was sixty-seven years old and had been retired five years when he was assigned to preside at the *Bakke* trial. The last thing he anticipated was a constitutional *cause célèbre*. "He walked in on this, expecting the usual run-of-the-mill cases," Reynold Colvin recalled. "From the look on his face I think he felt he had been done in."[16]

"Done in" or not, Judge Manker did conduct the *Bakke* trial and make the first decision in the case. The trial itself was relatively brief, since the facts in the case were virtually undisputed. The only witness was Dr. Lowrey. The chairman of the Davis admissions committee, who had played the key role in the decision to deny Bakke's second application, was questioned on the history and purposes of the special admissions program, as well as the circumstances concerning Bakke's applications. A deposition by Lowrey was also introduced, as well as Bakke's answers to written interrogatories and records documenting Bakke's attempts to get into the medical school.

Colvin's argument for Bakke was simple: equal protection means non-discrimination.[17] He claimed that the reason for Bakke's rejection was his race. "There is no question here but that Bakke's exclusion from the University of California Medical School at Davis was a result of a racial classification." Because of this, Colvin urged, Bakke had been the victim of racial discrimination. "If," Colvin's *Memorandum of Law* asserted, "the Constitution prohibits exclusion of blacks and other minorities on racial grounds it cannot permit the exclusion of whites on racial grounds." Bakke's exclusion on racial grounds violated his Fourteenth Amendment right to equal protection. "The admissions policy of the University of California School of Medicine at Davis must be struck down because it involves an unconstitutional racial discrimination in the form of a quota."[18]

The case for Davis was presented to Judge Manker by Donald L. Reidhaar, the university's general counsel. Reidhaar himself, like Colvin, had expressed doubts about the constitutionality of racial preferences. "In my opinion," he had written in a May 1974 memorandum to then University of California President Charles Hitch, "both the Equal Protection Clause of the Fourteenth Amendment to the United States Constitution and Title VI of the Civil Rights Act of 1964 and regulations issued thereunder prohibit a state university from granting preference in student admissions on the basis of race."[19]

Despite this, as the university's head attorney, Reidhaar, described as "a careful, meticulous man" in a contemporary account,[20] did his best to defend the Davis program. He argued that the program served rational and compelling interests, since it was a logical way to provide for minority physicians who "are likely to return to those disadvantaged areas from which they came." It would also provide for diversity in the medical school, so that faculty and students "will be exposed to the ideas, needs and concerns of minorities and thereby may be enlisted in meeting the medical needs of minorities."[21] Reidhaar also argued that Bakke would not have been admitted even if there had been no special program because other rejected applicants had higher ratings.

In addition, Reidhaar raised the issue that was to prove important in the Supreme Court's decision process in the case: that of the validity of the Davis program under Title VI of the Civil Rights Act of 1964. Under it,

"No person in the United States shall, on the ground of race, color, or national origin, be excluded from participation in, be denied the benefits of, or be subjected to discrimination under any program or activity receiving federal financial assistance."

Reidhaar argued that the Davis program did not violate this provision. Indeed, he urged, it had been interpreted to *permit* giving special consideration to minority group members in admissions for the purpose of increasing their participation in educational programs."[22]

From a broader point of view, Reidhaar asserted that equal protection was not violated when "the power of the state was used *affirmatively* to combat discrimination and make the promise of the Fourteenth Amendment a reality." In this case, the university was using its power "to achieve that same purpose in the Davis Medical School and in the medical profession. If such affirmative steps cannot be taken there will be few, if any, members of certain minority groups who will become doctors. And this will be the loss of both the school and society."[23]

JUDGE MANKER'S DECISION

Bakke came on for trial before Judge Manker on September 27, 1974. Two months later, on November 22, the judge issued a *Notice of Proposed Decision*, which was the opinion he proposed to issue in the case. In it, Manker indicated that he would hold the Davis program unconstitutional. He found that the evidence established that "the medical school had in fact established quotas for the so-called special program." Further, he found "that such program discriminates in favor of minority racial groups and against the white race." The necessary conclusion, according to the trial judge, was "that the special admissions program at the Davis Medical School as the same was in operation at the time of plaintiff's rejection as an applicant and as the school intends to continue it is violative of the Equal Protection Clause."[24]

However, while Bakke may have thus won the initial constitutional battle, he was not winning his personal war. Judge Manker found that Bakke had failed to prove that he would have been admitted if the special admissions program had not existed. On this point, the judge deferred to Dr. Lowrey's declaration on the matter, saying "The admission of students to the Medical School is so peculiarly a discretionary function of the school that the Court feels that it should not be interfered with by a Court, absent a showing of fraud, unfairness, bad faith, arbitrariness or capriciousness, none of which has been shown."[25] The court consequently refused to issue an order directing Davis to admit Bakke.

On March 6, 1975, on Colvin's petition, Judge Manker issued an *Addendum to Notice of Intended Decision*. He granted Colvin's request for injunctive relief "enjoining defendants from considering his race or the race of any other applicant in passing upon his application for admission to the medical school."[26] This order prohibiting consideration of race was, we shall see, to play a crucial part in the Supreme Court's decision process.

In addition, the addendum touched upon the Federal Civil Rights Act. Judge Manker concluded "that the same reasoning as set forth in the original opinion applies equally to the Federal Civil Rights Act."[27]

Judge Manker issued his judgment on March 6 as well. It denied the injunction Bakke requested ordering his admission to Davis. It also dealt with the consideration of race by the medical school:

"2. That plaintiff is entitled to have his application for admission to the medical school considered without regard to his race or the race of any other applicant, and defendants are hereby restrained and enjoined from considering plaintiff's race or the race of any other applicant in passing upon his application for admission."[28]

Finally, the Manker judgment ordered that Bakke "have judgment . . . declaring that the special admissions program at the University of California at Davis Medical School violates the Fourteenth Amendment to the United States Constitution, Article 1, Section 21 of the California Constitution, and the Federal Civil Rights Act."[29]

CALIFORNIA SUPREME COURT ARGUMENT

In a December 12, 1977, letter to Justice William J. Brennan, Justice John Paul Stevens would give his U.S. Supreme Court colleague a "brief procedural history of the [Bakke] case." He summarized Judge Manker's decision: "Judge Manker concluded that the special admissions program was illegal, but that Bakke would not have been admitted in 1973 or 1974 even if the program had not existed. . . . Accordingly, the judge denied an injunction ordering Bakke's application without regard to Bakke's race or the race of any other applicant."

The Manker decision was satisfactory neither to the university nor to Bakke, and both parties appealed. The appeal would normally have gone to a Court of Appeal, the state's intermediate appellate court. But the California Supreme Court decided to take the appeal directly. In a June 26 order, it transferred the case from the Court of Appeal to itself. *Bakke* thus next went for argument and decision to the highest California court.

The scene now shifted to the neo-Greek Temple in Sacramento which was the seat of the California Supreme Court when it sat in the state's capital. The building, erected in 1928, is five stories high and is made of granite. It was built as a memorial to those who died in World War I.

Bakke in the California Supreme Court began with the briefs submitted by the parties. They contained essentially the same arguments that had been made in the memoranda of law submitted to Judge Manker. There were also eight amicus briefs filed by organizations interested in the case, ranging from the American Federation of Teachers, which supported Bakke, to the Association of American Medical Colleges, which supported Davis.

Bakke's action in the trial court had attracted little attention. The university's counsel had been confident that Bakke's suit would be easily defeated, and there was no attempt to participate as amicus curiae. In fact, the NAACP, which had been invited to take part in the case, declined to do so. Like the university attorneys, the civil rights organization did not see the *Bakke* case as a real threat.[30] But now Manker's judgment on the invalidity of the Davis program and the California Supreme Court's decision to hear the appeal directly established the seriousness of Bakke's challenge.

At the time of *Bakke*, the California court was probably the most prestigious state court. Gone were the days when it could be said that "the California Supreme Court had been a traditional sanctuary for legal mediocrity."[31] Instead, under the leadership of one of this century's greatest judges, Chief Justice Roger J. Traynor, the California court became the most respected state bench. Although Traynor had retired in 1970, the court's reputation continued under his successor, Chief Justice Donald R. Wright. The court was also considered one of the most liberal in the country, as well as a leader in adapting the law to contemporary needs. From this point of view, the California court's *Bakke* decision surprised most observers.

Bakke was argued in the California court's first-floor courtroom in the Sacramento courthouse on Thursday, March 18, 1976. The seven Justices were all present when the session began at 9:30 A.M. They were seated on their leather chairs behind the traditional straight bench, still used in

appellate courts except for the United States Supreme Court, which had adopted a winged bench under Chief Justice Warren E. Burger. At precisely 9:30, Chief Justice Wright called the case and asked the two attorneys, Messrs. Colvin and Reidhaar, "will you please come forward to the counsel table."[32] Colvin informed the court that they had agreed that Reidhaar would argue first and the latter then began his presentation of the university's appeal.

Each attorney had half an hour to present his case. But the major part of their time was devoted to answering questions from the bench. The California Court, like the U.S. Supreme Court, peppers counsel with questions. Reidhaar had barely begun stating the case, telling the court how the special program reserved 16 percent of the Davis places "to be filled by qualified disadvantaged minority applicants," when Justice Mathew O. Tobriner interrupted and asked how they made sure that they were "qualified." Reidhaar began his answer, but was interrupted by Justice Stanley Mosk, who pointed out that, in regular admissions, no applicant with an average of 2.5 or less was even considered, while "among the 16 who were admitted on the preferential—under the preferential classification—there were many who had gradepoint averages as low as 2.1. How can you justify that?"

Mosk then asked whether this didn't show "that race is a factor which you considered." Reidhaar answered, "that's definitely correct Your Honor. . . . All applicants admitted through the special admissions program had been disadvantaged minority applicants."

But didn't that, queried the Chief Justice, pose directly the issue—"whether it is constitutional to use race as a classification for excluding students—that's what we really have, isn't it?"

Reidhaar conceded, "That certainly is a basic issue, Your Honor."

"It is the basic issue," replied Chief Justice Wright.

Reidhaar answered by referring to cases "holding that it is permissible to consider race and to make racial classifications for the affirmative purpose of promoting integration and promoting equality of opportunity." At this, Justice Mosk, anticipating the approach in his *Bakke* opinion, asked, "Is there any case that has held that discrimination against a minority is invidious, but discrimination against the majority is not?"

Mosk also indicated that he was troubled by the general nature of the exchanges between Reidhaar and the court. They discussed the Davis program and how the students were chosen under it; but there was no

indication of the effect on specific people. In particular, Mosk noted, "Counselor, there is one word we haven't mentioned here this morning, and that's Bakke. Mr. Bakke is the student who applied here."

Reidhaar responded by pointing out,

"Justice Mosk, you and other members of the Court may be interested to know that Mr. Bakke is in the courtroom this morning." He then stated, "It is indeed unfortunate that candidates with records as impressive as Mr. Bakke must be denied admission to the Medical School. But there has never been any suggestion or claim that Mr. Bakke is not qualified to undertake medical study. . . .

Justice Mosk: "Indeed about 20 to 30 points better qualified than the 16 who were given preferential treatment."

Mr. Reidhaar: "If one looks simply to a comparison of paper records."

By now Reidhaar's half hour had expired and the Chief Justice interrupted, "I believe, Counsel, that you have exhausted your alloted time— even your rebuttal time. I will, however, permit you to have the three minutes you requested"—i.e., for rebuttal.

The Chief Justice then called on Bakke's counsel. He was more nervous than Reidhaar and often was hesitant, even uncertain, in answering questions. But he was clear at the outset, stating flatly, "Your Honor, our position in this case is that what we have before us is a racial quota case." The record, Colvin urged, clearly supported this proposition.

Justice Tobriner asked whether Colvin was taking the "position that as a matter of principle generally you cannot take race into account in the selection of otherwise qualified persons?" Colvin was to be brought back to this question a number of times and never answered it clearly. He argued "that any racial classification is per se invidious." At the same time, he said, "Plaintiff in this case does not take the position that there can be no affirmative action steps." But he never indicated what these steps might be or how they could be taken without taking race into account.

Instead, Colvin urged, "I don't—I do not believe that people should get points by reason of the accident of ancestry." And, at the end of his presentation, Colvin went back to his categorical opening theme:

Justice Mosk asked, "Basically, do you object to having two separate admission programs? These factors all ought to be considered in one admission program, is that your—"

Colvin asserted, "That is our position, our position is that this is a flat out quota."

During his short rebuttal, Reidhaar was challenged by several of the

Justices. Chief Justice Wright asserted, "What you really did was just to simply take the lazy way out—just O.K., some certain percentage based on race and we make no other inquiry." Justice Sullivan expressed difficulty with the argument that students chosen by the special program were qualified: "Well you're just playing with the definition of 'qualified.' When you get over the one group your concept of qualified is different from qualified in the general admission group."

And Justice Mosk disagreed with Reidhaar's reliance on busing and segregation cases: "I don't see how you can equate bussing or segregation cases with this case because the white student . . . who might not want to go to an integrated school still gets his education one way or another. But Mr. Bakke here is excluded and does not get his medical education."

During his argument, Colvin had made one important point, which was to place the case in a different posture so far as Bakke personally was concerned. It will be recalled that the trial court had found the Davis special program unconstitutional but had refused to order Bakke's admission because he had failed to prove that he would have been admitted if there had been no special admissions program. During his presentation, Colvin pointed out that Judge Manker "decided Bakke's admission not on the basis of nonintervention—really on the basis of burden of proof."

At this, Justice Mosk asked, "you've now brought up another question—that is, where is the burden of proof? With regard to Mr. Bakke?"

Colvin replied that "Our position . . . is that once there is a case [which] holds that race is used on a discriminatory basis . . . the burden of proof shifts to the defendant." As we shall now see, the California Supreme Court was to agree with Colvin's view on the burden of proof. This, in turn, would lead to an order that Bakke be admitted to Davis.

BAKKE'S VICTORY IN SACRAMENTO

The highest California court issued its decision on September 16, 1976.[33] It constituted a complete victory for Bakke. The opinion of the court was written by Justice Mosk and joined by all except Justice Tobriner, who wrote a strong dissent. What was particularly striking to observers was that the polar views were expressed by the men who were considered the two foremost liberals as well as the most respected Justices on the court.

Mosk's opinion represented a complete rejection of the case for Davis. It contained four main themes:

1) "It is plain that the special admission program denies admission to some white applicants solely because of their race." The question posed by this fact was "whether a racial classification which is intended to assist minorities, but which also has the effect of depriving those who are not so classified of benefits they would enjoy but for their race, violates the constitutional rights of the majority."

2) For such a classification to be upheld, "not only must the purpose of the classification serve a 'compelling state interest,' but it must be demonstrated by rigid scrutiny that there are no reasonable ways to achieve the state's goals by means which impose a lesser limitation on the rights of the group disadvantaged by the classification." Nor should there be "a less demanding standard of review under the Fourteenth Amendment if the race discriminated against is the majority rather than a minority." The very concept of equal protection "is incompatible with the premise that some races may be afforded a higher degree of protection against unequal treatment than others."

3) The opinion rejects the claim that "the University has demonstrated that the special admission program is necessary to serve a compelling governmental interest and that the objectives of the program cannot reasonably be achieved by some means which would impose a lesser burden on the rights of the majority." In this respect the two major interests stated by the University "are to integrate the student body and to improve medical care for minorities. In our view, the University has not established that a program which discriminates against white applicants because of their race is necessary to achieve either of these goals."

4) "There is no evidence in the record to indicate that the University has discriminated against minority applicants in the past."

Mosk concluded that the Davis program was one that provided for racial quotas: "While a program can be damned by semantics, it is difficult to avoid considering the University scheme as a form of an education quota system, benevolent in concept perhaps, but a revival of quotas nevertheless." To uphold such a program "would call for the sacrifice of principle for the sake of dubious expediency and would represent a retreat in the struggle to assure that each man and woman shall be judged on the basis of individual merit alone, a struggle which has only lately achieved success in removing legal barriers to racial equality."

Judge Tobriner delivered a strong dissent. He asserted that the majority had ignored numerous precedents upholding "benign" racial classifica-

tions, intended to correct "Two centuries of slavery and racial discrimination [which] have left our nation an awful legacy, a largely separated society
in which wealth, educational resources, employment opportunities—indeed all of society's benefits—remain largely the preserve of the white-
Anglo majority." It was anomalous that "this court [which] has always
been at the forefront in protecting the rights of minorities" should hand
down this decision which precludes the state from implementing this
"affirmative action" program to provide for effective integration at Davis.

In an interview a year after the California court's decision, Justice Mosk
said that the majority had "had very little difficulty" in reaching its decision, once it had become evident that Davis was trying "to justify a quota
system." As Mosk put it, "The court saw quite clearly that this was a case of
racial discrimination, and it was our feeling that discrimination against a
person of any race is just bad."[34]

On September 30, counsel for Davis filed a petition for rehearing. It will
be recalled that, during the argument, Bakke's counsel had argued that the
University had the burden of proof on the issue of whether Bakke would
have been admitted if there had been no special admissions program.[35]
Now, with its petition for rehearing, the University filed a stipulation that
stated expressly, "The University concedes that it cannot meet the burden
of proving that the special admissions program did not result in Mr.
Bakke's failure to be admitted."[36] This concession placed the issue of
Bakke's admission in an entirely different posture. In denying the petition
for rehearing on October 28, the California court noted that "the University has conceded that it cannot meet the burden of proving that the special
admission program did not result in Bakke's exclusion. Therefore, he is
entitled to an order that he be admitted to the University."[37]

Why did the university make the concession which resulted in the
California court's order directing that Bakke be admitted to Davis? Bakke's
attorney said that it did so to ensure that the case could be taken to the
United States Supreme Court. The California Supreme Court had originally ordered the case sent back to the trial court to determine whether
Davis could meet its burden of proof. "Then," according to Colvin, "if
Bakke wasn't eligible for admittance—if he hadn't been discriminated
against—there would be no justiciable issue for the U.S. Supreme Court to
decide, and the California decision would stand. The University would
have to end its program."[38]

Be that as it may, the California Supreme Court decision not only agreed
with Judge Manker that the Davis program was unconstitutional, but also

directed the trial court to order Bakke to be admitted to Davis. What the highest California court did in this respect was summarized in Justice Stevens' already-quoted December 12, 1977 letter: "On appeal, the California Supreme Court reversed because the trial judge incorrectly placed on Bakke the burden of showing that he would have been admitted in the absence of discrimination. . . . The University conceded 'that it cannot meet the burden of proving that the special admission program did not result in Bakke's exclusion.' . . . Accordingly, the California Supreme Court directed the trial court to enter judgment ordering Bakke's admission." As will be seen in chapter 4, the order for Bakke's admission was to be stayed by the U.S. Supreme Court pending its review of the case.

TO APPEAL OR NOT TO APPEAL?

The question for the university after the adverse California Supreme Court decision was whether to appeal to the U.S. Supreme Court. Representatives of more than a dozen minority groups urged the regents not to do so. They argued that the university case was a poor vehicle for testing special admissions programs because the facts—particularly the flat 16 percent "quota"—were so strongly in favor of Bakke. Some went further and claimed that the regents were actually pleased with the *Bakke* result because they did not really want any preferential admissions. Anti-Bakke students hit hard on this theme in a debate with several regents at the Berkeley campus. One regent lost his temper and responded, "It makes me damn mad to . . . hear these paranoid rantings and ravings that are totally inaccurate."[39]

As a practical matter, the question—to appeal or not to appeal?—could only be answered one way by the university. The California courts not only had ruled the Davis program invalid but also had barred any consideration of race as a factor in admissions programs. This meant an end to programs seeking to secure minority students in the nation's largest state and perhaps to all other affirmative action efforts as well. The consequences of accepting the California courts' ruling were thus too great—both for the state itself and, because of the influence the ruling might have on universities and courts elsewhere, for the country as well.

At any rate, the regents voted in November 1976 to seek Supreme Court review. Soon afterwards, the university filed a petition for certiorari in the U.S. Supreme Court. Further disposition of the *Bakke* case was now in the hands of the nine Justices of the highest bench.

NOTES

1. 1 Alan Bakke versus Regents of the University of California 4–5 (Slocum ed. 1978).
2. Brown v. Board of Education, 347 U.S. 483 (1954).
3. Schwartz, *The Unpublished Opinions of the Warren Court* 446 (1985).
4. Wilkinson, *From* Brown *to* Bakke 82 (1979).
5. Schwartz, Swann's *Way: The School Busing Case and the Supreme Court* chapter 3 (1986).
6. Green v. County School Board, 391 U.S. 430, 437–438 (1968).
7. Swann v. Charlotte-Mecklenburg Board of Education, 402 U.S. 1 (1971).
8. Compare Tawney, Equality 139 (1931).
9. Executive Order No. 10925 (1961).
10. O'Neill, *Bakke and the Politics of Equality* 55 (1985).
11. DeFunis v. Odegaard, 507 P.2d 1169, 1199 (Wash. 1973) (dissent).
12. Infra, p. 54.
13. UJO v. Carey, 430 U.S. 144, 170 (1977).
14. DeFunis v. Odegaard, 507 P.2d 1169, 1182 (Wash. 1973).
15. Sindler, *Bakke, DeFunis, and Minority Admissions* 213 (1978).
16. Benfell, Should the Constitution Really Be Color Blind? *Barrister*, 11, 12 (Fall 1977).
17. O'Neill, supra note, 10, at 29.
18. Supra note 1, at 24–28.
19. O'Neill, supra note 10, at 28–29.
20. Benfell, supra note 16, at 13.
21. Supra note 1, at 116–117.
22. Id. at 120.
23. Id. at 118.
24. Id. at 177, 176, 190.
25. Id. at 191.
26. Id. at 194.
27. Id. at 196.
28. Id. at 206.
29. Ibid.
30. O'Neill, supra note 10, at 40.
31. Weaver, *Warren: The Man, The Court, The Era* 107 (1967).
32. The quotes from the argument are from 2 supra note 1, at 4 et seq.
33. Bakke v. Regents of the University of California, 553 P.2d 1152 (Cal. 1976). The quotes from the opinions are from this report.
34. O'Neill, supra note 10, at 42.
35. The argument had also been made in Bakke's brief. Supra note 1, at 279.
36. 2 id. at 53–54.
37. 553 P.2d at 1172.
38. Benfell, supra note 16, at 13.
39. Sindler, supra note 15, at 239.

THREE

From *Brown* to *Bakke*

T HE *Bakke* case was to present the Supreme Court with a new constitutional issue—that of the validity of programs such as Davis's, which are based upon racial classifications giving a preference to blacks and other specified minorities. By the time *Bakke* reached the Marble Palace, the issue had become a critical one, both to our law and to the society it served. In seeking to resolve it, the Justices had no precedent directly in point. But they did have at their disposal the prior caselaw on racial discrimination, starting with the 1954 *Brown* case—in many ways the watershed constitutional case of this century.[1]

BROWN ENFORCEMENT

Any discussion of the law governing racial discrimination must, of course, begin with *Brown v. Board of Education*.[2] The landmark decision ruled categorically that school segregation was unconstitutional. Yet, though the Court's May 17, 1954, decision established the unqualified principle that school segregation violated the Equal Protection Clause, it did not discuss the remedial question: how was the principle to be enforced? A separate decision—in *Brown II*—dealt with that issue a year after *Brown I* was decided.[3]

Brown II is remembered today mainly because of the statement in the opinion there that the *Brown I* no-segregation principle was to be enforced by the nondiscriminatory admission of blacks to schools "with all deliberate speed."[4] This oxymoronic phrase, so untypical of Chief Justice Warren's normal mode of expression, led to learned controversy on the phrase's origins. Papers recently made public indicate definitely that the phrase was used by the Chief Justice in response to a suggestion by Justice Frank-furter.[5]

More important than the origin of the phrase itself, however, was that it indicated that immediate relief was not to be granted for the constitutional violations suffered by segregated blacks. On the contrary, *Brown II* pro-vided time for enforcement of the no-segregation principle. It did so by requiring enforcement under the all-deliberate-speed language and by providing for what Justice Burton called decentralized enforcement of *Brown I*.[6] The Supreme Court would not itself perform the enforcement function. Instead, *Brown II* delegated that function to the federal district courts. It was those courts which were directed by *Brown II* "to take such proceedings and enter such orders and decrees . . . as are necessary and proper" to secure the admission of blacks "to public schools on a racially nondiscriminatory basis with all deliberate speed."[7]

The key factor in *Brown I* enforcement under the *Brown II* decision was the discretion vested in the federal courts. It is true, said the *Brown II* opinion, that the primary responsibility for resolving the problems "arising from the transition to a system of public education freed of racial discrimi-nation" was to be in the school authorities. But the courts would have to consider whether actions of the authorities constituted good-faith imple-mentation. The "courts which originally heard these cases can best perform this judicial appraisal,"[8] and they were vested with the broad discretion of courts of equity in exercising their enforcement function.

As it turned out, the *Brown II* enforcement approach meant delay in vindication of the constitutional right against segregation. As Justice Black had predicted at the *Brown II* conference,[9] there was to be only "glacial movement" toward desegregation in the South. "All deliberate speed" may never have been intended to mean indefinite delay, yet that is just what it did mean in much of the South—at least until the Supreme Court itself felt compelled to correct the situation, more than a decade after the *Brown* decisions.

FROM *BROWN* TO *GREEN*

A decade after *Brown*, the Supreme Court began to intervene more actively in desegregation enforcement.[10] It had become apparent that the *Brown II* formula in practice meant undue delay in the implementation of the *Brown I* principle. Justice Black's "glacial movement" prediction had proved all too accurate. If the desegregation pace were to be speeded up, the Marble Palace would have to take an active role in *Brown* enforcement.

The key cases in which such a role was assumed were the *Green* and *Swann* cases.[11] In *Green v. County School Board*,[12] the Court struck down a so-called freedom of choice plan, allowing a pupil to choose his or her own public school, adopted by a Virginia school board. The *Green* opinion was the strongest Supreme Court opinion on the subject since *Brown* itself. It stressed that what was required was elimination of the "dual [school] system, part 'white' and part 'Negro.' It was such dual systems that 14 years ago *Brown I* held unconstitutional and a year later *Brown II* held must be abolished."[13]

Green declared that the question in a school segregation case is whether the school authorities have "achieved the 'racially nondiscriminatory school system' *Brown II* held must be effectuated." It was not enough for school boards merely to remove the legal prohibitions against black attendance in white schools. Instead, "School boards such as the respondent then operating state-compelled dual systems were . . . clearly charged with the affirmative duty to take whatever steps might be necessary to convert to a unitary system in which racial discrimination would be eliminated root and branch."[14]

In addition, *Green* underlined the Court's impatience with continued delays in desegregation. The courts were no longer to tolerate school plans that might bring about desegregation at some future time. On the contrary, "The burden on a school board today is to come forward with a plan that promises realistically to work, and promises realistically to work *now*."[15]

SWANN AND REMEDIAL POWER

The far-reaching *Green* decision, the culmination of the Warren Court jurisprudence on school segregation, led directly to the Burger Court's most important decision on the subject: *Swann v. Charlotte-Mecklenburg Board of Education*.[16] *Swann* upheld the far-reaching desegregation order issued by the district court in the case, which included efforts to reach a 71%–29% white-black ratio in the different schools and provision for extensive busing to help attain that goal. The order required the busing of about 10,000 students solely for the purpose of desegregation—about one-fourth of the children attending schools in the district concerned.

The most important thing about the *Swann* decision was its recognition of broadside remedial power in desegregation cases. I have described the *Swann* decision process in detail in a recent book.[17] It shows how Chief Justice Burger's efforts to limit the district court's busing order were frustrated by other members of the Court who strongly supported a categorical affirmance of the lower court's order. In the first draft of his *Swann* opinion, the Chief Justice stated a most restricted view of the remedial power in this type of case, which the draft contrasted with what it termed "a classical equity case."[18] Later drafts modified this restricted approach and the final *Swann* opinion adopted a very broad conception of remedial power in such a case.

The *Swann* opinion specifically rejected the view stated in the Burger draft that the remedial power in this type of case was somehow less than that in the "classical equity case." As the *Swann* opinion put it, "a school desegregation case does not differ fundamentally from other cases involving the framing of equitable remedies to repair the denial of a constitutional right. The task is to correct, by a balancing of the individual and collective interests, the condition that offends the Constitution."[19]

The result is a broad statement of the reach of remedial power in such a case: "Once a right and a violation have been shown, the scope of a district court's equitable powers to remedy past wrongs is broad, for breadth and flexibility are inherent in equitable remedies."[20] Remedial discretion includes the power to attempt to reach a goal of racial distribution in schools comparable to that in the community and to order extensive busing if deemed appropriate to "produce an effective dismantling of the dual system."[21]

If we take *Green* and *Swann* together, they state a far-reaching theory of remedial power in racial discrimination cases which goes far beyond the no-segregation principle laid down in *Brown*. In *Green*, the Court changed the constitutional rule from the *Brown* prohibition against compelled segregation to an affirmative duty to immediately dismantle all dual school systems—a duty that required local authorities to "come forward with a plan that . . . promises realistically to work *now*."[22] If they did not come forward with such a plan, it was within the remedial power of the district courts to do so. From the *Brown* invalidation of prohibitions against blacks' attending white schools, the Warren Court had moved to the *Green* affirmative duty to provide a fully integrated school system, with the federal judges having the remedial authority to ensure that the conversion from a dual to a unitary system took place as soon as possible. The clear implication was that the district courts had the power to issue whatever orders were necessary to bring about an integrated system.

The *Green* opinion itself did not go beyond mentioning a modified "neighborhood school" concept as a possible remedy.[23] But that was only because the school district involved was a rural one with little residential segregation. The same suggestion would prove inadequate in urban areas with entirely different residential patterns. In such areas, would neighborhood schools be sufficient to meet the constitutional standard or would more drastic remedies be appropriate? Could those remedies include busing between white and black areas if the district courts determined that it was needed to ensure meaningful integration?[24]

Swann, of course, answered these questions in favor of the power to order more drastic remedies, including extensive busing. Indeed, as seen, *Swann* holds clearly that the remedial authority in these cases is the broad and flexible power traditionally exercised by courts of equity. As such, it includes the power to take any and all measures that may be deemed appropriate to attain the goal "of insuring the achievement of complete integration at the earliest practicable date."[25]

There is another point about *Swann* which is usually overlooked, yet which is most pertinent to any discussion of the *Bakke* case. Commentators on *Swann*, including this writer, focus on the Court's recognition of a very broad remedial power in the federal courts in desegregation cases. The *Swann* opinion did not, however, limit itself to judicial remedial power in such cases. It also dealt with the power of school authorities to further integration and indicated that, if anything, their authority in this respect was even broader than that possessed by the courts. According to *Swann*, "Remedial judicial authority does not put judges automatically in the shoes of school authorities whose powers are plenary."[26] Hence, the school authorities may frame remedies that may still be beyond the scope of judicial remedial power. "School authorities," the *Swann* opinion states, "are traditionally charged with broad power to formulate and implement educational policy and might well conclude, for example, that in order to prepare students to live in a pluralistic society each school should have a prescribed ratio of Negro to white students reflecting the proportion for the district as a whole. To do this as an educational policy is within the broad discretionary powers of school authorities."[27]

In *Bakke*, as already seen, the challenged admissions program was adopted by the Davis Medical School, not imposed by a federal court in the exercise of its remedial power. *Swann* implies that, if anything, even more deference should be given to measures adopted as a matter of educational policy by the relevant education authorities. But may such measures include preferential treatment for blacks and other minorities such as that provided under the Davis special admissions program? That was, of course, the question presented in *Bakke*. The same question had been before the Court four years earlier in the *DeFunis* case,[28] but the Justices had avoided answering it there by disposing of the case on mootness grounds.

DEFUNIS CASE

DeFunis v. Odegaard[29] had presented the Court with the *Bakke* issue during the 1973 term. Marco DeFunis, a white graduate of the University of Washington, had applied for admission to the university's law school. He had been turned down, even though 36 minority applicants, whose averages were below DeFunis's, had been accepted under a separate admissions procedure. Thirty of them had averages so low that they would have been summarily rejected had they been white. DeFunis brought suit in state court claiming that the Law School Admissions Committee had invidiously discriminated against him on account of his race in violation of the Equal Protection Clause. The trial court agreed with his claim and granted the requested relief. DeFunis was accordingly admitted to the law school. On appeal, the Washington Supreme Court reversed the trial court and held that the law school's admissions policy did not violate the Constitution. DeFunis was then in his second year at the law school.

DeFunis was argued in the U.S. Supreme Court on Tuesday, February 26, 1974. By that time, DeFunis had completed all but his last term at the law school. During the argument, the Justices asked DeFunis's attorney whether he had applied for admission to the final semester. "I don't know," was the answer. Justice Marshall then asked, "Is it possible for you to find out whether or not he has registered, and what happened if he did try to register, and let us know?"[30]

That same day, after the argument ended, the attorney sent a letter to the Chief Justice stating, "I wish to advise that Marco DeFunis, Jr. filed his registration with the University of Washington law school on Tuesday, February 26, 1974, which consisted of filling out a computerized form

listing the courses that he desired to take for his final quarter in law school."
Copies of this letter were immediately circulated to the other Justices.

When the *DeFunis* conference was held the following Friday, the Justices knew that DeFunis had registered for his final term at the law school. In addition, counsel for the latter had informed the Court that, if DeFunis did register, "that registration would not be canceled unilaterally by the university regardless of the outcome of this litigation."[31] This meant that DeFunis would be given the opportunity to complete his final semester and graduate, regardless of how the Supreme Court decided his case.

Despite this, Chief Justice Burger began the conference by discussing the merits of the case. "The question," he said, "is the extent to which race may be taken into account to exclude DeFunis." As the Chief Justice put it, "The premise seems to be that because blacks suffered oppression, there's a duty to redress the harm." Burger indicated that he doubted that that premise was enough to support DeFunis's exclusion.

Justice Douglas, who spoke next, displayed ambivalence on the merits. "Some things transcend race," the lanky Westerner declared. "I can't believe where aristocracy of talent is a problem, you can force a state university to take blacks in some jobs." But then Douglas went on to express a typically maverick view the other way, saying, "I'm suspicious of tests and maybe we ought to say that all at the bottom of the class must be taken in."

On the other hand, Justice Brennan expressed no doubts. He asserted that the courts had no business in limiting admissions policies so long as there was no clear racial discrimination, something not made out here. The Brennan view was supported by Justices White, Marshall, and Powell. "Race per se," said the latter, "is not an impermissible consideration in such a policy"—i.e., a statement of particular interest in view of Powell's later position in *Bakke*.

At the end of his conference statement, the Chief Justice had suggested that *DeFunis* could also be disposed of on mootness grounds. However, the strongest presentation in favor of the mootness approach was taken by Justice Stewart. "The case is moot," he stated flatly. This is "not a class action and not remotely akin to *Roe* or *Doe*." The Justice was referring to the two abortion cases the previous year, where the Court had rejected the mootness argument.[32] In this case, noted Stewart, "DeFunis is in law school and will graduate." Justice Blackmun also stated that he thought the case was moot.

In the weeks that followed the conference, Justice Stewart was able to secure the votes of Justices Rehnquist and Powell for disposition of *De-Funis* on mootness grounds. Five Justices, including the Chief Justice, now agreed to avoid the merits and their decision that the case was moot was announced in a per curiam opinion authored by Stewart. Justice Brennan, joined by Justices Douglas, White, and Marshall, issued a dissent protesting against what he termed "the Court's straining to rid itself of this dispute."[33] Justice Douglas also wrote his own dissent, which asserted the unconstitutionality of racial preferences in the admissions process. Only if the selection process was racially neutral could it be constitutional in the Douglas view.

Of course, the *DeFunis* decision did not enable the Justices to avoid permanently the crucial constitutional issues involved in the case. As the Brennan dissent put it, "Few constitutional questions in recent history have stirred as much debate, and they will not disappear. They must inevitably return to the federal courts and ultimately again to this Court."[34]

Brennan's prophecy was borne out when *Bakke* itself came before the Supreme Court.

UJO V. CAREY

Between *DeFunis* and *Bakke*, there was one case in the Supreme Court that raised the issue of racial preferences. Like the admissions programs challenged in *DeFunis* and *Bakke*, the law involved in *United Jewish Organizations v. Carey*[35] not only granted a preference to members of one racial minority, but also operated to exclude members of another ethnic group from the benefits conferred. As such the *UJO* case was a direct precursor of *Bakke*, insofar as the constitutionality of racially preferential programs was concerned.

UJO arose out of action taken by the New York Legislature to secure approval of the U.S. Attorney General to a reapportionment plan. Under section 5 of the Voting Rights Act of 1965, the approval is needed before such a plan may go into effect, unless the state obtains a declaratory judgment from a designated federal court. The Attorney General originally turned down the plan on the ground that, as to certain districts in the predominantly black Bedford-Stuyvesant area of Brooklyn, the state had not demonstrated that the redistricting had neither the purpose nor the effect of abridging the right to vote by reason of race or color. The Attorney

General objected to the plan because of what he called "an abnormally high minority concentration" in one state senate district "while adjoining minority neighborhoods are significantly diffused into surrounding districts."

To meet the Attorney General's objections, the state submitted a new plan which increased the size of the nonwhite majorities in four election districts to 65 percent. This directly affected an area where some 30,000 Hasidic Jews lived. They had been located in one assembly district and one senate district. The new plan split the Hasidic community between two senate and two assembly districts. Petitioners, on behalf of the Hasidic community, brought suit for injunctive and declaratory relief, alleging that the plan violated their rights under the Fourteenth and Fifteenth Amendments. They contended that the plan "would dilute the value of [their] franchise by halving its effectiveness," solely for the purpose of achieving a racial quota, and that they were assigned to electoral districts solely on the basis of race.

As Justice Brennan was to point out, in a November 23, 1977, MEMO-RANDUM TO THE CONFERENCE on the *Bakke* case, "There can be no question that the racial line used there [i.e., in the *UJO* case] disadvantaged the Hasidim." Did that, however, necessarily make the New York reapportionment plan unconstitutional? Brennan thought not. Though a racial line was used, "the use of race was not insulting or invidious and therefore not improper. . . . The redistricting therefore was upheld as a legitimate remedial step, notwithstanding its impact on the Hasidim."

The Brennan memo compared the *UJO* case to *Bakke*: "Bakke's claim for admission is of no more constitutional significance than the Hasidim's claimed right, in *UJO*, to vote as a single bloc." The question of whether the two cases were similar was discussed in the *UJO* conference on October 8, 1976—though, of course, the Justices then compared *UJO* to *DeFunis*, since *Bakke* had not yet come before the Court. Divergent views were expressed at the conference on the similarity issue. "What we ducked in *DeFunis*," asserted Justice White, "is here." The opposite view was stated by Justice Powell. "I can't see," he said, "a rub-off on employment or *DeFunis* type cases. This is legislative reapportionment and that's different."

On the merits, the majority agreed with the view expressed by Justice Stevens that it was "not impermissible to take into account race in drawing district lines." Justice White, who was to author the *UJO* opinion, also stated that there could be an express racial classification here—"but on the ground of compliance with the Attorney General and section 5" of the Voting Rights Act. Anticipating the first draft of his opinion, White stressed, "I'll tie it as closely as I can to section 5."

Justice Stewart, on the other hand, put forward an even narrower view on judicial review power in such a case than that expressed in his concurring *UJO* opinion. "There's no case at all here," Stewart asserted. "Courts cannot get into legislative reapportionments unless there's a violation of one-man, one-vote or of section 5."

With Justice Marshall not participating, none of the Justices favored reversal of the state court decision upholding the New York plan. The Chief Justice assigned the opinion to Justice White, who soon circulated a draft opinion of the Court. As White had indicated at the conference, the draft was based entirely on section 5 of the Voting Rights Act. Petitioners' argument, said the draft, "fails to appreciate the role of the Voting Rights Act in this case. This is not a case, as petitioners would have it, of 'affirmative action' or 'benign discrimination'; nor is it even a case of 'remedial' discrimination designed to eliminate the effects of past discrimination. It is rather a case involving the application of the screening procedures of the Voting Rights Act to ensure that a change in voting procedures—here a new reapportionment statute—does not discriminate against racial minorities."

Respondents had urged that, wholly aside from the Voting Rights Act, it was constitutionally permissible for a legislature to draw district lines deliberately in such a way as to achieve a proportion of majority white and of majority nonwhite districts roughly approximating the proportion of each racial group in the countywide population. The White draft conceded, "This argument may have considerable merit." However, the draft went on, "we do not need to reach it because we dispose of this case on a narrower ground"—i.e., the validity of the state's action under section 5 of the Voting Rights Act.

Justice Brennan wrote to Justice White stating, "I agree with the basic approach of your present circulation because I think we ought to avoid if possible reaching the broader question of the constitutionality of 'quotaizing' districts in the reapportionment process."

The others, however, refused to go along with White's narrow rationale. This was soon recognized by White himself. In a December 2, 1976, MEMORANDUM TO THE CONFERENCE, he wrote, "The risk of circulating a draft in this case with a rationale for which there was little

enthusiasm at conference has perhaps been verified." Referring to his draft
and a later "circulation taking essentially the same course," White conceded, "it is doubtful that it will garner the necessary votes." If it did not,
the White memo concluded, "I shall redo the opinion and reflect what I
understand to be the majority view—which I share—that a State may,
without relying on the Voting Rights Act, use racial consideration in
districting at least to the extent necessary to validate New York's actions in
this case."

White then circulated what became the ultimate *UJO* opinion, shorten-
ing the part on section 5 of the Voting Rights Act and adding two additional sections (parts III and IV of the final opinion of the Court) upholding
the constitutionality of the New York plan. This proved too much for Chief
Justice Burger, who had voted for affirmance at the conference. On January 3, 1977, the Chief Justice sent a "Dear Byron" letter, telling of his
"difficulty" with the redraft. "I hope," the Burger letter went on, "to
circulate a memo articulating my problems with any fixed 'numbers' which
seem to give tacit approval to a 'quote' [sic] concept. We unanimously
rejected racial balance in school desegregation in *Swann* and I fear the
proposed disposition seems counter to that in spirit."

"I will have my thoughts ready this week," the Burger letter concluded.
The "thoughts" were circulated in a January 4 eight-page typed memorandum. This memo is much stronger than the Chief Justice's *UJO* dissent
and contains a clear statement of Burger's view on both the racial considerations which led to the New York plan and other programs involving racial
preferences. As such it foreshadowed the Chief Justice's constitutional
approach in the *Bakke* case.

"In my view," the Burger *UJO* memo began, "the State of New York has
engaged in a very questionable type of legislation in which literal discrimination—the establishment of racial or ethnic quotas is used. It has done so
on the basis of assumptions not supported by the record and thereby
achieved what, for me, is a very questionable result."

In the first place, the memo declared, it could not be said that New York
had considered race as "merely one of several political characteristics" in
drawing up the reapportionment plan: "Race appears to be the one and
only criterion applied." In effect, as Burger saw it, the state had used the 65
percent nonwhite majority as a virtual "quota" in the districts concerned.
"'Racial quota' and 'racial balance,'" wrote the Chief Justice, "are emo-
tionally loaded terms and to be used with caution. Yet the 65 percent figure

for nonwhites, was viewed as so concretely fixed a criterion by the reapportionment committee that even the slightest deviation was deemed impermissible. This cannot, I think, be characterized in any other way. This is a 'lily' that will not hold the gilt sought to be applied to it."

The Burger memo asserted that "the 65 percent quota" was based upon the assumption of racial bloc voting. "Since this concept seems now to have the formidable combination of support by the federal, executive and the New York legislative branch—and now the approval of this Court—is it not a way of saying that the historic American 'Melting Pot' is passe?"

The memo argued that the New York plan reached an unconstitutional result. "Of course," the Chief Justice conceded, "petitioners are not constitutionally entitled to remain unified within a single political district. But does it not have a constitutional protection against being carved up to deliberately create a bloc of some other favored group?"

Nor does "[t]he fact that the assumed motive of the state legislature was to benefit, rather than to harm, a racial minority . . . , in my judgment, constitutionally insulate the racially discriminatory apportionment scheme. . . . If 'benign' discrimination has a place, this case does not now seem to call for it."

Burger's memo referred to "various programs favoring the victims of past discrimination in employment and education. Such programs are rationalized as compensation for harm such victims have suffered in the past, and to benefit society by promoting the long-overdue benefits of an integrated society." The Chief Justice noted that such programs had "come under serious challenge from the individuals in the majority group who have been harmed by the imposition of such reverse discrimination." The memo cited *DeFunis* and *Bakke* (recently decided by the California Supreme Court). Burger then asserted, "Whatever the merits of those controversies—a question the Court need not decide today—'reverse racial gerrymandering' is a dubious remedy for dealing with the problem of past *voter* discrimination."

On the contrary, "Manipulating the racial composition of electoral districts to assure one minority or another 'deserved' representation" involved an invalid consideration of race in the electoral process. "While it certainly is permissible for a legislature to consider the race of its constituents, along with other factors, in drawing up district lines, racial gerrymandering, *i.e.*, the drawing of district lines with the purpose of achieving a predetermined racial concentration, cannot withstand constitutional scrutiny." The record shows that this is what occurred in this case.

Burger concluded with a warning that the Court's *UJO* decision was eroding the progress that had been made in achieving integration. "If minority 'blocs' are to be rewarded by being artificially reinforced what is the incentive for them to seek the suburbs with true integration in every city block, precinct and ward, to give effect to our boast of a 'Melting Pot.' Minorities in Washington have almost total political power; if they spread into neighboring suburbs of Virginia and Maryland they dilute that power in the new setting and risk losing it in Washington."

Though the Chief Justice did dissent in *UJO*, his dissent was but a pale version of his January 4 memo, with almost all the extreme language eliminated. The other Justices joined in the decision that the challenged reapportionment plan was valid. Yet there is no doubt that, as the already quoted Brennan memo points out, "the racial line used [in *UJO*] disadvantaged the Hasidim."

From this point of view, as the Brennan memo put it, "*UJO* is a paradigm example of what the Fourteenth Amendment does not condemn." It means that the law does not require the automatic invalidation of all decisionmaking which takes race into account. According to Brennan, "We long ago crossed that bridge in cases that approved race-sensitive policies and remedies, and thus firmly settled the principle that not every remedial use of race is constitutionally forbidden. Last Term's *United Jewish Organization* v. *Carey*, 430 U.S. 144, definitely imbedded that principle in concrete."

As the *Bakke* decision process was to show, however, the concrete was to prove less firm than Brennan indicated.

NOTES

1. Brown v. Board of Education, 347 U.S. 483 (1954).
2. 347 U.S. 483 (1954).
3. Brown v. Board of Education, 349 U.S. 294 (1955).
4. Id. at 301.
5. Schwartz, *The Unpublished Opinions of the Warren Court* 468 (1985).
6. See Schwartz, *Super Chief: Earl Warren and His Supreme Court—A Judicial Biography* 93 (1983).
7. 349 U.S. at 301.
8. Id. at 299.

9. Schwartz, *Super Chief*, supra note 6, at 118.
10. Goss v. Board of Education, 373 U.S. 683 (1963).
11. Green v. County School Board, 391 U.S. 430 (1968); Swann v. Charlotte-Mecklenburg Board of Education, 402 U.S. 1 (1971).
12. 391 U.S. 430 (1968).
13. Id. at 435.
14. Id. at 437–38.
15. Id. at 439.
16. 402 U.S. 1 (1971).
17. Schwartz, Swann's *Way: The School Busing Case and the Supreme Court* (1986).
18. Id. at 114.
19. 402 U.S. at 15–16.
20. Id. at 15.
21. Id. at 30.
22. Supra note 15.
23. 391 U.S. at 442, n.6.
24. Compare Wilkinson, *From* Brown *to* Bakke—*The Supreme Court and School Integration* 117 (1979).
25. United States v. Montgomery County Board of Education, 395 U.S. 225, 231 (1969).
26. 402 U.S. at 16.
27. Ibid.
28. DeFunis v. Odegaard, 416 U.S. 312 (1974).
29. 416 U.S. 312 (1974).
30. 80 Kurland and Kasper, "Landmark Briefs and Arguments of the Supreme Court of the United States: *Constitutional Law*" 509 (1975).
31. 416 U.S. at 316, n.3.
32. Roe v. Wade, 410 U.S. 113 (1973); Doe v. Bolton, 410 U.S. 179 (1973).
33. 416 U.S. at 349.
34. Id. at 350.
35. 430 U.S. 144 (1977).

FOUR

Before the Supreme Court

O<small>N</small> February 18, 1977, the Supreme Court voted to grant certiorari in the *Bakke* case. Though it is not apparent from the *United States Reports*, which states only that the writ was granted, the Justices were closely divided on whether to take the case. The opposition to certiorari was led by Justice Brennan. At first glance, this may seem paradoxical, since the Justice had issued a strong dissent in the *DeFunis* case, which severely rebuked the Court for ducking the constitutional issue in that case. In *DeFunis*, Brennan had declared, "I can . . . find no justification for the Court's straining to rid itself of this dispute." In fact, Brennan asserted, "in endeavoring to dispose of this case as moot, the Court clearly disserves the public interest."[1] Now, in *Bakke*, Brennan himself strongly urged the Justices not to grant certiorari.

Brennan's position can be easily explained. At the time of *DeFunis*, the Justice had tentatively concluded that affirmative action programs were constitutional. He thought that a majority of the Court would take the position that race may be treated as a positive factor in making admissions decisions, but he could not, particularly because of Justice Douglas's *DeFunis* opinion, be sure.

Most important to Brennan was to have the constitutional question raised in *DeFunis* and *Bakke* dealt with by the Court in a sympathetic case. Brennan feared that *Bakke* was a risky vehicle for the purpose. The most troublesome feature of the Davis program was that it set aside 16 places for members of minority groups. Brennan was afraid that a majority of the Justices might be so repelled by the existence of such a "quota" that they would not only strike down the program but also indicate that race could never be considered in the admissions process. Because of this, Brennan strongly urged the others not to grant certiorari in *Bakke*. He was supported by Justices Marshall, Blackmun, and the Chief Justice. There were, however, five votes against Brennan's view and it was announced that certiorari was granted in *Bakke* on February 22, 1977.[2] The order of the California court directing Bakke's admission to Davis was stayed pending disposition of the case by the Supreme Court.[3] Argument was scheduled for the beginning of the Court's next term, in October 1977.

THE JUSTICES PREPARE

After certiorari was granted, the Justices began to look ahead to the *Bakke* case. Justice Brennan, in particular, wrote some of his 1976 term opinions with *Bakke* in mind. In *UJO v. Carey*, the Justice issued a concurrence which expressly considered, although it did not resolve, the question of the constitutional permissibility of what he called "benign discrimination."[4] Then, in *Califano v. Webster*, the per curiam was authored by Justice Brennan, who stated specifically that Congress could grant greater social security benefits to women in order to compensate them for past societal discrimination.[5] Brennan told his law clerks that when he wrote this opinion, he hoped that he might be deciding *Bakke* as well.

As soon as the Justices returned from their summer recess, they immersed themselves in the *Bakke* case. Most of them put aside as much of their other work as possible, because they wanted to give the case the fullest consideration even before the oral argument, which was scheduled for October 12, 1977. Thus, Justice Brennan—the one Justice who personally read certiorari petitions during each term—deviated from his normal practice and had his law clerks handle all the certiorari work during the first two weeks of the term, so that the Justice's time might be freed for *Bakke* preparation.

Soon after Brennan's mid-September return from his vacation on Nantucket, he discussed *Bakke* during lunch with Justice Marshall. The latter told Brennan that he could count five votes against quotas—the "Nixon four" and Justice White. Marshall suggested that they find some pretext to get rid of the case because he believed that quotas were often indispensable to affirmative action programs. Brennan replied that, in light of his *De-Funis* dissent, he simply could not be a party to any such action and that he would prefer losing on the merits to seeing the Court once again avoid decision of this issue after having granted certiorari. In any case, Brennan said that he did not share Marshall's pessimism. He thought all the Justices—with the possible exception of the Chief Justice—were genuinely open to upholding the constitutionality of the Davis program.

As will be seen, the Justices began to prepare memoranda on the case even before they first discussed *Bakke* at the conference after oral argument. They also had their law clerks work on what one Justice called "the formidable pile of briefs," as well as analyses of the record and findings below. Because of the importance of the case, Justice Brennan deviated from his normal practice of letting his view of the case crystallize at oral argument and prepared, over the weekend preceding argument, a memorandum to himself outlining his own tentative view of the case. Written out in Brennan's own hand on thirteen yellow legal-size pages, it was headed *Bench Notes—Bakke*. It is of particular interest for what it reveals about the thinking process of a Justice at the outset of a crucial case.

Most of the memo focused on the facts of the case, both summarizing them and raising questions with regard to them. At the end of his factual summary, Brennan wrote: "*NOTE PARTICULARLY*: Record shows medical faculty is convinced that 'special admissions program is the only method whereby the school can produce a diverse student body which will include qualified students from disadvantaged backgrounds,' that few, if any, blacks, Chicanos, Indians or Orientals would be able to get into Davis or any other medical school, without the special or similar program. The record is barren of any other evidence of availability of alternative means."

Brennan's bench notes devoted their last few pages (about two out of eight in the typed copy) to the merits of the case. The discussion here reached a result which foreshadowed the treatment of the matter in Brennan's *Bakke* opinion. The Justice began by stating, "Surely this Court's decisions have settled that not every remedial use of race is constitutionally forbidden. Although of course not as numerous as decisions remedying specific instances of discrimination, use of race to remedy the effects of *societal* discrimination has been sustained." After citing three cases[6] to support this statement, Brennan wrote, "*QUESTION*: Should taking of *race* into account be *a fortiori* permissible?"

Brennan next asked, "If there is nothing to suggest, and it does not appear that there is, that the program actually aims to demean or insult whites or indeed any racial group, may we infer that it was indeed benign to redress societal discrimination as claimed, and does not disguise a policy intended to discriminate, or having the effect of discriminating against whites as whites, or disguises a policy intended to perpetuate disadvantageous treatment of the plans supposed beneficiaries?"

The Justice then went into the review standard in such a case: "should heightened standard or rationality be applied? Either portends I suppose considerable litigation but I lean to the rationality standard at least when as here there is not the slightest evidence in the record of any invidious motive against whites, or any basis for an inference that what is presented as an instance of benign race assignment in fact is something else." This was, of course, a narrower standard of review than that adopted in the Brennan *Bakke* opinion.[7]

The bench notes continue with the concession, "the social reality is I suppose that even a benign policy of assignment by race is viewed as unjust by many in our society especially by those individuals who are adversely affected by a given classification." But that did not, in Brennan's view, require a different result: "should that require the judiciary to do more than demand of the decision-maker, here the admissions committee, that these concerns be weighed against the need for effective social policies promoting racial justice in a society beset by deep-rooted racial inequities?"

Brennan stressed again that the Davis program did not "demean or insult whites." As he put it, "I have difficulty finding the basis in this record for an inference, let alone a conclusion, that the special program constitutes a classification that penalizes a vulnerable subgroup of whites—rather it spreads the costs among whites generally." He also stressed, "This program is not of course governmentally mandated but was voluntarily instituted by Davis." A decision here need not go beyond such a program: "to hold that voluntary minority admissions programs are consistent with the Equal Protection Clause would not establish the validity of mandated programs."

Brennan's bench notes ended by a summary of the role of the Court in such a case: "I should think that our duty ends when we have inquired into, and satisfied ourselves that (1) the use of race is noninvidious; (2) that the program was adopted to counter the effects of past societal discrimination and secure the educational, professional and social benefits of racial diversity and (3) that the program is tailored to such objectives."

GOVERNMENT BRIEF

Toward the end of his bench notes, Justice Brennan wrote, "Despite the paucity of the record as to the why of the 16 places, I hope we can reject the Government's suggestion that we remand for an examination into the reasons for adopting that particular means, into why one non-minority applicant was admitted who had a lower benchmark than another non-minority applicant; into the effect of the individuality of the evaluators upon benchmark scores; into whether the Dean and faculty at Davis were right in thinking that the admission of more fully qualified students from minority communities would tend to increase the availability and use of medical services in the communities from which they were drawn."

The Government's suggestion, to which Justice Brennan referred, was contained in the brief submitted by the United States as amicus curiae in September 1977. In addition to the briefs filed by the parties, 62 amicus briefs were filed in the Supreme Court in the *Bakke* case. Of these, the most important was that filed by the Government. The key question in the case, according to the Government brief, was "Whether a state university admissions program may take race into account . . . ?"[8]

This was to be a crucial issue in the case on which, as we shall see, Justice Brennan was to secure a bare majority for an affirmative answer. The Government brief itself answered the question by urging, "Insofar as the judgment of the Supreme Court of California declares that the Medical School may not consider the race of applicants for the purpose of operating a properly administered affirmative action admissions program, the judgment should be reversed."[9] The brief also asked the Court to vacate the judgment so far as it ordered Bakke's admission and remand the case to examine, among other things, the questions summarized in the Brennan bench notes, since it was not clear from the record exactly how the Davis program operated.

More interesting, however, than the substance of the Government's brief was the politically charged manner in which it was prepared. Briefs for the United States in the Supreme Court are submitted by the Solicitor General—whose office has prided itself on the independent manner in which it operates. The Solicitor General has always exercised his own judgment, free of political and other influences, on how to handle cases in the Supreme Court. Indeed, the first opportunity of then-Assistant Attorney General Warren E. Burger to argue before the highest tribunal came when the

Solicitor General refused to argue a loyalty case because he disagreed with the Government's position.

In *Bakke*, however, the Government brief was prepared as much in the White House as in the Solicitor General's office. The brief's first draft was written by the Civil Rights Division in the Department of Justice, and revised by the Solicitor General's assistant, with further redrafts during August 1977. At this point, the White House became concerned about a document that they felt would be taken as a statement of President Carter's policy on a crucial and sensitive issue. The two Solicitor General aides working on the brief then conferred at the White House with Robert Lipshutz, the President's counsel, and Stuart Eisenstat, his chief assistant for domestic policy. Then on September 1, Attorney General Griffin B. Bell took the current draft of the brief to the White House and handed it to President Carter in the presence of Eisenstat and Lipshutz. The President turned the draft over to the latter and told them to review it. Eisenstat wrote a memorandum criticizing the draft as badly organized, badly written, and containing language that could be used against many of the Government's own affirmative action programs. The brief was then rewritten to reflect the White House views and ultimately approved by Eisenstat and the President himself.

What is striking about the writing of the Government brief was, in addition to the unusual White House interference in the work of the Solicitor General's office, the extent to which the intrusion was concealed from Solicitor General Wade H. McCree, Jr., a firm believer in the tradition of complete independence for his office. McCree told a reporter just before the *Bakke* argument that he knew nothing about and had never seen the Eisenstat memo that constituted the most extensive White House intervention in the brief-drafting process.[10]

The Justices were also apparently upset by the reports of the Government's brief-drafting process that appeared in the press. According to one account,[11] the Chief Justice and Justice Blackmun told McCree that the entire Court was offended by the press leaks on the matter. McCree reported to Attorney General Bell that he was informed that the Justices felt that the newspaper accounts subjected them to improper public pressure when they were about to hear oral argument.

On September 19, after the Government brief had been filed, the Attorney General denied at a press conference that the President had been "centrally involved" in preparing the brief. Bell also said, "we don't want to get into the contents of the brief . . . because we don't want to get crossed up with the Supreme Court and be accused of arguing our case before the media and the nation."[12]

ORAL ARGUMENT

Oral argument in *Bakke* was scheduled for Wednesday, October 12. The courtroom was, of course, packed. Interest in the case was so intense that a Justice, recalling the case, says, "I understand that spectators desiring to see a portion of the argument began to line up about 5:00 P.M. on the afternoon of the 11th." By the time dawn broke, more than 100 would-be spectators were huddled together on the Court's granite steps, stamping their feet to ward off the morning chill. Soon, before the argument was to begin, celebrities began arriving: senators and congressmen, high executive officials, distinguished lawyers, and judges. Unobtrusive in the audience was Mrs. Earl Warren, widow of the Chief Justice who had delivered the historic school desegregation decision in 1954.[13]

The Justice already quoted says that "the interest of the outside world was reflected within the Court as well. The excitement and intense anticipation on the Court was apparent to me the instant I entered the courthouse that morning."

Like all Supreme Court sittings, the October 12 session began at precisely 10 A.M. When the hands of the clock behind the bench indicated the hour, the nine black-robed Justices stepped through the red velour draperies and took their places. At the sound of the gavel the crowded courtroom lapsed into absolute silence. All rose and remained standing while the Court clerk intoned the time-honored cry, "Oyez! Oyez! Oyez! All persons having business before the Honorable, the Supreme Court of the United States, are admonished to draw near and give their attention, for the Court is now sitting. God save the United States and this Honorable Court."

The room is dominated by the Justices' long raised bench. It used to be the traditional straight bench, but in 1970 Chief Justice Burger had it altered to its present "winged," or half-hexagon, shape. In a February 4, 1971 *Memorandum to the Conference*, Burger had informed the others that everyone was in favor of the "change with the possible exception of Justice Black whose position can probably be described as 'take it or leave it.'"

Like all the furniture in the courtroom, the bench is mahogany. Behind the bench are four of the room's massive marble columns. The large clock hangs on a chain between the two center ones. In front of the bench are seated, to the Court's right, the pages and clerk, and, to the Court's left, the marshal. Tables facing the bench are for counsel. Behind the tables is a section for members of the bar and a much larger general section for the public, with separate areas for the press and distinguished visitors.

Goose-quill pens are placed on counsel tables each day that the Justices sit, as was done at the earliest session of the Court. The practice had been interrupted by World War II, when the prewar supply ran out, and then again in 1961, when the quills were temporarily replaced by more modern writing instruments. But traditions die hard at the Supreme Court. The quills soon found their way back to the counsel tables, and there are still spittoons behind the bench for each Justice and pewter julep cups (now used for their drinking water).

The *Bakke* argument began just after the Justices sat down in their plush high-back black-leather chairs. The audience also sat down and the Chief Justice began, in his deep bass, "The first case on today's calendar is No. 76–811, Regents of the University of California against Bakke. Mr. Cox, you may proceed when you are ready." At this Archibald Cox strode briskly to the podium, put on his reading glasses, and began presenting the case for the university. Cox, a Harvard law professor, former Solicitor General, and special Watergate prosecutor, was resplendent in a black cutaway, striped tie, and the crew-cut grey hair that had become his trademark.

According to the Justice who has been quoted, the *Bakke* argument "was not only substantively useful, but produced some high comedy as well." Thus, at one point, Justice Blackmun wondered if the Davis program could be compared to athletic scholarships. Cox said that there was a parallel, since such scholarships represented the faculty's choice to promote the school and "the aim of some institutions does seem to be to have athletic prowess."[14]

"It's the aim of most institutions, isn't it? Not just some," Blackmun countered.

"Well, I come from Harvard, sir," Cox quipped. "I don't know whether it's our aim, but we don't do very well." At this, the audience erupted in laughter.

Cox had begun his presentation by getting to the nub of the case, as he saw it. "This case . . . presents a single vital question: whether a state university, which is forced by limited resources to select a relatively small

number of students from a much larger number of well-qualified applicants, is free, voluntarily, to take into account the fact that a qualified
applicant is black, Chicano, Asian or native American in order to increase
the number of qualified members of those minority groups trained for the
educated professions and participating in them—professions from which
minorities were long excluded because of generations of pervasive racial
discrimination."

Cox tried to place the answer in broader perspective: "The answer which
the Court gives will determine, perhaps for decades, whether members of
these minorities are to have the kind of meaningful access to higher education in the professions, which the universities have accorded them in recent
years, or are to be reduced to the trivial numbers which they were prior to
the adoption of minority admissions programs."

For, Cox asserted, there was one reality "which, I say, I think the Court
must face when it comes to its decision": .... "There is no racially blind
method of selection, which will enroll today more than a trickle of minority
students in the nation's colleges and professions."

After a few minutes, Justice White interrupted Cox with a question
about the record. And then the queries came from all sides of the bench. So
thick and fast did they come that, at the end of Cox's presentation, the Chief
Justice said, "we've taken a good deal of your time, so we'll enlarge your
time five minutes."

A number of Justices appeared troubled by what seemed a racial quota at
Davis. Cox tried to meet this concern. "I want to emphasize," he declared,
"that the designation of 16 places was not a quota, at least as I would use
that word. Certainly it was not a quota in the older sense of an arbitrary
limit put on the number of members of a non-popular group who would be
admitted to an institution which was looking down its nose at them."

Justice Stewart: "It did put a limit on the number of white people, didn't
it?"

Cox: "I think that it limited the number of non-minority, and therefore
essentially white, yes. But there are two things to be said about that.

One is that this was not pointing the finger at a group which had been
marked as inferior. .... So I think it was not stigmatizing in the sense of the
old quota against Jews was stigmatizing, in any way."

Justice Stewart: "It did put a limit on the number of non-minority people
in each class?"

Cox: "It did put a limit, no question about that. .... But I would emphasize that it doesn't point the finger at any group, it doesn't say to any group, 'you are inferior.'"

Justice Rehnquist asked Cox how he could distinguish between the setting aside of 16 seats and the setting aside of 50 seats. "Would that be any more infirm than the program that Davis has?"

The distinguished professor toyed with his spectacles and ceded, "I would say that as the number goes up, the danger of invidiousness or the danger that this is being done not for social purposes but to favor one group . . . is great."

But Cox stubbornly continued to insist that what was involved was not a "quota"—at least not in the pernicious sense of that term. Justice Powell then interposed,

"Mr. Cox, the facts are not in dispute. Does it really matter what we call this program?"

Cox: "No. I quite agree with you, Mr. Justice. I was trying to emphasize that the facts here have none of the aspects, that there are none of the facts that lead us to think of 'quota' as a bad word."

After further intensive questions, Cox tried to get back to his main theme. "We submit, first," he declared, "that the Fourteenth Amendment does not outlaw race-conscious programs where there is no invidious purpose or intent, or where they are aimed at offsetting the consequences of our long tragic history of discrimination, and achieving greater racial equity."

But Cox could get no further. "Mr. Cox," interposed Justice Stevens, "may I interrupt you with a question that's always troubled me? It's the use of the term 'invidious,' which I've always had difficulty really understanding. You suggested, in response to Mr. Justice Rehnquist, that if the number were 50 rather than 16, there would be a greater risk of a finding of invidious purpose. How does one—how does a judge decide when to make such a finding?"

Cox: "If Your Honor is asking me what do I mean by 'invidious,' I mean primarily stigmatizing, marking as inferior, shutting out of participation."

Justice Stevens persisted: "Mr. Cox, let me make my question a little more precise. Can you give me a test which would differentiate the case of 50 students from the case of 16 students?"

Cox: "Well, if the finding is that this was reasonably adapted to the purpose of increasing the number of minority doctors, and that it was not an arbitrary, capricious, selfish setting—and that would have to be decided in the light of the other medical schools in the state and the needs in the state; but if it's solidly based, then I would say 50 was permissible."

Toward the end of Cox's allotted time, the Chief Justice asked, "Are you going to address the question of other alternatives, Mr. Cox?"

To this, Cox replied, "In our view, the other alternatives suggested simply won't work."

Any program which did not take race into account, Cox asserted, would not succeed. "If we are talking about realities, race is a fact; it is something that all kinds of social feelings,contacts, a vision of one's opportunity, are related to. And if one is going to meaningfully direct these programs in social objectives, it is simply stultifying to disregard a reality that we hope will stop having significance in these areas, and which will have more— and which we have a best chance of depriving of its present unfortunate significance if these programs are permitted to continue and succeed."

The Justice who has been quoted has said that Cox's argument was "very good." He went on to say, "In my opinion, he faltered only once." That came midway through Cox's presentation, when Justice Stevens interposed: "Mr. Cox, may I ask you a question? The trial court found a violation of Title VI of the 1964 Civil Rights Act. Do you think we have to consider the Title VI question before getting to the constitutional question?"

Cox: "No, because the Supreme Court of California ruled only on the federal Constitution, and I would think the other questions were not before this Court."

According to my informant, Cox was "apparently unprepared for this question" and he "attempted to argue that it would be improper for the Court to affirm on a ground that had not been the basis for the judgment below. When the members of the Court expressed skepticism, Cox went on to observe that, while Davis was subject to Title VI, there were a number of unresolved questions that the parties had not focused upon. He mentioned in particular the question whether Title VI could be privately enforced."

Cox's responses, the Justice I have been quoting tells us, "did nothing to dissuade those who were inclined to consider an affirmance on statutory grounds." Looking back at it, says the Justice, "Although I doubt, in retrospect, that it would have made any difference, Cox, I think, would have done better if he had argued the paramount importance of the consti-

tutional question and noted that this Court had, in comparable circumstances, e.g., the *Arlington Heights* case[15] from the 1976 term, declined to
consider nonconstitutional grounds which had not been relied upon in
support of the lower court's judgment."

As will be seen in the next chapter, Cox's inadequate Title VI answer
gave the Justices no help on the statutory issue. The same was true of the
responses given by the other two attorneys to questions on the matter. The
Solicitor General also indicated that the Court should not address the Title
VI issue and counsel for Bakke was unclear in his answers to the Justices'
questions on the matter.

After Cox had finished, Mr. McCree, in the Solicitor General's traditional morning coat, rose and addressed the Court. His performance, the
same Justice has said, "was only fair." This assessment stemmed in part
from the fact that McCree spent much of his time defending the Government's assertion[16] that the case should be remanded for consideration of
whether Asian-Americans should have been included in the special admissions program—an issue that was largely irrelevant to the *Bakke* decision.

On the principal issue in the case, McCree urged "this Court to reject the
holding of the Supreme Court of California, that race or other minority
status may not constitutionally be employed in affirmative action and
special admissions programs, properly designed and tailored to eliminate
discrimination against racial and ethnic minorities as such discrimination
exists today, or to help overcome the effects of past years of discrimination."

The Chief Justice interjected, "Mr. Solicitor General, is there any evidence in this record that this University, its Medical School at Davis, has
ever engaged in any exclusion or discrimination on the basis of race?"

McCree had to concede, "There is no evidence in the record that this
University has, and, indeed, I would be surprised to have found it, according to the state of this record." However, the Solicitor General declared,
"the school need not be restricted to eliminating the effects of its own acts of
discrimination, but may take into account society's discrimination, because
of the pervasiveness of its impact."

McCree, himself only the nation's second black Solicitor General,[17]
stressed "the extent and duration of racial discrimination in America,"
which "continues until the present day." Indeed, he noted in an untypically
eloquent passage, "many children born in 1954, when *Brown*[18] was decided, are today, 23 years later, the very persons knocking on the doors of

professional schools, seeking admission, about the country. They are persons who, in many instances, have been denied the fulfillment of the promise of that decision because of resistance to this Court's decision that was such a landmark when it was handed down." In such a situation, "to be blind to race today is to be blind to reality."

The last to speak at the argument was Bakke's lawyer, Reynold Colvin. Arguing his first case before the Court, Colvin was, as the Justice who has been quoted put it, "plainly in over his head. In view of the importance of the case, this was unfortunate. However, he did provide us with comic relief." What happened was summarized by the Justice: Colvin "began his argument by explaining, at great length, that he was Alan Bakke's lawyer, and by summarizing all the steps that were taken to commence the lawsuit. After three or four minutes of these essential [sic] irrelevancies, Bill Rehnquist interrupted and brought down the house" with the observation, "But no one is charging you with laches here, Mr. Colvin."

"Undaunted," the Justice goes on, Colvin continued to treat the Justices like a trial jury and belabored "the undisputed facts concerning the operation of the program." Finally, Justice Powell, normally the most courteous Virginia gentleman, could stand it no longer. He interrupted Colvin and pointed out that "the basic facts" were neither denied nor disputed. "We are here," Powell caustically commented, "—at least I am here—primarily to hear a constitutional argument. You have devoted twenty minutes to laboring the facts,[19] if I may say so. I would like help; I really would, on the constitutional issues. Would you address that."

"Colvin then," according to the Justice who was my source, "turned to the constitutional merits, doing the best he could. But that proved to be very poor indeed." At one point, this Justice notes, "I heard Byron White whisper 'this is unbelievable' and I did not disagree."

One who reads the argument transcript is bound to conclude that the Justice's comments about Bakke's counsel are not overdrawn. After the argument, the Justice learned that several of the amici who supported Bakke had tried to persuade Colvin to allow Philip B. Kurland, an eminent law professor, to use some of his argument time, but Colvin had refused.

Colvin found himself in a corner throughout his presentation because of his constant assertion that any consideration of race in the admissions process was invalid: "to the extent that the preference is on the basis of the race, we believe that it is an unconstitutional advantage." Moreover, declared Colvin, the 16 seats set aside by Davis constituted an invalid racial quota. Justice Marshall, the one black Justice and the man who, as NAACP counsel had successfully argued the *Brown* school segregation case,[20] asked, "Now, would your argument be the same if one, instead of sixteen seats, were left open?"

Colvin replied: "Numbers are unimportant. It is the principle of keeping a man out because of his race that is important."

This led to the following colloquy:

Mr. Justice Marshall: "You are arguing about keeping somebody out and the other side is arguing about getting somebody in."
Mr. Colvin: "That's right."
Mr. Justice Marshall: "So it depends on which way you look at it doesn't it? . . .
Mr. Colvin: "If I may finish. The problem——"
Mr. Justice Marshall: "You are talking about your client's rights. Don't these underprivileged people have some rights?"
Mr. Colvin: "They certainly have the right to compete——"
Mr. Justice Marshall: "To eat cake."

After Colvin sat down, Cox spent some minutes on a brief rebuttal. He stressed: (1) "that there is no per se rule of color-blindness incorporated in the Equal Protection Clause"; (2) "that the educational, professional and social purposes accomplished by a race-conscious admissions program are compelling objectives, or to put it practically, they are sufficient justifications for those losses, those problems, that are created by the use of race"; and (3) "we submit that there is no other way of accomplishing those purposes."

Cox ended with a plea that the courts not become the supervisors of admissions policies. "I think," he declared, "if you set a lot of rules that would draw the federal courts into scrutinizing the details of what is done would invite constant litigation and, as I say, it would abandon a source of creativity. It would destroy important autonomy, in wrestling with which I and, I am sure all, the Court recognize is an extraordinarily sensitive and difficult problem, but a search for justice for all to which this country has always been committed, and which I am sure it still is."

At this, the Chief Justice leaned forward and said, "Thank you, gentlemen, the case is submitted."

"Whereupon," the official transcript concludes, "at 11:58 o'clock, A.M., the oral argument in the above-entitled matter was concluded."

NOTES

1. DeFunis v. Odegaard, 416 U.S. 312, 349 (1974), supra p. 32.
2. 429 U.S. 1090 (1977).
3. 429 U.S. 953 (1976).
4. 430 U.S. 144, 170 (1977), supra p. 14.
5. 430 U.S. 313, 318 (1977).
6. UJO v. Carey, 430 U.S. 144 (1977); Morton v. Mancari, 417 U.S. 535 (1974); Califano v. Webster, 430 U.S. 313 (1977).
7. Infra p. 47.
8. Government brief, p. 6.
9. Id. p. 79.
10. Osborne, "White House—Carter's Brief," *New Republic*, March 15, 1977, p. 13, from which much of the account in the text is derived.
11. Ibid.
12. Ibid.
13. Brown v. Board of Education, 347 U.S. 483 (1954).
14. Quotations from the argument are taken from the transcript and 46 *U.S. Law Week* 3249–56.
15. Arlington Heights v. Metropolitan Housing, 429 U.S. 252 (1977).
16. Government brief, pp. 75–76.
17. Justice Marshall had, of course, been the first.
18. Supra note 13.
19. The transcript reads "a fact," but this seems erroneous.
20. Supra note 13.

FIVE

Title VI and First Conference

Lᴵᴷᴱ the reports of Mark Twain's death, the typical reports on the value of Supreme Court oral argument are greatly exaggerated. True, virtually everyone who has written on the subject, including the Justices themselves, have stressed the importance of the argument to the Court's decision process. A lifetime's study of the high bench has, however, convinced me that the principal purpose of the argument before the Justices is a public-relations one—to communicate to the country that the Court has given each side an open opportunity to be heard. Thus not only is justice done, but it is also publicly seen to be done.

But the cases are rare where the arguments of counsel—brilliant though they may appear to the courtroom audience—really influence the decision in an important case. The oral argument in *Bakke* itself well illustrates this point. It may be doubted that the statements by counsel there played any part in the Court's decision process. Without question, Professor Cox was far more effective than the other two attorneys who argued. Bakke's lawyer, as just seen, was strikingly inept in his presentation. Yet it is all but certain that the argument itself did not influence one vote on the Court. On the important issue of Title VI, indeed, the unhelpful answers of counsel led the Justices to seek additional briefs on the matter.

FOCUS ON TITLE VI

"In spite of prodding from the Bench," asserted an October 13 letter from the Chief Justice to Justice White, "we did not get much help from the parties on the Title VI issue." As seen in the last chapter, counsel for Bakke did not respond to the Justices' queries on the matter and Professor Cox and the Solicitor General both urged the Court not to address the Title VI issue. At the conclusion of the argument, Justice Brennan, for one, did not believe that there would be any sentiment among the Justices—even among those who opposed the Davis program—to consider the Title VI issue seriously. The day after the argument, however, it was common knowledge among the law clerks that Justice Stevens was devoting his attention to Title VI and that several other Justices had directed their clerks to do research on the statute.

Among the latter was Justice Brennan, who had concluded from the flurry of activity on the matter that Title VI would, indeed, be a major issue before the Justices. Brennan was one of those who had a clerk look into Title VI. His preliminary investigation suggested that, (1) though a private right of action could be inferred under Title VI, (2) Title VI would not forbid a bona fide affirmative action program if the Constitution permitted it. The clerk stressed that regulations promulgated under Title VI explicitly authorized affirmative action and the legislative history indicated that Congress never intended to prohibit it. The clerk's research confirmed Justice Brennan's own view—that Title VI would be no more restrictive than the Constitution.

When they arrived at the conference room on October 14, the Friday after the *Bakke* argument, the Justices knew that the first conference on the case would focus on Title VI even more than the constitutional issue. It was also known that some of the Justices intended to move that the Court request supplemental briefs on Title VI.

WHITE'S MEMORANDUM

The day before the conference, the Justices received a three-page single-spaced MEMORANDUM FOR THE CONFERENCE from Justice White. "Although not in accord with practice," the memo began, "I thought I would spare you listening to what I would initially say about the *Bakke* case in conference tomorrow in the event I was not dissuaded by the views of those who precede me."

The White memo first of all stated his disagreement with the argument in some of the *amici* briefs that Bakke had no standing to attack the Davis program. "His claim is that he was disqualified for racial reasons from competing for the 16 seats reserved for the task force program. It is not that his application should have been considered by the task force committee but that there should not have been a racially discriminatory special program at all and that the 16 seats should have been filled through the general admissions procedure. Bakke is entitled to have this claim adjudicated."

The memo then referred to "suggestions in one or more briefs *amici* that the task force program is *required* by the Fourteenth Amendment as a remedy for past discrimination against minorities in this country." White categorically stated, "I do not accept that position." As the Justice saw it, "The California Supreme Court declared that the Fourteenth Amendment *forbids* the special program and the validity of that conclusion seems to be the constitutional issue tendered by the University."

The major part of the White memo was devoted to the Title VI issue. It referred to Bakke's claim "that he is entitled to his judgment because the task force program is forbidden by Title VI of the Civil Rights Act." Even though the California Supreme Court did not decide that issue, wrote White, "We are at least *entitled* to consider the statutory ground which Bakke requests; and because we usually prefer to deal with a possibly dispositive statutory ground before reaching a constitutional issue, I think we *should* deal with the Title VI argument."

White then referred to the argument "by some of the *amici* that Title VI and the regulations under it *require* precisely what the University has done," as well as the position of the Government "that federal statutory policy at least *authorizes* affirmative action programs taking race into account in admitting students even though this may result in preempting some seats on the basis of race." In the Justice's view, "If either of these positions is valid, the Congress has expressly or implicitly asserted that the Fourteenth Amendment does not bar racial preference in university admissions. For some, perhaps, this would be an important consideration in resolving the Fourteenth Amendment issue." White supported this statement by citing *Katzenbach* v. *Morgan*,[1] where the Court had construed Congressional power to enforce the Fourteenth Amendment most broadly to include even the power to expand the substantive scope of the Equal Protection Clause.

White next went into the merits of the Title VI issue. He began with a dig at the Government's performance at the argument. "Despite the position of the United States," wrote White, "whatever that might be, I doubt that Bakke's statutory claim is frivolous." On the contrary, the memo went on, "It is just not that clear that a statute which on its face forbids racial exclusions from government sponsored programs nevertheless permits or requires exclusions based on race."

White then indicated his view on additional briefs. "Before concluding that national statutory policy is to authorize racially preferential admissions policies in universities, I would want as much help from the parties as possible. The difficulty is that the University has not briefed the issue, and Bakke's brief is quite inadequate. . . . I think we should call for further briefs on the Title VI issue."

In a trenchant paragraph toward the end of his memo, Justice White summarized his overall view of the case: "If we were to decide that Title VI forbids what the University is doing, this particular case would be over. Congress has simply forbidden something that the Fourteenth Amendment might permit. If on the other hand we were to decide that Congress has authorized racially sensitive admissions policies, then the constitutional issue must be reached. Against such a statutory background, I would reverse the Fourteenth Amendment judgment of the Supreme Court of California. I agree with Bakke that he has been excluded from competing for the 16 seats on racial grounds; but as I see it the state interests are sufficiently important to warrant the preference, and there are no satisfactory alternatives for achieving the University's goals. Nor do I—although I am not adamant about it—see much difference between the open reservation of seats for minorities at issue here and a 'racially sensitive' program which in the end would often make race the determinative factor in administering a seemingly neutral set of qualifications."

On the other hand, the memo concluded, the Court could find that Title VI was not determinative and deal with the constitutional question. "Conceivably we could decide that the federal statutes and regulations neither forbid, require nor authorize what the Medical School has done. This would bring us to the constitutional issue unencumbered by and without guidance from congressional action. In that event, it is probable, but I'm not sure, that I would arrive at the same conclusion."

BURGER'S AND POWELL'S RESPONSES

"For me," Justice White declared at one point in his memo, "these are not easy conclusions to come to, to say the least." Presumably, every member of the Court agreed with this statement, as shown by the intense activity that went on in all the chambers throughout the *Bakke* decision process.

After he had read White's memo, the Chief Justice sent its author a brief letter, also dated October 13. Copies were received by the other Justices the next morning just before they left for the conference. "I have your memorandum of today," the Burger letter began. The Chief Justice stated that he thought that "there may be some sentiment to ask the parties to brief this." The letter concluded with a sentence stating, "The language of the statute bears rather startling resemblance to the situation presented by this case." This indicated that Burger might be willing to affirm on the basis of Title VI alone.

The next morning, Friday, October 14, shortly after the Justices entered the conference room, they received a three-page MEMORANDUM TO THE CONFERENCE from Justice Powell, which, he wrote, "is prompted by Byron's suggestion that we consider special briefing or a remand [on]² Title VI. I would oppose this suggestion." In Powell's view, "the arguments on both sides of the Fourteenth Amendment issue are as fully developed as they will ever be. Any action by us that may be perceived as ducking this issue for the second time in three years would be viewed by many as a 'self-inflicted wound' on the Court."

The Powell memo asserted that additional briefing was not necessary since "my brief Chambers' check of the law indicates that the Howard University amicus brief about covers the field." In addition, the memo stated, "If a majority of the Court is of the opinion that Title VI at least does not forbid this program, then sending it back or requiring rebriefing would be futile as a practical matter." That was true because "one's view of what is permitted under the statute is almost certain to be the same as one's opinion of the reach of the Fourteenth Amendment. If the prevailing sentiment is that the Equal Protection Clause permits the special program, the same conclusion almost certainly will be reached under Title VI. Thus, the constitutional issue would not be avoided."

"On the other hand," Powell went on, "a decision that Title VI forbids the program, made merely to avoid a decision that the Fourteenth Amendment may permit it, would be futile. Futile, because the next case will present the Fourteenth Amendment issue anyway. It also may seem irrational because if one really believes that special preferences are permissible under the Fourteenth Amendment, there seems to be no reason to reach a different result under a similarly Delphic Title VI."

As Powell saw it, the Court should not try to take the easy way out by seeking to avoid the constitutional issue. Since Title VI and the Fourteenth Amendment had the same substantive content, a decision on the one would necessarily be a decision on the other. "In sum," the Powell memo concluded, "a holding either way on Title VI almost surely will presage quite clearly the Court's views on the constitutional issue."

FIRST CONFERENCE

The first *Bakke* conference began soon after Powell's memo was distributed on Friday morning, October 14. The conference room itself was a large rectangular chamber at the rear of the Court building, behind the courtroom. One of the longer walls had two windows facing Second Street. The other, with a door in the middle, was covered with bookshelves containing reports of decisions of the Supreme Court and federal courts of appeals, as well as copies of the *United States Code* and *U.S. Code Annotated*. Along one of the shorter walls was a fireplace, above which hung a Gilbert Stuart portrait of Chief Justice John Marshall in his robes. To the left of the portrait was a forest painting by John F. Carlson. On the opposite wall hung two landscapes by Lily Cushing, a beach scene and another forest scene. Chief Justice Burger told me that he originally had these paintings hung for Justice Douglas, always noted for his love of the outdoors.

In the center of the conference room ceiling was an ornate crystal chandelier, and at one end of the room stood a table around which the Justices sat, with the Chief Justice at the head and the others ranged in order of seniority, the most senior opposite the Chief, the next at the Chief's right, the next at the Senior Associate's right, and so on. In the ceiling above the chandelier were bright fluorescent lights—one of the improvements installed by Chief Justice Burger.

In his October 13 letter to Justice White, the Chief Justice had stressed the importance of the Title VI issue: "I have spent considerable time in the last few days on the Title VI matter and expect to devote some time to it in my opening summary tomorrow."

At the conference itself Burger's emphasis on Title VI set the theme for the discussion that followed. The Justices were sharply divided both on the effect of Title VI and the need for additional briefs. The strongest view on Title VI was stated by Justice Stevens. He announced that he was of the tentative view that Title VI prohibited the Davis program. He said that the statutory language seemed so clear that resort to legislative history was inappropriate, but he also believed that the legislative history supported his interpretation.

The conference voted five (the Chief Justice and Justices White, Black-mun, Rehnquist, and Stevens) to four (Justices Brennan, Stewart, Marshall, and Powell) in favor of further briefing. Though the point was raised, there was no sentiment for scheduling a reargument on the matter. The conference closed with the Chief Justice's suggestion that the chambers of each Justice should share research with the others and exchange views on the case.

NOTES

1. 384 U.S. 641 (1966).
2. The original reads "in," but this is clearly an error.

SIX

The Right Takes the Lead

IN a 1986 speech, Justice Blackmun analyzed the divisions within the Supreme Court. As he saw it, there were three principal blocs among the Justices. "I had always put on the left," he said, Justices Brennan and Marshall. "Five of us," he noted, were "in the middle"—referring to Justices Stewart, White, Powell, Stevens, and himself. On the right, according to Blackmun, were the Chief Justice and Justice Rehnquist.[1]

Few would disagree with this analysis, particularly so far as the Justices at the two extremes are concerned. Now, in the *Bakke* case, it was the two on the right who took the lead after the conference. Both the Chief Justice and Justice Rehnquist circulated memoranda giving their views on how the case should be decided and their memos dealt with the constitutional merits, though the Burger memo also discussed the Title VI issue on which the conference had largely focused.

Before the Burger and Rehnquist memos were circulated, there were several other developments. On October 17, the Court issued an order directing each party in *Bakke* to submit, within thirty days, a supplemental brief "discussing Title VI of the Civil Rights Act of 1964 as it applies to this case."[2] While they were waiting for the supplemental briefs on Title VI to arrive, the Justices exchanged views on issues in the case.

As already stated, the memoranda exchange began with memos circulated by the Chief Justice and Justice Rehnquist. Mention should, however, also be made of two less important memos circulated by Justice

Stevens on October 19. They were largely follow-ups to the Justice's conference presentation on Title VI. Stevens's first memo argued that the statutory question had to be addressed and suggested that the case be remanded to the California Supreme Court with instructions to decide whether Title VI barred the program—a suggestion which received no support from any member of the Court and was soon abandoned by its author. The second Stevens memo was by his law clerk. It dealt with both the substantive reach of Title VI and the issue of whether a right of action could be inferred. On both points, the memo supported the view Justice Stevens had stated at the conference.

BURGER MEMORANDUM

On October 21, a week after the conference, a more significant MEMO-RANDUM TO THE CONFERENCE was circulated by the Chief Justice (Appendix A). Headed "CONFIDENTIAL," this memo of six single-spaced pages was really an outline for an opinion affirming the decision below. It is of particular interest as a statement by the Chief Justice of his view of the case—particularly since he ultimately issued no opinion in *Bakke*. "I have," the Burger memo began, "made a tentative and preliminary analysis of what this case appears to be at the present stage." He had, the Chief Justice went on, acted "on the assumption that a way can be found to affirm the decision of the California Supreme Court without putting the states, their universities, or any education institutions in a straitjacket on the matter of broader based admissions programs."

The Chief Justice then rejected the notion that the courts could do more than act negatively in such a case. As the memo put it, "Establishing fixed ground rules for educators is not the business of courts except when, as in desegregation cases, we are confronted with a pattern of affirmative *de jure* conduct, based exclusively on race. We have far more competence to say what cannot be done than what ought to be done."

Despite the reference to desegregation cases as an exception to this negative approach, the Chief Justice had tried to adopt the same negative posture in his Court's most important desegregation case—the *Swann* school busing case in the 1970 term.[3] His draft opinion there had asserted that any guidelines the Court could fashion in that case would be "inescapably negative." The Chief Justice had eliminated this negative approach in

Swann only when it met with strong opposition from the Justices—and then only in his third draft opinion in the case.[4]

In his *Bakke* memorandum, the Chief Justice next referred to the objectives of the Davis program. "The Regents," the memo conceded, "adopted this program to accomplish a number of commendable, long-range objectives." But that did not mean the program had to be upheld, since, "as presently structured, the program is one of the more extreme methods of securing those objectives." That was true because "The program excluded Bakke from the medical school on the basis of race and this is not disputed. I am open to being shown how, consistent with the prior decisions of the Court, we can escape the significance of this fact." This last sentence hardly indicated a readiness to uphold the Davis program.

Instead, the problem, as the Burger memo saw it, was the "tactical" one "of how best to structure and shape a result so as to confine its impact and yet make it clear that the Court intends to leave states free to serve as 'laboratories' for experimenting with less rigidly exclusionary methods of pursuing desirable social goals."[5] The Chief Justice wrote that "My inclination at this point is" to favor a negative decision striking down the Davis program, without indicating affirmatively what type of program would pass constitutional muster—"to emphasize the particularly troubling aspects of the Regents' Program and the difficult statutory and constitutional problems they raise, but to go only a little beyond that point in addressing the question of what alternatives might be devised."

Burger concluded the first part of his memo with a summary of the "basic facts" in the case, which he asserted, were not disputed:

(1) Bakke was not allowed to compete for any of the 16 seats reserved for the Regents' Program solely because of his race.

(2) Bakke's individual qualifications were such that he would have been admitted if all 100 seats had been open and free from any arbitrary exclusion based on race.

(3) The university evaluated minority applicants as a separate group and did not compare their individual qualities with those of other applicants.

STANDARD OF REVIEW

The second part of the Burger memo was headed STANDARD OF REVIEW. "The first question for the Court," it began, "is what level of scrutiny should be applied in this case." For the reader to understand this issue of the proper standard of review, a word must be said about the standards developed by the Supreme Court. Justice Holmes once characterized the Equal Protection Clause as "the usual last resort of constitutional arguments."[6] That was true because, when Holmes wrote, judicial scrutiny of governmental action challenged on equal protection grounds was normally governed by the traditional rational-basis test.

The rational-basis test is an extremely deferential one, requiring only that the classification at issue have a reasonable basis in fact and that it "rest upon some ground of difference having a fair and substantial relation to [the] object of the legislation."[7] The Court need determine only that the particular classification was the product of a rational legislative choice.[8] Under the rational-basis test, "it is only the invidious discrimination, the wholly arbitrary act, which cannot stand."[9] Virtually all laws emerge untouched from such scrutiny: The rationality test, "when applied as articulated, leaves little doubt about the outcome; the challenged legislation is always upheld."[10]

Over the years, however, the Court had developed a stricter level of scrutiny to be applied in certain cases. In them, the mere showing that it is rationally related to a legitimate governmental objective is not enough to sustain a challenged classification. In those cases, the test of mere rationality gives way to one of strict scrutiny[11] under which the classification will be held to deny equal protection unless justified by a "compelling" governmental interest.[12] Strict scrutiny is required under the compelling-interest test when the classification (1) interferes with the exercise of a fundamental right; or (2) operates to the peculiar disadvantage of a suspect class.[13] The Court has said that these are the only equal protection cases where strict scrutiny, rather than review under the rational-basis test, is demanded.[14]

The suspect-classification concept is the one that is relevant to the *Bakke* case, on the basis of the proposition that, as Justice Brennan was to put it in his *Bakke* opinion, the Equal Protection Clause's "assertion of human equality is closely associated with the proposition that differences in color or creed, birth or status, are neither significant nor relevant to the way in which persons should be treated."[15] These differences should all be constitutionally irrelevant—mere accidents of birth or condition, which fade into insignificance in the face of our common humanity. To such differences, the law should remain blind, not distinguishing on the basis of who a person is, or what he is, or what he possesses. From this point of view, the best examples of suspect classifications are those based upon race, ancestry, alienage,[16] or indigency.[17]

When we say that a classification is suspect, we mean that it must be supported by a *compelling* state interest or it violates equal protection no matter how reasonably it may seem related to a legitimate public purpose. This may be seen from cases involving classifications based upon race. Racial and ethnic distinctions are inherently suspect and call for the most exacting judicial examination.[18] Governmental action that singles out members of a race for discriminatory treatment may not be justified upon the ground that it is reasonably related to maintenance of public order.[19] Similarly, a law that operates to curtail the legal activities of an organization formed to vindicate the rights of a racial minority may not be sustained, though it might otherwise be valid under the state's power to regulate the legal profession and improper solicitation of legal business.[20]

From this point of view, Chief Justice Burger was plainly correct when he asserted in his October 21 memo, "Although I have long been uneasy with the 'slogans' that have evolved in equal protection analysis, I think that the Court must give the very closest look possible—essentially 'strict scrutiny'—to any state action based on race. No member of this Court, so far as I recall, has ever had any question but that racial classifications are suspect under all circumstances."

But this assertion alone did not resolve the *Bakke* issue. Unlike the racial classifications condemned in previous cases, that in *Bakke* did not single out members of a minority for discriminatory purposes. Instead, so far as those favored under the Davis program were concerned, the racial classification was a protective one, designed to redress the inequality in educational opportunities that had prevented them from enjoying the real benefits of the equality guaranteed by the Constitution. Is a program based on racial classification equally "suspect" when its purpose is not discrimination against any minority, but "to remove the disparate racial impact"[21] that might otherwise exist in the given field?

An affirmative answer must be given to this question, according to the Chief Justice. Any other answer ignores the fact that however "benign" its purpose, a program such as the Davis program inevitably discriminates against members of the white majority. "I can find no principled basis," Burger asserted, "for holding that this program is exempt from close scrutiny because it only excludes members of the 'majority.' We cannot assume that individuals who appear to be part of a 'majority' have consented to racial discrimination against themselves." This was plainly true of Bakke, who never consented to the discrimination against him.

The Burger memo stressed "the 'no person' language of Title VI and the 'any person' language of the Fourteenth Amendment." Given this, the Chief Justice asserted, "I become confused by the glib attribution of either a benign or invidious purpose to an exclusionary classification solely on the basis of whether it appears to a reviewing court that minorities are favored thereby." Such an "analysis proceeds on the dubious assumption that minorities are readily identifiable 'blocs' which in some way function as units and are generally harmed or benefited in roughly the same degree by the same external forces such as social programs like the one at issue here. That is a superficial and problematic characterization of intent that does not satisfy me as the 'trigger' for one level or another of equal protection scrutiny."

This part of the Burger memo concluded by raising the question "whether the university's sound and desirable objectives provide sufficient justification for the rigid, plainly racial basis of the Regents' Program." The Burger answer was, "I do not think they do. The university desires to remedy the general effects of broad historic social discrimination, not discrimination by the university or by the state but by society at large, in and outside California."

At this point, the Chief Justice also expressed a doubt on whether the Davis program would achieve its goal—"to produce doctors who can and will serve areas and patients who currently lack adequate medical care, and to erode racial stereotypes."

"Parenthetically," the memo asserted on this point, "the program seems deficient in not *binding* the admittees *by contract* to carry out the commitment to serve the blighted, neglected areas. A contracted, five-year commitment is a familiar mechanism in other areas."

ALTERNATIVES

The next section of Burger's memo was entitled "Alternatives." It began with the assertion, "There are many ways that the University can pursue these goals short of completely excluding whites from competing for a certain number of places in its entering class." The defendants had argued that their program was the only practical way to accomplish their goal, but the Chief Justice rejected their claim. "On this record," Burger wrote, "I must reject the Regents' assertion that there are no realistic alternatives to their program. They can't *know* because they have not tried any alternatives."

The memo rejected the notion that it was for the Court to indicate what such alternatives might be. "The task of setting standards for admission to the medical school, I repeat, is beyond judicial competence." What the Court should do here was to provide "only the limited constraint imposed by a narrow affirmance here—that race *alone* can never be a permissible basis for excluding an applicant. *Brown I* settled that and I cannot believe anyone wants to retreat."

Next was a statement of the Chief Justice's belief that there were practical alternatives to the Davis program. "I am convinced," the memo stated, "that remedial educational programs can be devised to give 'disadvantaged' applicants an opportunity to compete successfully for admission to medical schools." The Chief Justice referred to a recent desegregation case as an illustration of what could be done. "In *Milliken II*, the Court endorsed special training for disadvantaged children whose 'habits of speech, conduct, and attitudes' reflect 'cultural isolation' from the mainstream of society. *Milliken* v. *Bradley*, 76–447, 45 L.W. 4873, 4879. Similar measures ought to be explored and might be applied in the context of higher education."[22]

The Chief Justice ended this section with the statement that he was "not convinced that the Court should forbid efforts to establish programs primarily for those who have sustained deprivations which closely correlate with race but might affect anyone isolated from the cultural mainstream." In such alternative programs, even race might be considered as a factor. "I am not ready to say now that in evaluating 'disadvantage' race may not be given some consideration." This was, of course, close to the view to be taken in Justice Powell's *Bakke* opinion, which received the support of a bare majority on this point, though not the Chief Justice.

DISPOSITION

The Burger memo's last section was headed "Disposition." "As of now," it began, "I would say only that this rigidly cast admissions program is impermissible on this record because it does precisely what has long been condemned by this Court—it excludes applicants on the basis of race. On this record there is nothing to suggest any inquiry into alternatives was made. I simply cannot believe the Regents' frankly race-based program is the least offensive or least intrusive method of promoting an admittedly important state interest."

The memo now turned from the constitutional to the statutory issue. Burger's conclusion here was that "the Regents' program surely appears to be in plain conflict with the explicit language of Title VI." That was true because the constitutional and statutory prohibitions were congruent. "Since the Fourteenth Amendment and Title VI are cast in similar terms except that Title VI is more specific and is a summary mechanism for federal regulation of its grants of money, I have some difficulty reading their respective prohibitions on racial discrimination differently."

Under this approach, the case should be decided under Title VI. "If, after receiving the requested briefs, we conclude that Bakke is covered under Title VI, it seems to me, as of now, that our long practice and policy has been to base our decision on the statutory ground."

But the crucial point which he intended to make in the memo, the Chief Justice continued, was that of "exploring the idea of a very narrow affirmance, making clear that other avenues are open." This meant that "we do not have to pass on the constitutionality of the possible alternative admissions programs. Acknowledging the plain and obvious proposition that there are other alternatives does not require us to bless them in advance."

The memo then returned to the possible consideration of race as an admissions factor. "For now," the Chief Justice wrote, "I would leave open whether and to what extent indirect consideration of race is compatible with constitutional or statutory proscriptions. I find that articulating this concept is far from easy but I am optimistic that a way can be found."

Again, however, the memo returned to its stress on the desirability of a narrow affirmance. "Confining ourselves to a narrow affirmance along these lines would seem both prudent and generally consistent with our traditional method of developing principled approaches to complex social issues through a case by case process rather than by wholesale, uninformed pronouncement."

Now came the peroration, which deserves a full quotation:

With all deference to the distinguished array of counsel who have been plunged into a very difficult case on a record any good lawyer would shun, I see no reason why we should let them (aided by the mildly hysterical media) rush us to judgment. The notion of putting this sensitive, difficult question to rest in one "hard" case is about as sound as trying to put all First Amendment issues to rest in one case.

Brown I[23] bears date May 17, 1954 and case by case evolution has followed up to our recent *Milliken II* last June.[24] I see no signs of abatement in the refinement process there.

If it is to take years to work out a rational solution to the current problem, so be it. That is what we are paid for.

REHNQUIST SUPPORTS THE CHIEF JUSTICE

The second step in the effort of the conservative Justices to take the lead in *Bakke* was a November 11 memorandum by Justice Rehnquist (Appendix B). Before it was circulated, an eleven-page memo had been sent around by Justice Marshall on October 28. The Justice wrote that it was prepared by one of his law clerks and analyzed the legislative history of Title VI. That memo had tried to show that, while ambiguous in many respects, portions of the legislative history specifically suggested that bona fide affirmative action programs were consonant with the statute.

I have been told that the Brennan law clerks had confidently predicted that Rehnquist would vote to uphold the Davis program. It is hard to see the basis for their belief, given Rehnquist's reflex toward the right in cases involving racial classifications. At any rate the Court community saw clearly where Rehnquist stood in *Bakke* when he circulated his November 11 memo expressing strong support for the Burger view that the Davis program was invalid.

The Rehnquist memo was accompanied by a brief covering letter. "As Byron said in his circulation just before our first Conference on the case," the letter stated, "it is not the 'usual practice,' but I think I have derived some benefit from his and other's subsequent written circulations." In addition, Rehnquist wrote, "I also think that some written comments before Conference on a case this complicated and multifaceted could save a lot of time in what is bound to be a long Conference discussion anyway."

The memo itself consisted of nineteen typed pages. The assertion at its beginning indicated clearly what the Justice's conclusion would be: "The University's admissions policy in this case seems to me to make its 'affirmative action' program as difficult to sustain constitutionally as one conceivably could be."

For him, Rehnquist wrote, "Two factual elements in particular stand out, and the Regents make no bones about them." First was the fact that "the limitation of the special admissions programs to blacks, Hispanics, native Americans, and other minorities is not simply a shorthand method of finding people who may have been 'culturally deprived' or 'disadvantaged' in such a way that, although they might be very good medical students or doctors, they would not do well on standardized tests." Instead, "the University's ultimate goal is to place additional members of these ethnic minorities in the medical school."

Justice Rehnquist then stated what he saw as the central goal of the equal protection guaranty. "I take it as a postulate that difference in treatment of individuals based on their race or ethnic origin is at the bull's eye of the target at which the Fourteenth Amendment's Equal Protection Clause was aimed." This did not necessarily mean that there might never be valid racial classifications. "I don't think the Court has ever held foursquare with the first Mr. Justice Harlan's view that the Constitution was 'color blind,' and therefore forbade every conceivable differentiation in treatment on the basis of race. But certainly the cases are too numerous to require citation that differentiation between individuals on this basis is 'suspect,' subject to 'strict scrutiny,' or whatever equivalent phrase one chooses to use."

"The second factual aspect of the program," the memo went on, "is that the actual individualized determination made by the University of who is admitted and who is excluded is, with respect to these sixteen seats, made to depend on racial or ethnic classifications." This fact, said Rehnquist, made *Bakke* "substantially different" from *UJO v. Carey*[25] (supra chapter 3). "There it was undisputed that the legislators, in making their decision, had taken race into account in redistricting for the New York legislature; the Court nevertheless upheld the redistricting statute, pointing out that no individual was deprived of the right to have his vote counted."

"I would think," Rehnquist wrote, "that most, if not all, legislators consider racial or ethnic factors in voting on bills that come before them." But that does not necessarily make laws passed by them invalid. "So long as the resulting statute does not make race or ethnic status the determining factor in whether an individual receives a benefit or is denied one, I don't think the Fourteenth Amendment speaks to these sort of deliberations." (Rehnquist did not explain why the redistricting in *UJO* that denied the Hasidim's ability to vote as a bloc did not deny a "benefit.")

The memo also asserted that the Davis program could not be brought under the holdings in *Swann v. Charlotte-Mecklenburg Board of Education*[26] and other school desegregation cases. Indeed, asserted Rehnquist,

"While it certainly cannot be said that we start with a clean slate, I find little in our previous cases upon which I would feel comfortable in resting if I were to uphold the Davis admissions program."

The Rehnquist memo then went into a subject it had already touched upon—the proper standard of review. "Need the Davis scheme pass only a rational basis equal protection test (which it clearly does—obtaining doctors to serve in ghetto areas is certainly a permissible state concern and the Davis system, though not perfectly tailored to that end, is close enough)? And, if more rigorous scrutiny is mandated, are the proffered justifications sufficiently 'compelling' to sustain the program?"

Justice Rehnquist agreed with the Chief Justice's conclusion that strict scrutiny was required in such a case. "I think," he wrote, "one can avoid strict scrutiny only if it is said that whites who are in the majority may not assert a claim for denial of equal protection by reason of a classification based on race. But I find that notion ultimately quite unsatisfying."

The Justice rejected "the view that the [Fourteenth] Amendment protects only members of a minority class." On the contrary, "I see nothing in our prior cases to suggest different Fourteenth Amendment analysis should be applied to Caucasians as opposed to members of minority groups."

CAROLENE FOOTNOTE

At this point the Rehnquist memo discussed the footnote in the 1938 *Carolene Products*[27] case, which has been considered one of the foundations of strict-scrutiny review. *Carolene Products* itself dealt with economic regulation, which is reviewed under the rational-basis test. However, in what has been called the "famous footnote four"[28] in his otherwise obscure opinion, Justice Stone questioned whether "more exacting judicial scrutiny" might not be appropriate in cases involving restrictions on the personal rights guaranteed by the Fourteenth Amendment. In particular, Stone asked "whether prejudice against discrete and insular minorities . . . may call for a correspondingly more searching judicial inquiry."[29]

It should be stated parenthetically for those concerned with the growing role of the law clerks in the drafting of opinions that the first draft of the footnote was written by one of Stone's law clerks. "The ideas originated with me," the clerk later recalled. Stone, he said, "adopted it almost as drafted."[30] The second most celebrated footnote in Supreme Court history[31]—upon which the strict scrutiny review standard has been based—was thus conceived and drafted by a law clerk, rather than the Justice in whose name the opinion was issued.

Justice Stone himself explained the note to Chief Justice Hughes, while the Justices were considering his *Carolene* opinion. "It seemed to me desirable," Stone wrote "to file a caveat in the note" to the rational-basis standard applied in "the ordinary run of . . . cases" for "these other more exceptional cases." What he was trying to state, Stone informed the Chief Justice, was "The notion that the Court should be more alert to protect constitutional rights in those cases where there is danger that the ordinary political processes for the correction of undesirable legislation may not operate."[32]

In his November 11 *Bakke* memo, Justice Rehnquist recognized that the proponents of the Davis program relied on the *Carolene* footnote's singling out of "discrete and insular minorities" to support the view that strict scrutiny was not required in cases involving action favoring such minorities. To Rehnquist, however, the *Carolene* doctrine could not be relied on to support the Davis program. "I do not think it has been held or even suggested that this doctrine lends support to the limitation of claims of racial discrimination to the non-Caucasian races."

Such a limitation would undercut the purpose of the equal protection prohibition. In Rehnquist's view, "The reason for this prohibition is not because minority ethnic and racial groups are the most frequent victims of such discrimination, although in fact they are; the reason for the prohibition is that classification of individuals on the basis of race is, except in the rarest of cases, not a permissible basis of governmental action."

MINORITIES, MAJORITIES, AND COMPELLING INTEREST

The equal protection prohibition, says Justice Rehnquist, was undoubtedly placed in the Constitution to prevent racial discrimination. "It was in order to make the principle that race is an invalid basis for differentiation among individuals secure against the vicissitudes of legislative pulling and hauling that it was put in the Constitution. The benefit to minorities resulting from placing it in the Constitution is that it prohibits the enactment of laws in violation of it which majority-dominated legislatures might otherwise be quite willing to enact."

But that did not mean that the constitutional protection was limited to racial minorities. As the Rehnquist memo saw it, "because its placement in the Constitution confers a benefit on minorities which 'majorities' do not need as much does not mean that on those occasions when a Caucasian dominated legislature chooses to discriminate against a Caucasian, the principle contained in the Equal Protection Clause does not likewise apply to that discrimination."

Since, in Rehnquist's view, this was to be treated as a case of racial discrimination, even though it was discrimination against the majority, the proper review standard was that of strict scrutiny. "Thus for me this is a case requiring 'strict scrutiny.'" This meant that the Court had to determine whether the Davis program was supported by a "compelling state interest." The Rehnquist memo expressed doubt about the usefulness of that phrase. "If by strict scrutiny we mean that sort of justification which will avail to sustain a racial classification such as this, the phrase 'compelling state interest' really asks the question rather than answers it, unless we are to revert simply to what Holmes called our own 'can't helps.'"

At any rate, Justice Rehnquist rejected the proffered goals as sufficient to support the Davis program. First of all, he wrote, "I am inclined to agree with the Chief that it would be very difficult to view as constitutionally sufficient most of the proffered non-race goals, such as more doctors in the ghetto. Not that these interests are illegitimate or unimportant, but by definition all are based on notions of administrative convenience and I think our cases indicate that under the rubric of 'strict scrutiny' it generally takes something more to justify a classification based on race." In addition, "as the Chief suggests, there are other, much less troubling methods of accomplishing these goals."

The same is true of "racial diversity in the student body rationale." Perhaps it would be desirable to have more members of racial minorities in the student body. "But I would think that the Fourteenth Amendment holds that for governmental purposes nobody 'has' anything simply by virtue of their race. Members of minority groups are not less valuable human beings simply because of their minority status and, it would seem to me, are not more valuable either."

That leaves "only the notion that past societal discrimination justifies these affirmative action programs." To Rehnquist, "This is not an unappealing rationale. But I ultimately think it also unacceptable."

Under the prior cases, says Rehnquist, race may be taken into consideration in implementing a remedy against past discrimination. "But these principles have thus far been limited in cases from this Court to remedying wrongs at the behest of identifiable victims of particular discriminatory practices." Consequently, "it should not be enough here for the state to say that the applicants admitted under the minority program were victims of generalized past discrimination." That is true because "the right not to be discriminated against is personal to the individual, and in this case Bakke's right to equal protection of the laws cannot be denied him simply because at some other place or at some other time minority group members have been discriminated against."

What the state is doing here is to treat "racial groups *en bloc* rather than individually. The state proposes to remedy past discrimination against blacks as a group by present discrimination in favor of individual blacks and against individual whites. Nothing in our cases . . . holds that this sort of practice is consistent with the Equal Protection Clause."

To Justice Rehnquist, remedial schemes like the Davis program "are based on assumptions that are, in my opinion, impermissible predicates for governmental action in light of the Fourteenth Amendment." They assume that every minority applicant has been discriminated against. "While it is clear," Rehnquist asserts, "that every person who has suffered racial discrimination on account of being a member of a minority is, by definition, a member of a minority, I am unwilling to agree that every member of a minority has been discriminated against, in the sense that under the Fourteenth Amendment it is permissible for the state to provide a remedy. The fit between the two groups (members of minority groups and persons who have been discriminated against on account of membership in a minority group) is far from exact and thus an insufficient basis for use of racial classifications."

Justice Rehnquist, then made an interesting comparison between *Bakke* and *Buckley v. Valeo*[33] where the Court struck down Congressional limitations on campaign spending by candidates from their own funds as violative of their First Amendment rights. "I think," Rehnquist wrote, "there is some resemblance in the argument of petitioners and the *amici* who support it to the Court of Appeals' opinion in *Buckley v. Valeo*, which we largely rejected when we decided that case. The Court of Appeals there, it seemed to me, appeared to say that in order to achieve the 'compelling state interest' of allowing everybody to be heard to some extent, Congress did not abridge the First Amendment by preventing some people from talking as much as they wanted."

The Rehnquist memo gave the Justice's reaction to this approach and its counterpart in *Bakke*. "This seemed to me like something out of George Orwell, or like Rousseau's idea that people would be forced to be free, and I have something of the same feeling, though perhaps to a lesser extent, about the idea that discrimination based on race can be justified because the opposite type of discrimination has been and probably still is practiced in other places."

"In short," the Rehnquist memo summed up, "I don't think the Davis plan is valid under the Equal Protection Clause of the Fourteenth Amendment." It then discussed the question also raised in the Chief Justice's memo (which was to acquire such importance under Justice Powell's *Bakke* opinion)—that of "whether even though race may not be used as the sole factor, it may be used as one of a number of factors." Rehnquist stated that he would "certainly reserve the question," but went on to say, "I think it would probably be difficult under the foregoing line of reasoning to allow express consideration of race as a substantial factor at all." He supported this conclusion by reference to a case where the Court struck down a Louisiana law requiring the race of candidates to appear opposite their names on the ballot.[34] "What if," Rehnquist asked, "in addition to race, Louisiana had required the listing of six additional factors which were at least arguably relevant to a voter's decision as to which candidate should be elected? Would the law then have been upheld?"

The Rehnquist memo ended with the statement, "Since we are awaiting briefs on Title VI, and the sort of research that has been done in Thurgood's and John's chambers has not been done in mine, I withhold judgment on that question."

NOTES

1. *N.Y. Times*, March 8, 1986, p. 7.
2. 434 U.S. 900 (1977).
3. Swann v. Charlotte-Mecklenburg Board of Education, 402 U.S. 1 (1971).
4. See Schwartz, Swann's *Way: The School Busing Case and the Supreme Court* 116, 147 (1986).
5. The Chief Justice was referring here to the famous Brandeis passage in New State Ice Co. v. Liebmann, 285 U.S. 262, 311 (1932), which had been quoted earlier in the Burger memo.
6. Buck v. Bell, 274 U.S. 200, 208 (1927).
7. Reed v. Reed, 404 U.S. 71, 76 (1972).

8. Alexander v. Fioto, 434 U.S. 634, 640 (1977).
9. New Orleans v. Dukes, 427 U.S. 298, 303–304 (1976).
10. Massachusetts Board v. Murgia, 427 U.S. 307, 319 (1976) (dissent).
11. Id. at 318.
12. Shapiro v. Thompson, 394 U.S. 618, 658 (1969) (dissent).
13. Massachusetts Board v. Murgia, 427 U.S. 307, 312 (1976).
14. Ibid. But compare Craig v. Boren, 429 U.S. 190 (1976) (intermediate level of scrutiny in sexual classification cases).
15. 438 U.S. at 355.
16. These three classifications are listed as suspect in Massachusetts Board v. Murgia, 427 U.S. 307, 313 (1976).
17. San Antonio School District v. Rodriguez, 411 U.S. 1, 61 (1973).
18. Regents v. Bakke, 438 U.S. at 291, per Powell, J.
19. Wright v. Georgia, 373 U.S. 284, 293 (1963); Cooper v. Aaron, 358 U.S. 1, 16 (1958).
20. NAACP v. Button, 371 U.S. 415 (1963).
21. Regents v. Bakke, 438 U.S. at 369, per Brennan, J.
22. Milliken v. Bradley, 433 U.S. 267 (1977).
23. Brown v. Board of Education, 347 U.S. 483 (1954).
24. Supra note 22.
25. 430 U.S. 144 (1977).
26. 402 U.S. 1 (1971).
27. United States v. Carolene Products Co., 304 U.S. 144 (1938).
28. So characterized in Mason, "The Core of Free Government, 1938–40," 65 *Yale Law Journal* 597, 598 (1956).
29. 304 U.S. 144, at 152, n.4.
30. Mason, *Harlan Fiske Stone: Pillar of the Law* 513 (1956).
31. The most celebrated footnote was in Brown v. Board of Education, 347 U.S. 483, 494, n.11 (1954). The Brown footnote 11 was also drafted by a law clerk. See Schwartz, The *Unpublished Opinions of the Warren Court* 459 (1985).
32. Mason, supra note 30, at 514.
33. 424 U.S. 1 (1976).
34. Anderson v. Martin, 375 U.S. 399 (1964).

SEVEN

Powell's Draft Opinion

I~N~ Justice Blackmun's analysis of the Justices summarized at the beginning of the last chapter,[1] two were at either extreme and five "in the middle." The votes of those at the two extremes were clearly predictable in a case such as *Bakke*. The Chief Justice and Justice Rehnquist would vote to strike down the Davis program and their memoranda discussed in the last Chapter confirmed their positions in this respect. Similarly, Justices Brennan and Marshall could be expected to vote to uphold the Davis program.

This meant that the crucial *Bakke* votes would be cast by the center Justices. In this respect *Bakke* bears out the conclusion stated some years ago by Justice Blackmun that there was a "centrist balance" in the Burger Court, with the decisions usually turning on the votes of the center Justices.[2]

Of the Justices "in the middle," two had indicated what their votes would be. Justice White has tended to vote more with the conservative Justices than with Justices Brennan and Marshall—with one important exception. As explained by Justice Blackmun in 1986, "One gets into racial problems . . . and Byron is distinctly to the left of center. I think it's the old John F. Kennedy influence, if you like."[3]

White's October 13 memorandum (supra p. 57) indicated that the Justice would follow his normal voting pattern and come down in favor of the Davis program and "would reverse the . . . judgment of the Supreme

Court of California." Justice Stevens, on the other hand, had announced at the conference that, in his view, Title VI prohibited the Davis program. Though he stated that this was only his "tentative" view, it foreshadowed a vote against the Davis program.

A decision either way would need the votes of two of the remaining three Justices—Justices Stewart, Blackmun, and Powell. At this point, they had given no indication of how they would vote. As will be seen in the next chapter, however, Justice Stewart would announce at the next *Bakke* conference his strong opposition to the Davis program. On the other hand, those who were pro-Davis hoped for the support of Justice Blackmun. Though Blackmun was not to make his view on the case known until the following May, his law clerks had told Brennan's clerks months earlier that he would vote with their Justice.

This left the deciding vote up to Justice Powell. No one could predict with confidence how he would come down in the case. His October 14 memorandum (supra p. 60) had urged only that the Court should not avoid the constitutional issue; it had not indicated what his position was on its merits.

POWELL'S MEMORANDUM OPINION

The Justices had not yet met in conference to discuss the merits in *Bakke*. All they had done thus far was to deal with Title VI and request supplemental briefs on that issue. At the October 14 conference, however, the Chief Justice had suggested that the Justices exchange their views through memoranda circulated even before the conference on the merits. The Burger and Rehnquist October 21 and November 11 memos (supra pp. 64, 71) had begun the exchange even before the Title VI briefs had been submitted. Those briefs arrived on November 16 and were followed on November 22 by Powell's draft opinion which was to play the crucial role in deciding *Bakke*.

The Powell draft was accompanied by a covering MEMORANDUM TO THE CONFERENCE. It pointed out that the accompanying draft "addresses only the constitutional issue." His review of the Title VI issue, Powell went on, confirmed the view expressed in his October 14 memo. There is, he wrote, "little doubt that there was no legislative intent to have Title VI depart from the dictates of the Fourteenth Amendment. The principles by which the validity of the action are to be judged are the same."

Powell's conclusion was that, in these circumstances, "the narrower mode of decision would be to avoid reaching out for the statutory ground. A decision under Title VI would require resolution of the several significant questions not argued or addressed below, e.g., whether there is an implied private right of action under Title VI, whether such a right would entail private remedies, and whether it would require exhaustion of administrative remedies."

Thus, the Powell memo asserted, "there is no reason to avoid the constitutional issue. This was the basis of the holding in the California supreme court, was the issue that prompted us to grant certiorari, and was—until we requested Title VI briefing—the only substantive issue addressed by the parties."

The accompanying draft was headed MEMORANDUM TO THE CONFERENCE from MR. JUSTICE POWELL. It consisted of twenty-six printed pages and was, despite its title, the first draft of what would be his *Bakke* opinion. It is reprinted in Appendix C. As the covering memo indicated, the draft was devoted solely to the constitutional issue; it concluded categorically that the Davis program violated the Equal Protection Clause of the Fourteenth Amendment.

In a 1986 interview, Justice Brennan described the exchange of drafts and memoranda which plays so important a part in the Court's decision process. "It's startling to me every time I read these darned things," he said, "to see how much I've had in the way of exchanges and how the exchanges have resulted in changes of view, both of my own and of colleagues. And all of a sudden at the end of the road, we come up with an agreement on an opinion of the Court."[4]

The process described by Justice Brennan was not, however, what happened in *Bakke*. The exchanges there led neither to an agreement on an opinion of the Court, nor to substantial changes in the drafts that were circulated. The positions taken by the Justices in the first conference on the merits, on December 9, remained unchanged throughout the *Bakke* decision process.

In particular, the constitutional discussion in Justice Powell's November 22 draft opinion was virtually identical with that in the opinion he ultimately issued. Because of the critical role played by Powell's opinion in the final *Bakke* decision, his first draft should be analyzed in detail, both to understand his constitutional views (which most commentators accept as those adopted by the *Bakke* decision) and to point out the changes made in the draft by his final opinion.

STRICT SCRUTINY

Powell begins with what would become Part III of his opinion. He does not include the statement of facts and history of the case and the discussion of Title VI, which would become Parts I and II of his final opinion. The draft is, in accordance with the view expressed in Justice Powell's October 14 memo, devoted entirely to the constitutional question. And it answers it almost entirely in favor of Bakke.

The "crucial battle" says the draft, is that "over the proper scope of judicial review." The parties disagree as to the proper level of scrutiny. Petitioner, relying on the *Carolene Products* footnote (supra p. 73),[5] argues that strict-scrutiny review "should be reserved for classifications disadvantaging 'discrete and insular minorities.'" Bakke claims that the level of scrutiny accorded a racial classification does not turn upon membership in a discrete and insular minority. Instead, the rights established by the Fourteenth Amendment are personal rights.

Justice Powell comes down squarely behind Bakke's approach. He, too, stresses that Fourteenth Amendment rights are guaranteed to the individual. It follows that "equal protection cannot mean one thing when applied to one individual and something else when applied to a person of another color." Both are entitled to the same protection.

In this case, Powell goes on, it makes no difference whether the Davis program establishes a "goal" or "a racial quota." What is clear is "it is a line drawn on the basis of race," in this case, declares the Powell draft (in a passage omitted from the final opinion) "the classification is not neutral on its face; the intention to restrict competition by whites is evident and not denied."

Justice Powell rejects the claim that strict scrutiny should not be applied here because white males such as Bakke "are not a 'discrete and insular minority' requiring extraordinary protection from the majoritarian political process." Powell refers to the *Carolene* footnote, but notes that, before 1970, the decisions did not refer to "discreteness and insularity." Instead, as he sees it (in a statement also left out of his final opinion) "Prior citations to 'footnote 4' generally concerned the 'preferred' position of First Amendment freedoms."

The Powell draft flatly rejects the view "that discreteness and insularity constitute necessary preconditions to strict scrutiny of otherwise sensitive classifications." On the contrary, "Racial and ethnic classifications . . . are odious without regard to these additional characteristics." It follows that "Racial and ethnic distinctions of any sort are inherently suspect and thus call for the most critical[6] judicial examination."

Justice Powell then goes into the history of the Fourteenth Amendment and concludes that it confirms "a reading of the Equal Protection Clause which states a principle of universal application and is responsive to the racial, ethnic and cultural diversity of the Nation." The clause's reach does not depend upon "discrimination by the 'majority' white race against the Negro minority."

Powell characterizes the pro-Davis argument as "a more restrictive view of the Equal Protection Clause," which would "hold that discrimination against members of the white 'majority' can never be suspect" (the final opinion inserts "if its purpose can be characterized as benign"). To Powell, this would make for a "two-class" theory that would turn back the "clock of our liberties" to 1868.[7]

For Justice Powell, the whole notion of "varying the level of judicial review according to a perceived 'preferential' status of a particular racial or ethnic minority" is untenable. In the first place, "There is no principled basis for deciding which groups will merit 'heightened judicial solicitude' and which will not." Certainly, courts cannot properly evaluate the extent of the prejudice suffered by different minority groups. "The kind of variable sociological and political analysis necessary to produce such rankings simply does not lie within the judicial competence."

The very idea of preference, according to the Powell draft, gives rise to "serious problems of justice." In particular, "there is no warrant in the constitution for forcing innocent persons in respondent's position to bear the burdens of redressing grievances not of their making." All this is avoided, "If it is the individual who is entitled to judicial protection against classifications touching upon his racial or ethnic background because such distinctions impinge upon personal rights, rather than the individual only because of his membership in a particular group."

Justice Powell then finds that preferential classifications based upon race are not supported by the cases involving school desegregation, employment discrimination, and sex discrimination. "Each of [those] cases . . . presented a situation radically different from the facts of this case."

"The school desegregation cases are simply inapposite" ("simply" was omitted in the final opinion). To hold otherwise, Powell asserted (in a passage left out of his final opinion), and "to analogize petitioner's special admission program to a remedy in a desegregation case and suggest that it should therefore be judicially 'approved' is to transform a remedy fashioned to correct a wrong, into a right in and of itself."

Similarly, the employment cases are not relevant to a case where there are no proved constitutional or statutory violations. "Where the preferential classification is not tailored as a remedy for a proven constitutional or statutory violation, proper analysis requires the application of strict scrutiny" (a sentence also not in the Powell *Bakke* opinion).

The sex classification cases also do not support preferential racial classifications. Apart from the fact that "women are the *majority* sex group" (a point Powell removed from his final opinion), gender-based distinctions are less likely to create the problems present in preferential racial programs. "In any event, we have consistently declined to view gender-based classification as suspect or as comparable to racial classifications for the purpose of equal protection analysis."

In addition, the other cases relied upon[8] do not support the *Davis* program. Unlike the programs in other cases, that at issue here totally forecloses individuals not from the designated minority groups from the sixteen special admission seats. "Because of that foreclosure, some individuals are excluded from enjoyment of a state provided benefit—admission to the medical school—they would otherwise receive. When a classification denies an individual opportunities or benefits enjoyed by others solely because of his race or ethnic background, it must be regarded as suspect."

NO COMPELLING INTEREST

If the Davis classification is "suspect," it is subject to strict scrutiny review and may be upheld only if supported by a "compelling interest." Are the purposes served by the Davis program substantial enough to meet this requirement?

Justice Powell next goes into the purposes advanced to support the Davis program. "The special admissions program purports to serve the purposes of: (i) 'reducing the historic deficit of traditionally disfavored minorities in medical schools and the medical profession,' . . . (ii) countering the effects of societal discrimination; (iii) obtaining the education benefits that flow from an ethnically diverse student body; and (iv) increasing the number of physicians who will practice in communities currently underserved."[9] According to Powell, none of these purposes "is substantial enough to support the use of a suspect classification." This conclusion is supported by a detailed analysis of the four purposes to show that racial preference is not necessary to further those purposes.

This is particularly true with regard to the claim that reservation of seats for those from the preferred interest groups is the only effective means to secure diversity in the student body. "The diversity that furthers a substantial state interest encompasses a far broader base of qualifications and characteristics of which racial or ethnic origin is but a single element." Justice Powell gives the example of Harvard to show how an admissions program, which considers race among other factors, may be "designed to achieve meaningful diversity in the broad sense of this term." Such a program permits race to be considered but, at the same time, "specifically eschews quotas." That is not true of the Davis program. As the Powell draft puts it, "A facial intent to discriminate, however, is evident in petitioner's preference program and not denied in this case. No such facial infirmity exists in an admissions program where race or ethnic background is simply one element—to be weighed fairly against other elements—in the selection process."

This reference to race as one of the factors which may be considered by an admissions program turned out to be crucial to the *Bakke* case. It was to serve as the bridge between Powell's initial rejection of the Davis program and the final decision, which enabled the four pro-Davis Justices to join a significant portion of Powell's final opinion.

But the November 22 Powell draft ended with a categorical rejection of the Davis program. "In summary," began the draft's concluding section, "it is evident that the Davis special admission program involves the use of an explicit racial classification never before countenanced by this Court. It tells applicants who are not Negro, Asian, or 'Chicano' that they are totally excluded from a specific percentage of the seats in an entering class."

The Davis program, Powell concludes, disregards the individual rights guaranteed by the Fourteenth Amendment. "When a State's distribution of benefits or imposition of burdens hinges on the color of a person's skin or on his ancestry, he is entitled to a demonstration that the challenged classification is necessary to promote a substantial state interest. Petitioner has failed to carry this burden."

NOTES

1. *N.Y. Times*, March 8, 1986, p. 7.
2. *N.Y. Times* Magazine, February 20, 1983, p. 20.

3. Supra note 1.
4. *N.Y. Times*, April 16, 1986, p. B8.
5. United States v. Carolene Products Co., 304 U.S. 144, 152, n.4.
6. The final opinion uses the word "exacting" instead of "critical."
7. When the Fourteenth Amendment was ratified.
8. Lau v. Nichols, 414 U.S. 563 (1974) and UJO v. Carey, 430 U.S. 144 (1977).
9. In the final opinion, iii and iv in the quoted paragraph are reversed.

EIGHT

Brennan's Reply and Conference on Merits

H AD Powell's November 22 draft come down as his final *Bakke* opinion, it would have meant a final decision far different than that ultimately rendered. As the Justice was to state in the December 9 conference on the merits, his draft pointed to an unqualified affirmance—which would have struck down the Davis program without any holding that race might be considered as one factor in a flexible admissions program. Such a decision could have meant the end of affirmative action programs in higher education, including the Harvard program Powell had referred to favorably in the draft. All such programs, and any others which took race into account, would have been condemned as "reverse discrimination," outlawed by the Fourteenth Amendment.

BRENNAN ATTEMPTS TO PERSUADE POWELL

For the Justices who favored the Davis program, the Powell draft in its initial form was a disturbing development. It indicated that they could secure a decision upholding the Davis program only through a coalition of Justices Brennan, Stewart, White, Marshall, and Blackmun. But, as they were soon to learn, such a coalition would not be possible. Justice Stewart, for one, would state flatly at the next conference on the case that he intended to vote against Davis, and Justice Blackmun was not to state his position definitely until the following May. This meant, at most, four votes for the Davis program unless Justice Powell could be persuaded to change his vote.

The position in this respect was plainly apparent to Justice Brennan, the senior associate on the Court and the leader of the pro-Davis Justices. As his memorandum of November 23 was to show, Brennan disagreed completely with the reasoning in Powell's draft. However, Brennan thought that there was a possibility that Powell could be persuaded to uphold the Davis program. Brennan hoped that Powell would ultimately see that the difference between the Davis minority set-aside and the Harvard program considering race as a factor was largely one of form.

Brennan soon found out, however, that Powell could not be moved. When Brennan made overtures, Powell reminded his colleague of his extensive experience in educational administration. Powell told Brennan, politely but firmly, that his views were fixed. This was reaffirmed by a second draft of the Powell *Bakke* opinion, which was circulated on December 1. This was essentially unchanged from the original November 22 draft, particularly in its categorical conclusion that the Davis program was unconstitutional.

Later in the term Justice Powell talked with Brennan's law clerks about *Bakke,* noting that he believed universities could seek to have specific percentages of minorities in each entering class but he didn't think that they should "look so bad" as Davis did under its program.

BRENNAN'S MEMORANDUM

Justice Brennan had sent around his views on *Bakke* in a November 23 MEMORANDUM TO THE CONFERENCE (Appendix D). This nineteen-page memo dealt with both the constitutional and Title VI issues and concluded in favor of the Davis program on both grounds. From this point of view, Brennan's memo is a rough first draft of his final *Bakke* opinion. "I fully share the hope," Brennan began, "that circulation of views in advance of conference will be helpful in deciding this significant case." The memo then noted why it was devoted largely to the constitutional issue. "I've concluded," Brennan wrote, "that Title VI affords no escape from deciding the constitutional issue. Specifically, I agree . . . that decision of this case can no more easily be made on the 'delphic' wording of

Title VI than on the language of the Fourteenth Amendment. My discussion of the constitutional problem therefore precedes my Title VI discussion."

On the constitutional issue, the memo was firmly in favor of Davis. First of all, Brennan stated, "If Davis' program is unconstitutional, I am clear that this is not because the law requires the automatic invalidation of all decisionmaking which, like Davis' admissions decisions, takes race into account. We long ago crossed that bridge in cases that approved race-sensitive policies and remedies, and thus firmly settled the principle that not every remedial use of race is constitutionally forbidden."

As Brennan saw it, "Last Term's *United Jewish Organization v. Carey*, 430 U.S. 144, definitely imbedded that principle in concrete, and Bakke's claim for admission is of no more constitutional significance than the Hasidim's claimed right in *UJO*, to vote as a single bloc."

The memo rejected the famous Harlan dictum that "Our Constitution is color-blind":[1] "to read the Fourteenth Amendment to state an abstract principle of color-blindness is itself to be blind to history." The consequence, in Brennan's view, was that it was "clear that states are free to pursue the goal of racial pluralism in their institutions in order to afford minorities full participation in the broader society."

Brennan then pointed to the justification for the Davis program, emphasizing that before such programs "the numbers in which minorities were admitted to medical schools were so niggling as to severely embarrass the nation's determination that minorities should fully participate at all levels of society." With such a situation, "I think that medical educators, who stand at the gateway to the profession, are entitled to embark upon affirmative action programs in order to achieve the participation of minorities in the profession as an end in itself."

But were the means which Davis selected constitutional? In answering this question, Justice Brennan agreed that the Fourteenth Amendment surely protects whites as well as blacks. The memo then stressed what, to the Justice, was the key factor in the Davis program—that it was not intended to insult or demean anyone. "If I thought for a moment that Davis' failure to admit Bakke represented a governmental slur of whites—for example, a statement from Davis that Bakke was being denied admission because 'whites are too dumb to be good doctors,' or because 'Bakke is Mick Irish, or Jew, or Hungarian, or Englishman'—then I would not hesitate to apply the strictest of scrutiny."

Everyone knows, however, that the Davis program did nothing like this. Instead, "I think I'm right that all nine of us agree that Davis in this case did *not* use race with ill will toward Bakke or anyone."

To Justice Brennan, the cases that struck down racial classifications, starting with *Brown*[2] itself, "are primarily about stigma and insult." On the contrary, "the element that is missing from this case (and would be fatal to the Davis program if present) has had several labels during my 21 years here: stigma, insult, badge of inferiority, invidiousness,—to name some."

Thus, as Brennan saw it, the governing "constitutional principle . . . can be summarized as follows: government may not on account of race, insult or demean a human being by stereotyping his or her capacities, integrity, or worth as an individual. In other words, the Fourteenth Amendment does not tolerate government action that causes any to suffer from the prejudice or contempt of others on account of his race."

The memo referred to *UJO v. Carey*[3] (supra chapter 3) as "a paradigm example of what the Fourteenth Amendment does not condemn." In Brennan's view of *UJO*, "There can be no question that the racial line used there disadvantaged the Hasidim." But the crucial fact in *UJO* was "that the use of race was not insulting or invidious and therefore not improper."

Brennan referred to the cases involving "classifications disadvantaging 'discrete and insular' groups" and asserted that they also turned upon his governing principle, "because the history and political weakness of the group convinced the Court that the classifications were intended to insult them and do them harm."

This was definitely not true of the Davis program: "I feel, and I doubt any of my colleagues disagree, that Davis' admissions policies as applied to Bakke are *not* of that nature." Bakke may not have been admitted to Davis. "But he was never stereotyped as an incompetent, or pinned with a badge of inferiority because he is white. Therefore, we would simply ignore the history of our country and of the Fourteenth Amendment, as well as the University of California's true purposes in adopting the Davis program, if we were to conclude that the child in *Brown* in 1954 and Alan Bakke in 1977 appear before this Court on the same footing."

Justice Brennan then went on to assert that, whatever standard of review was used, the Davis program should be upheld. "Moreover, under any standard of Fourteenth Amendment review other than one requiring absolute color-blindness, the Davis program passes muster." That was true because "All would agree that the alternatives suggested by the California

Supreme Court are fanciful." In actuality, "the medical profession is only on the threshold of developing admissions standards that can fairly be applied to all races."

Brennan then considered an alternative that had been debated within his chambers—the development of an admissions system "which accurately predicts the abilities of minority applicants to be good doctors so that minority and nonminority applicants may be chosen from a single pool solely on the basis of 'merit.'" Such a system, the Justice assumed, would avoid the *Bakke* problem. But Brennan's examination of the relevant literature concerning medical school admissions persuaded him that such a system was not a realistic alternative. The reality was that "at this point educators have not been able to devise ameliorative programs other than a race-conscious admissions system such as Davis employs."

The memo underlined the "apparently unanimous conclusion" of educators and professional associations "that without programs like Davis' qualified minorities would essentially disappear from their institutions. Their view is that an affirmance here will deny them any use of race as a factor in admissions with the result that they will be unable to fulfill what they take to be their responsibilities to the nation." Brennan's conclusion was that "Such a result would truly be a national tragedy, and I cannot accept that legal doctrine points in that direction."

The Justice then explained what he thought was the proper judicial role in cases like *Bakke*. "I believe that a court must assure itself that the decision maker relying on race intends no insult or slur to whites—that the reliance is in fact a benign attempt to remedy discrimination in our society." Then, said Brennan, a modified version of the rational-basis test should be applied. "Once this is done, however, any further inquiry, in my view, should be limited to whether the affirmative action policy actually adopted is a reasonable and considered one in light of the alternatives available and the opportunities that it leaves open for whites."

Under this approach, the Davis program should be upheld. "Turning to Davis' program, I cannot say that the decision to set aside 16 places out of 100 for *qualified minority* students (the emphasis is very important for Davis would not fill the number of places set aside unless there were 16 minority applicants it considered clearly qualified for medical education) is an unreasonable one, especially in California where far more than 16% of the population is minority."

This is true even if the Davis program may have the undesirable side effect "of promoting thinking in racial terms." To Brennan, "such short-term race consciousness is a necessary and constitutionally acceptable price to pay if we are to have a society indifferent to race, in which blacks and whites have equal access to both the medical profession and medical services, in the long run."

Brennan then referred to the crucial point upon which the pro-Davis Justices were later to join Powell's *Bakke* opinion and which Brennan's was to characterize as the central meaning of the *Bakke* decision—namely, the use of race as one factor in admissions decisions.[4] In his memo, Justice Brennan candidly conceded "that we are just deluding ourselves if we think that there is a meaningful, judicially enforceable distinction between setting aside a reasonable number of places for *qualified minorities* and a process that accomplishes the same end by taking race into account as one of several admissions factors." That is the case because, "If admissions officers understand that they may increase the number of minorities in school they obviously will manage to make the various subjective judgments necessary to accomplish their goal, whether or not that goal is explicitly stated in terms of a set number." In such a case, the subjective admissions decisions will scarcely be subject to meaningful judicial review. As Brennan put it, "Unless we want to throw every admissions decision into federal court for a judge somehow to decide whether race was taken too much or too little into account, we should support a school faculty that acts honestly in adopting the type of reasonable affirmative action plan it views as appropriate for its school."

Justice Brennan concluded his constitutional discussion by asserting, "When educators with virtually one voice tell us that only programs like Davis' offer any significant promise of achieving that goal, and that if they are declared unconstitutional then only a handful of minority students will make medical or other professional schools in the foreseeable future, we turn a deaf ear at our peril."

The last two and a half pages of the memo were devoted to a brief discussion of Title VI. Here the Justice argued "that reasonable affirmative actions programs were not barred by Title VI—so long of course as the programs were constitutional." The qualification of constitutionality was required by the conclusion that Title VI was congruent with the Equal Protection Clause. As Brennan put it at the end of his memo, "Title VI essentially incorporates Fourteenth Amendment standards and treats affirmative action as does the Amendment."

DECEMBER 9 CONFERENCE

A few days after Justice Brennan circulated his memo, Justice White told him that his own views were very close to those Brennan had stated. This meant that there were now three definite votes to uphold the Davis program—Brennan's, White's, and Marshall's (who would, without a doubt, follow the approach in the Brennan memo). The pro-Davis Justices had also hoped to be able to count on Justice Powell, but his November 22 draft showed that he was in the anti-Davis camp. This meant that a decision for Davis could be secured only if Justices Stewart and Blackmun joined the Brennan bloc. Stewart, however, soon showed—in his presentation at the first conference on the merits—that he agreed with the Chief Justice and Justice Rehnquist, while Blackmun was, at this point, rendered *hors de combat.*

Following the November sitting of the Court, Justice Blackmun had gone to the Mayo Clinic for surgery, therefore missing the Court's December sitting; he was not expected back in Washington until Christmas. Before he left, Blackmun had told the Chief Justice that the *Bakke* conference scheduled for December 9, at which the merits of the case were to be thoroughly discussed, should take place without him.

Justice Blackmun confirmed what he had told the Chief Justice in a December 5 MEMORANDUM TO THE CONFERENCE sent from Rochester, Minnesota. "I think," Blackmun wrote, "the conference and the discussion of the case should go on even though I am not back in Washington at the time. My absence should not defer conference discussion (without me) and the development of the analysis and thinking of the *Bakke* case." Though, as already noted, Blackmun's clerks had told the others that he would vote with the pro-Davis bloc, the memo indicated that the Justice had not yet made up his mind on the case: "I can swing into place one way or the other after my return." Blackmun also suggested that, because of his surgery, he had not yet been able to devote the necessary attention to the case. His memo concluded with the statement, "My presence, if I were there, would be of little assistance anyway for I am frank to say that I have not thus far had the energy to get into the supplemental briefs that were requested."

In retrospect, a Justice has said, "the best course would have been to postpone the Bakke conference, for Harry's idea of 'after his return' ended up being on May 1." Despite this the conference took place, as scheduled and without Blackmun—on the morning of Friday, December 9. The Justices gathered in their oak-paneled book-lined conference room and exchanged their customary handshakes. The formal greetings did not, however, conceal their underlying division on the merits of the case.

BURGER AND BRENNAN BEGIN THE CONFERENCE

The Chief Justice led off the conference by repeating the view expressed in his October 21 memo that the Davis program was subject to strict scrutiny review and that, under that standard, "this rigidly cast admissions program is impermissible." Burger stated that, in his opinion, "Diversity is a desideratum but it ought to be sought at lower levels than graduate school." The Chief Justice also said that the Court "could affirm on Title VI."

Justice Brennan, who spoke next as the senior Associate, expressed an entirely different view. He also repeated the position taken in the memo that he had circulated November 23. As seen in our discussion of the memo, Brennan's position was that heightened scrutiny was inappropriate where, as here, the purpose or effect of the racial classification was not to insult or demean anyone. In addition, as Brennan saw it, whatever the standard of review, the program was valid. As far as Title VI was concerned, it was congruent with the Equal Protection Clause. This meant that Title VI could not prohibit an affirmative action program that satisfied constitutional standards.

STEWART OPPOSES DAVIS

Justice Stewart, who followed, was considered a critical vote by the pro-Davis Justices. Without Stewart, they knew, they had little chance of upholding the Davis program. Stewart began by stating that there was "nothing in the Equal Protection Clause that forbids a state from barring admission to . . . applicants based on geography, alumni, athletics, etc." He then said that he would decide this case on the Fourteenth Amendment, rather than on Title VI, for three reasons: (1) that had been the basis of the California Supreme Court's decision; (2) because Title VI applied to private parties, it would be a broader decision than a constitutional one; and (3) Congress could not have meant to forbid what the Equal Protection Clause permitted.

Justice Stewart then addressed the constitutional issue. "If the Equal

Protection Clause does nothing else," he said, "it forbids discrimination based on a person's race alone." As Stewart saw it, "That's precisely what the Davis program does and injurious action based on race is unconstitutional." The principle categorically stated by Stewart was, "No state agency can take race into account" (though he indicated that the same might not be true of a federal agency, saying "my view on the Fifth [Amendment] might be different").

Justice Stewart's extreme position came as a surprise to the Justices who favored upholding the Davis program. They had originally hoped to secure Justice Powell's support, but his November 22 draft showed that such support would not be forthcoming. Having lost Justice Powell, the only hope for the pro-Davis bloc, as already seen, was a coalition of Justices Brennan, Stewart, White, Marshall, and Blackmun. But now Stewart was indicating that the pro-Davis view could at best obtain four votes. Indeed, to at least one of the pro-Davis Justices, Stewart's conference position seemed identical, in all relevant respects, to that taken in Justice Rehnquist's November 11 memo. This Justice at least knew by the close of Stewart's statement that he and his pro-Davis colleagues had lost their chance for a decision clearly upholding the Davis program. Their efforts thenceforth would have to be concentrated on preventing an affirmance that would ban all racial considerations in university admission programs.

WHITE AND MARSHALL SUPPORT BRENNAN

The statements of the other Justices at the conference followed predictable lines—particularly in view of the pre-conference memoranda that they had circulated. Justice White, as the order of seniority continued, spoke next. White began by stating, with regard to Title VI, "I think there's no private cause of action." On the other hand, "If Congress thought the Constitution required color-blindness when Title VI was written, that would cement its meaning even if [it was a] wrong understanding of the Fourteenth [Amendment]." He said, however, that Title VI "is congruent with the Fourteenth," which meant that the Court must reach the constitutional issue.

On that issue, Justice White went on, his view was in favor of the challenged program. "Davis," he declared, "may set this quota and fill it with qualified Negroes." In conclusion, White apparently relied on the *Katzenbach v. Morgan* approach taken in his October 13 memo, saying,

"I'll rely on the legislative-executive view of what's permissible under the Fourteenth [Amendment]."

Justice Marshall, the next to speak, said that he agreed substantially with Justices White and Brennan, "although I'm not sure there isn't a private cause of action under Title VI." In discussing the constitutional issue, Marshall made the point that he was to repeat later in the *Bakke* decision process: "this is not a quota to keep someone out, it's a quota to get someone in."

JUSTICE POWELL'S CONCESSION

The last three Justices to speak at the conference were for affirmance of the California Supreme Court. One of them, however, made a crucial concession that led to the ultimate resolution of the case. The concession was made by Justice Powell, who delivered the key opinion that determined the ultimate *Bakke* holding.

Powell began with a statement that he agreed that Title VI and the Fourteenth Amendment are congruent. He then repeated the views expressed in his November 22 draft. "I can't," Powell declared, "join Thurgood, Byron, and Bill in their holding that 16 or 84 or any quota was okay." Under their view, "the effect of the Fourteenth [Amendment] is completely lost." Then Powell stated the approach on which his *Bakke* opinion was to turn: "While admissions policy should be left to the university, the colossal blunder here was to pick a number. Diversity is a necessary goal to assure a broad spectrum of Americans an opportunity for graduate school. . . . Each applicant should be able to compete with others and taking race into account is proper—but never setting aside a fixed number of places."

In view of what he had just said, Justice Powell announced, he would vote to affirm. At this, Justice Brennan interjected that he thought that, under the approach to the case he had just stated, Powell should vote to affirm in part and reverse in part. Brennan explained that the judgment of the California Superior Court seemed to require that Davis adopt a color-blind admissions system for the future. Justice Powell went along with this new approach (which had initially been suggested by one of Brennan's law clerks). "I agree," Powell concluded his conference presentation, "that the judgment must be reversed insofar as it enjoins Davis from taking race into account."

Justice Brennan himself, of course, immediately saw the significance of Powell's agreement. He stressed its importance to his law clerks, pointing out to them that if the case were to come down as a partial reversal, public attention was likely to be focused on what he saw as the positive aspect of the decision—that the principle of affirmative action was being upheld.

THE CONFERENCE ENDS

Justice Rehnquist, who spoke next, stated that he basically agreed with Justice Stewart. However, "I don't agree with Lewis that race can be taken into account." As for Title VI, said Rehnquist, that is "more difficult for me. I'm not sure there is a private cause of action. I'm not sure either that Title VI and the Fourteenth [Amendment] are congruent."

The last conference presentation was by Justice Stevens, then the junior Justice. "I would decide on Title VI," he began. "If Bill, Byron, and Thurgood prevailed, we'd have a permanent conclusion that blacks can never reach the point where they'd not be discriminated against." Stevens then declared that, while "affirmative action programs have performed a fine service, they ought to be temporary. I can't believe that the day won't come when two-track systems will be unnecessary."

In Stevens's view, the Court should "duck the constitutional holding" and rely on Title VI. "I think," Stevens concluded, "Title VI gives a private cause of action and that [under it] less than Fourteenth Amendment proof is required. No intent need be proved, for example. I would hold that Title VI is violated by the two-track quota system."

After the Justices had concluded their conference presentations, it was clear that they were sharply split. The tally sheet of a Justice present at the conference which I have used lists the vote as five (the Chief Justice and Justices Stevens, Powell, Rehnquist, and Stevens) for affirmance and three (Justices Brennan, White, and Marshall) for reversal. But the majority was not united upon the grounds for decision—i.e., on whether to base it upon the Fourteenth Amendment, Title VI, or both. And Justice Powell's concession meant that the majority was even further fragmented.

During the remainder of the conference, there was a discussion back and forth on the views presented. Justices Brennan and White discussed the possibility, if Justice Blackmun joined either them or Justice Powell, of joining parts of a Powell lead opinion. The Chief Justice interjected at this point that no one had yet made any assignment to Justice Powell. On the other side, Justice Stewart told Justice Stevens not to count him out definitely on Title VI, suggesting that, if needed to make a Court, Stewart could go along on Title VI. Justice Rehnquist then told Justice Stevens that the burden was on Stevens to allay Rehnquist's doubts on whether a private right of action existed under Title VI. Finally, Justice Stevens indicated that he was going to look very carefully at the California Superior Court judgment to see if Brennan's interpretation of it was correct. From his statements, Stevens wanted, if at all possible, to avoid making any comment under Title VI or otherwise concerning the permissibility of a Harvard-type program.

NOTES

1. Plessy v. Ferguson, 163 U.S. 537, 559 (1896).
2. Brown v. Board of Education, 347 U.S. 483 (1954).
3. 430 U.S. 144 (1977).
4. Bakke, 438 U.S. at 325.

NINE

December Deluge

T HE December 9 conference was followed by what one Justice termed "the deluge of memoranda of December." Memos were sent back and forth as the Justices sought to deal with the issues raised at the conference and in the prior memoranda that had been circulated, and to persuade each other to adopt their authors' views. In particular, there were efforts to reach the two men who were now seen as the key "swing votes"—Justices Powell and Blackmun.

One familiar with the work of the Warren Court cannot help but note an important difference between that tribunal and its successor. In Warren's day, a major part of the exchanges between the Justices was oral, especially in the form of Justice-to-Justice politicking designed to obtain votes for a given point of view. Chief Justice Warren was notably effective in such efforts, and his persuasive powers enabled him to secure key votes in a number of important cases. Several Justices told me how hard it had been to withstand the Chief Justice when he was able to operate in a one-on-one setting.

In the Burger Court, the situation was different. Chief Justice Burger was not able to serve as the catalyst in the decision process the way his predecessor could. Moreover, Powell's characterization of the Justices as operating like nine separate law firms[1] was particularly appropriate for the Burger Court. In it, the Justices tended to exchange their views in writing. There was much less of the personal give-and-take that played the crucial role in the Warren Court's decision process. In part this was a natural consequence of the Xerox copier, which was first installed in the Court soon after Burger took office. It was so much easier to exchange memos that it was not necessary to have as much discussion among the Justices on cases before the Court.

BRENNAN INTERPRETATION DISPUTED

At the December 9 conference, Justice Brennan had secured Powell's key concession by stressing that the original judgment in the case by the California Superior Court had required Davis to adopt a colorblind admissions system. Justice Stevens had indicated, however, that he questioned the Brennan interpretation of the California judgment. When Brennan returned to his chambers after the conference, he immediately checked the California Superior Court's judgment. Its second paragraph—enjoining Davis from "considering plaintiff's race or the race of any other applicant in passing upon his application for admission"—appeared to the Justice to prohibit a Harvard-type program and hence to support his position.

On Monday, December 12, when Justice Brennan went to his chambers, there was a letter to him dated that day from Justice Stevens disagreeing with Brennan's interpretation. "After reflecting on your comments at conference," Stevens began, "I have concluded that the trial court's decree does not force us to consider the legality of a Harvard-style program prematurely." Stevens stressed that the California Superior Court had denied an injunction ordering Bakke admitted to Davis, but had held that he was entitled to have *his* application considered without regard to race. This meant, wrote Stevens, that "Bakke's is not a class action, and the 'color-blind' relief applied only to Bakke's application."

Stevens then quoted the entire second paragraph of the Superior Court's judgment:

"2. [P]laintiff is entitled to have his application for admission to the medical school considered without regard to his race or the race of any other applicant; and defendants are hereby restrained and enjoined from considering plaintiff's race or the race of any other applicant in passing upon his application for admission."

"By straining mightily," the Stevens letter conceded, "one could find an ambiguity in this injunction. The final 'his' could arguably apply to 'any other applicant.'" Such an interpretation was, however, unwarranted. As

Justice Stevens saw it, "the consistent use throughout the paragraph of the pronoun to refer to Bakke militates against such a reading, as does the failure of the trial court to suggest that it was issuing relief to applicants who were not parties to the suit."

WHITE SUPPORTS BRENNAN

A December 12 MEMORANDUM TO THE CONFERENCE was circulated by Justice White in answer to Stevens's letter. White supported the Brennan interpretation of the California judgment. "Contrary to John's memorandum," it began, "I am inclined to think that in passing on the injunction ordering Bakke's admission to the Medical School, we must decide whether the Regents of the University of California may employ race in any way as a factor in making admissions decisions."

White also quoted paragraph two of the Superior Court judgment: "On appeal, the Supreme Court of California left this portion of the judgment standing. It viewed the central issue in the case as being 'whether the rejection of better qualified applicants on racial grounds is constitutional,' Petn. App. 16a, and answered the question in the negative—'no applicant may be rejected because of his race, in favor of another who is less qualified, as measured by standards applied without regard to race.'" This meant, wrote White, that "the University was forbidden from considering the race of any applicant to be the determinative factor in passing upon Bakke's application."

"The breadth of the California courts' rulings," White asserted, "makes it necessary for the Court to consider the constitutional propriety of racial preferences in order to determine whether Bakke was entitled to an order directing his admission." This was true, according to White, because "A decision limited to a holding that the Medical Schools' special admissions program was unconstitutional would not resolve the question of Bakke's admission. The reason for this is that even if that program as presently administered is unconstitutional, the University is entitled to an opportunity to demonstrate that Bakke would have been denied admission even in the absence of the defect which rendered the program unconstitutional."

To support this statement, the White memo cited *Mt. Healthy City School District v. Doyle*,[2] which had been decided at the beginning of 1977. That case arose out of an action by a teacher, who claimed that he had not been rehired because he had relayed the contents of an intraschool memorandum to a radio station. The Court held that that action by the teacher constituted speech protected by the First Amendment. Nevertheless, as explained in a more recent federal case,[3] the Court noted plaintiff's history of objectionable behavior during his employment and remanded the case for a determination as to whether defendant had shown by a preponderance of the evidence that it would have reached the same decision even in the absence of the protected conduct. As summarized by Justice Powell in his soon-to-be-discussed memorandum, the case was remanded for the district court to determine "whether the First Amendment activity in fact had been the 'but for' cause of Doyle's discharge."

White argued that Davis's concession "that it could not establish that, but for the existence of the special admissions program, Bakke would not have been admitted" did not require a different result. In light of the decisions by the two California courts, "the University must have understood that it could not grant any preference based on race in the course of passing on Bakke's application." On the other hand, White went on, if "the California courts were wrong and race does have legitimate uses in making admission decisions, the University would be entitled to an opportunity under *Doyle* to establish, upon remand, that Bakke would not have been admitted if the special admissions program had been administered in a manner conforming to constitutional requirements."

Such an approach, in White's view, "would place the University in a much more favorable posture, because it might be able to prove that under a constitutionally administered special admissions program Bakke's chances of admission would be remote." The necessary conclusion, according to the White memo, was that "the question of whether Bakke is constitutionally entitled to a judgment ordering his admission seems inextricably linked to the question of whether special consideration may be given in any form to racial minorities."

BRENNAN'S DECEMBER 13 MEMORANDUM

After he had read White's memo, Justice Brennan prepared his own MEMORANDUM TO THE CONFERENCE elaborating on Justice White's views. This six-page memo, prepared by one of Brennan's law clerks and circulated December 13, began, "I fully agree with Byron's conclusion that in deciding whether Bakke was entitled, under the federal constitution, to the judgment ordering his admission to the Davis medical school we must answer the question whether race can ever be a permissible consideration in making admissions decisions."

Justice Brennan then made a statement designed to attract a coalition that would go at least as far as Justice Powell in upholding race as a factor in admissions decisions: "After conference, I thought that on one view or another the Chief Justice, Byron, Thurgood, Lewis, and I believed it could be constitutionally permissible to give consideration to race." Despite its concession below that it could not prove that Bakke would not have been admitted, Brennan asserted, Davis should not be foreclosed "from attempting to make that showing upon remand if we take the position that race may be given 'weight' in the admissions process."

In Brennan's view, the Davis concession was made in light of the California courts' decisions that race could never be made a positive factor in the admissions process. "If, on the other hand, the California Supreme Court had taken the view that race can constitutionally be made a positive factor in an admissions decision—but can not be decisive—I doubt the University would have conceded that Bakke would have been admitted if the unconstitutional aspects of the program had been eliminated." In such a case, Brennan went on, "even if Bakke would have been admitted under the colorblind system required by the state courts, it might have been possible for Davis to show that he would not have been admitted if Davis had modified its admissions criteria to eliminate the quota and run a Harvard type program. Indeed, there is much in the record suggesting that, even if the quota had been abolished, Bakke would have been rejected."

That was true because "The committee could, consistent with a Harvard type program, have preferred slightly 'less qualified' minority applicants— i.e. ones with somewhat lower benchmark scores—to nonminority applicants like Bakke in order to attain the constitutionally permissible goal of integration. In short, it is possible that Davis could easily demonstrate that Bakke would not have fared any better under a Harvard type program than he did under Davis's 'quota' system."

Brennan concluded that "if we were to agree that the Davis program is unconstitutional but were to conclude that the California Supreme Court erred in ruling that race may never be made a positive factor in making an admissions decision, simple fairness requires that Davis be given a chance to show that Bakke would not have been admitted under a constitutional program." It followed that, "if we believe that race is a permissible consideration, I think we must say so, reverse the judgment in part, and remand the case for proceedings not inconsistent with our decision."

"Of course," Justice Brennan ended his memo, "my preference remains—as I voted at Conference—to reverse outright. But if that view does not carry the day, I think the Court is dutybound to decide whether race can ever be a permissible consideration."

BURGER AND POWELL REPLY

In his memorandum Justice Brennan had indicated that a coalition in favor of the Powell approval of race as a factor to be considered in the admissions process could be put together, consisting of himself, the Chief Justice, and Justices White, Marshall, and Powell. Presumably, he had included the Chief Justice in the projected majority because Burger's October 21 memorandum (supra p. 69) had stated expressly, "As of now, I am not convinced that the Court should forbid efforts to establish programs primarily for those who have sustained deprivations which closely correlate with race but might affect anyone isolated from the cultural mainstream. I am not ready to say now that in evaluating 'disadvantage' race may not be given some consideration."

The Chief Justice, however, quickly disassociated himself from the Brennan coalition effort. In a December 19 "Dear Bill" letter, Burger put to rest the notion that he would be willing to join the Powell "race as a factor" approach. "Your memorandum of December 13," Burger asserted, "does not quite reflect my position on the use of race as criteria for admission or exclusion." In his October 21 memo, the Chief Justice wrote, he had "indicated my sympathy with leaving maximum 'elbow room' to educators but stopping short of use of race as such to admit or exclude. This led me to an affirmance but not, as I thought I made clear at conference, on the route Lewis would go."

To Burger, Brennan's approach could not be followed. "As I see the record the University cannot now show that it acted in a way which, for me, is foreclosed by its position in this case. Hence there is no purpose in a remand to explore this."

On the same day, December 19, Justice Powell circulated an important MEMORANDUM TO THE CONFERENCE. Its significance for the ultimate *Bakke* decision lay in Powell's indication that he agreed with the concession he had made to Justice Brennan at the December 9 conference—that, on his view of the case, he had to vote to reverse in part. "As I stated at Conference," Powell wrote, "(when Bill Brennan put the question as to the form of a judgment under my view), I had not considered the scope of the trial court's injunction. If it can be read as enjoining Davis from ever including race or ethnic origin as *one* element, to be weighed *competitively* with all other relevant elements in making admissions decisions (i.e., from adopting what I shall refer to herein as the 'Harvard'—type admissions policy), then—as I stated—I would certainly favor a modification of that injunction."

This meant, Powell stated, that, "in the unlikely but welcome event that a consensus develops for allowing the competitive consideration of race as an element, I think we should affirm as to the Davis program, but reverse in part as to the scope of the injunction."

Justice Powell went on to say that he did not support the Brennan and White suggestion that would require a remand for a determination whether Bakke was entitled to the judgment ordering his admission. "I do not agree," Powell wrote, "that this is a case that properly could be remanded for the retroactive application by Davis of a Harvard-type admission program that was not in existence in 1973 or 1974, and that could not possibly be structured and applied fairly some four to five years after the discriminatory action."

In Powell's view, "*Mt. Healthy* [upon which the White memo had relied] simply does not apply to such a situation." The Powell reasoning here was similar to that in Note 54 of his published *Bakke* opinion. Powell distinguished *Mt. Healthy* because in it, there was "considerable doubt" as to whether the teacher would have been discharged without his First Amendment activity. "Here, in contrast, the University has represented to us that this particular racial classification was *essential* to the admission of the minority students in question."

According to Powell, here "The relevant inquiry concerns Davis' interest and purpose *at the time* it excluded Bakke, not the reasons it conceivably could have entertained, but did not. The answer is not speculative." The Davis action at issue was, on its face, racially motivated. "Here the improper racial purpose was the *sole* motivation for the dual admissions program." It follows that "Mt. Healthy is wholly inapposite."

In this case, we know how the Davis program was applied. However, it would be "sheer speculation to say how—or even if—Davis would have operated its admission program if it had known that the Harvard-type program was permissible and its Task Force program was unconstitutional." To determine how Davis would have decided Bakke's application under a Harvard-type program would, the Powell memo asserted, "be a fictitious recasting of the facts." The same would be true of the action on remand under the White-Brennan suggestion. "In practical terms, if—on remand—Davis reaffirmed the admission of all 16 minority applicants in both years and adhered to its exclusion of Bakke, it would appear to all the world as a self-serving charade. No one would accept it as bona fide."

"For these reasons," Powell concluded his memo, "I think it would be improper to remand the case under *Mt. Healthy*. Certainly it would set a dangerous and far-reaching precedent."

STEVENS AND TITLE VI AGAIN

On December 19, Justice Stevens wrote Justice Powell, "I agree completely with your analysis of *Mt. Healthy*." In the remainder of his letter, Stevens indicated his disagreement with the view that the Court should consider the "race as one factor" question. As Stevens saw it, the Court should "construe the injunction as merely prohibiting the consideration of the race of any applicant in the processing of *Bakke*'s application." If that were done, Bakke "will be admitted to medical school and there will be no outstanding injunction forbidding the consideration of racial criteria in processing other applications." Under this approach, "neither Bakke nor the University can be adversely affected by the failure to render an advisory opinion on the validity of a Harvard-type program."

Stevens concluded that "the facts (1) that the judgment, fairly read, only relates to Bakke's right to be admitted and (2) that this reading cannot harm either litigant, are persuasive reasons for not reaching out to discuss a profoundly difficult constitutional issue that is not necessary to the resolution of the controversy between the litigants before us."

At the end of his letter, Justice Stevens noted, "I am working on an additional memorandum relating to the statutory question which I hope to circulate in a few days." Stevens circulated the promised memorandum, 32 pages in length, on December 29. It was devoted to Title VI and most of it (27 pages) dealt with the question of whether there was a private right of action under the statute. Its strong "conclusion that an individual may maintain a cause of action under Title VI" was supported by a detailed analysis of the purposes of Title VI and that statute's legislative history. In

Stevens's view, "Bakke's suit is clearly the sort of private action that Congress envisioned [to] further the remedial purposes of the Title." I have been told that Stevens's primary purpose here was to persuade Justice Rehnquist, who had expressed doubts on the matter, that a private right of action could be inferred from the statute. By now Stevens realized that Rehnquist's vote was essential to his efforts to persuade the Court to avoid the constitutional issue and decide the case under Title VI.

In the last two pages of his memo, Justice Stevens eloquently gave his reasons for wishing to avoid decision of the constitutional issue:

"'The most substantial argument against resting the decision in this case on Title VI is not that there is no private cause of action under the statute, but that the Court has an obligation to decide important constitutional issues such as this. Although I fully appreciate the force of this argument, I cannot believe that we should abandon our normal principles of restraint to reach an issue that will have potentially far reaching and unforeseeable consequences on future social legislation. It is true that Title VI was, in large part, intended to echo the constitutional prohibition against racial discrimination. But we are not bound by Congress' view of the Constitution in 1964, and the language of the statute may well independently proscribe conduct that the Constitution does not. The critical point is that a decision based on Title VI leaves room for legislative and executive flexibility in areas where that is badly needed. '. . . much of [legislation] is evanescent, and meant to be. Principle is intended to endure, and its formulation casts large shadows into the future.' A. Bickel, The Least Dangerous Branch 131. While the question of reverse discrimination obviously involves enduring principles, I am convinced that it also poses problems unique in our history and that the faults and virtues of many of the proposed solutions can only be adequately judged on an 'empirical' basis. The legislative arena is the proper forum for this sort of experimentation. A constitutional decision, regardless of the final result on the merits, poses the danger, eloquently expressed by Justice Jackson in his dissent in *Korematsu*, that the rationalizing principle will 'lie about like a loaded weapon ready for the hand of any authority that can bring forward a plausible claim. . . . A military commander may overstep the bounds of constitutionality, and it is an incident. But if we review and approve, that passing incident becomes the doctrine of the Constitution. There it has a generative power of its own, and all that it creates will be in its own image.' "[4]

NOTES

1. *Congressional Quarterly's Guide to the U.S. Supreme Court* 754 (1979).
2. 429 U.S. 274 (1977).
3. Weinstein v. University of Illinois, 628 F. Supp. 862, 866 (N.D. Ill. 1986).
4. Citing Korematsu v. United States, 323 U.S. 214, 242, 246 (1944).

Outward Calm

According to the Justice quoted at the beginning of chapter 9 on the December deluge of memoranda, it "was followed by a period of relative outward calm, which lasted until the middle of April." Only two memoranda were circulated between December 29 and April 13, but of course this did not mean a complete hiatus in the *Bakke* decision process. There were behind-the-scenes activities among the anti-Davis Justices which led to their agreement to join a Title VI opinion, as well as a rejection of that approach in the one memorandum circulated during the period. Much of the time was spent waiting for Justice Blackmun, who was still recuperating from his surgery. As it turned out, his was the crucial vote for the ultimate decision in the case. But Blackmun was to keep the others waiting until May 1, when he finally announced his vote to the conference.

POWELL REPLIES TO STEVENS

After Justice Brennan received Powell's December 19 memorandum rejecting his suggestion of a remand for a determination of whether Bakke would be entitled to admission under a Harvard-type program, he considered responding, but decided that there was no point in doing so. Without Justice Powell's support, there was no chance of getting five votes for a remand. When Stevens's December 29 memo was circulated, however, it seemed to call for a reply from those who disagreed with it. After the memo had been digested in the different chambers, one of Powell's law clerks came to see one of Brennan's to discuss the possibility of a response to the last part of the Stevens memo (that quoted on p. 107). Justices Powell and Brennan discussed the matter through their law clerks and decided that what they termed the Stevens "hymn to *Ashwander*"[1] (the leading case on the desirability of avoiding constitutional issues if a case could be decided on nonconstitutional grounds) might, if unanswered, be persuasive to Justice Blackmun. Powell and Brennan, therefore, agreed that a responding memorandum should be prepared. They also agreed that, since Brennan was then undergoing medical treatment, the memo should be written by Powell.

Powell's MEMORANDUM TO THE CONFERENCE consisted of nine pages and was circulated January 5, 1978. It was divided into two parts. Part I began by referring to the December memoranda deluge. "The combination of the Chief's invitation to circulate memoranda and our deferral of a definitive Conference vote have resulted in an unprecedented volume of circulations in this case. Although my first impulse is to cringe when I see another one, each memorandum has been educational for me and—in a case of this importance—the exchange of views has been a welcome supplement to our usual truncated Conference discussion." Powell wrote that he was "hesitant to impose upon you yet another memorandum. But John's thoughtful essay of December 29 (that enlightened my New Year's weekend) emboldens me to do so."

Taking issue with the Stevens approach, Powell stressed "that we could not responsibly follow a Title VI route to avoidance of the constitutional problem." Powell recognized that since briefs on Title VI had been requested the opinion had to address the statutory problem. "I continue to believe, however, that invoking *Ashwander* principles in support of affirmance under Title VI alone reads too much into Justice Brandeis' admonition. It is not a license for invariable recourse to statutory interpretation."

"Nor," as Powell saw it, "do our 'normal principles of restraint' invariably counsel the decision of difficult statutory issues not passed upon by the court below, in order always to avoid a properly presented constitutional question."

Powell summarized "John's position on the substance of the Title VI argument" by saying, "he agrees that 'Title VI was, in large part, intended to echo the constitutional prohibition against racial discrimination.'" In Powell's view, "that conclusion is clearly correct." That being the case, the memo went on, "The next question is whether—because of prudential considerations—we should read a broader meaning into the legislative history or rely on a perceived 'plain meaning'* of §2000d [of Title VI], in order to avoid reaching the Fourteenth Amendment issue." "It seems to me," the memo went on, "that either of these approaches would present a departure from the normal decision-making processes of this Court and could be justified only by a basic judgment about the nature of the racial problem in this country and the institutional role of this Court."

To interpret Title VI as going beyond the Equal Protection Clause would, Powell asserted, "be quite a judicial *tour de force*. . . . A disregard of Congress' apparent purpose ('to echo the constitutional prohibition') and the expanding of Title VI into an independent, broad-gauge prohibition would—as I view it—be quite difficult to justify."

Powell concluded "that the decision to affirm on the basis of Title VI alone *would* represent a departure from our usual methods of adjudication. It would be 'worth the candle' only if it furthered some extremely important prudential consideration."

The memo then noted, "John believes that it does. The prudential considerations that he advances for avoidance of a constitutional decision are based upon his view—as I understand it—that reverse discrimination 'poses problems unique in our history,' . . . problems that may work themselves out in the short run, obviating any need to make a constitutional judgment at this time."

The memo conceded, "If there were reasonable assurance that this 'unique' problem would resolve itself in the foreseeable future, there would be more force to John's counsel of avoidance." To Powell, however, "there is no evidence that this problem will 'go away'."

The memo then referred to the *DeFunis* case[2] where the Court avoided the constitutional issue. "We were criticized then for leaving the hundreds of state colleges, universities and graduate schools without guidance. The need for resolution of the issue certainly has not lessened."

The same thing would happen here if the Stevens view were followed. "If the Court now were to affirm this case on Title VI without reaching the Fourteenth Amendment, again we will have resolved finally exactly noth-

---

*There was a footnote here in Powell's memo: "I place this phrase in quotation marks to emphasize that the only thing even close to being 'plain' about the meaning of § 2000d is that Congress seemed to think it meant the same thing as the Equal Protection Clause, which is far from 'plain.'"

ing." Such an opinion on the statutory ground alone "would hold only that the language of Title VI proscribes the precise type of reverse discrimination found to exist by the courts below."

The memo then described the effect of such a Title VI opinion. "Every state institution of higher learning in our country would then have to terminate forthwith all Davis-type programs. Institutions with Harvard-type programs, or some variation thereof, would have no idea whether they were in compliance with the law." The consequence would be that, "Inevitably, after some presently indeterminate time—perhaps another two to three years—the constitutional issue will again be before us."

"It seems to me," therefore, Powell's Part I concluded, "that the relevant prudential considerations weigh heavily in favor of our resolving the constitutional issue that is before us, which was the issue that prompted us to take the case." Or, as Powell summed it up at the end of his memo, "prudential considerations—the desirability of resolving a constitutional issue of national importance and one that will not 'go away'—weigh strongly in favor of staying on the course that we charted when we granted certiorari."

Part II of the memo was devoted to the "race as a factor" issue that was to be a crucial part of the final *Bakke* decision. Powell began this section by referring to the argument "that if the Court were to affirm the judgment of the California Supreme Court, any indication in the Court's opinion that race properly may be one element to be weighed in admission decisions would be mere dictum and therefore inappropriate." Powell stated his disagreement with this argument: "Again, I respectfully differ from those who hold this view."

The judgment of the California court, Powell stressed, "draws meaning from the opinion supporting it, and that meaning is that race may never be considered to any extent in admitting students to a university. Certainly the opinion of the California court has been read that way, and I do not see how it can be read any other way." To Powell, of course, "this holding is erroneous."

Powell now asserted that the view on which Justice Brennan had persuaded him at the conference was the correct approach. "It would not suffice for us merely to state that we do not read the California judgment as necessarily prohibiting all use of race in admissions decisions, or to say that we reserve judgment on other types of race conscious plans." On the contrary, "In view of the opinion below . . . , such an unenlightening statement by this Court would merely perpetuate the confusion and doubt that now exists."

Justice Powell wrote that, as stated in his November 22 draft opinion, "I agree that diversity of the student body, as that term is now used, is now generally recognized as a state and educational interest of the highest importance." However, the Justice did not agree that the Davis program was the only effective means of serving this interest. "Accordingly, it would be essential to demonstrate that other less restrictive means not only are available, but are employed successfully by leading universities."

Thus, not only should the Court decide the constitutional issue, but, "in view of my perception as to the correct analysis of the constitutional issue, I consider it both necessary to a reasoned opinion, as well as prudential, to negate petitioner's basic position by demonstrating that valid and less restrictive means are available to further the asserted state interest."

WHITE ON TITLE VI AGAIN

Between the Powell January 5 memo and the middle of April, only one memorandum was circulated. It was a 41-page printed Memorandum of MR. JUSTICE WHITE, circulated on February 10, and devoted entirely to the Title VI issue. It was accompanied by a covering MEMORAN-DUM TO THE CONFERENCE: "Since I have concluded most of my research concerning the application of Title VI to *Bakke*, I thought it might be useful to circulate my conclusions in written form."

White started by noting that a holding that the Davis program violated Title VI would dispose of *Bakke* on the statutory basis alone. If that was the case, White declared, "I am firmly of the view that the Court should not, particularly in this case, ignore or abandon its time-honored rule that statutory grounds should be addressed first and constitutional issues not at all if the statutory rationale is dispositive."

White then stated why the Justice held this view. "To put aside a statute that may forbid or affirmatively permit the very conduct at issue is to ignore the views of that branch of the Government having exclusive legislative power, as well as those of the President, who has signed the legislation, and of the Executive Branch that enforces the law and necessarily interprets it in the process. It is also to assume a prescience, a power and a public influence that history has indicated the Court does not and should not have."

As White saw it, however, "the statutory issue presented—namely, whether Bakke is entitled to relief under Title VI—is shortly disposed of because in my view there is no private right of action available under Title

VI." In this respect, wrote White, "I am unable to agree with JOHN STEVENS' thorough memorandum and with what I suspect will be the views of a majority of the Court with respect to private actions under Title VI."

White went on to say that, "whether private actions under Title VI are permissible is not for the purposes of this case very important—and could even be assumed, *arguendo*,—if a majority of the Court is of the view, as I am, either that the legal standard under Title VI is not stricter than the constitutional rule and would thus not forbid what the Constitution permits, or, on its own bottom, does not proscribe the medical school's admissions scheme." If either view were adopted, "dealing with the constitutional issue would be essential."

Despite his view on this, White wrote, "Because the Title VI standard remains unresolved, however, I shall address the private cause of action question, which is in any event an important matter in the overall administration of the statute."

After the introductory section just summarized, the White memo was divided into two parts. Part I argued that there was no "private cause of action under Title VI." White had reached this conclusion both from the statutory language and the legislative history. As far as the former was concerned, White declared, "There is no express provision for private action to enforce Title VI, and it is quite incredible that Congress, after so carefully attending to the matter of private actions in other titles of the Act, intended silently to create a private cause of action to enforce Title VI." And the memo quoted passages in the Congressional debates "where it is explicitly stated that a private right of action under Title VI does not exist."

Part II of the memo was devoted to White's view that "Title VI prohibits only those uses of racial criteria that are in violation of the Fourteenth Amendment; it does not bar the preferential treatment of racial minorities as a means of remedying past societal discrimination to the extent that such action is consistent with the Fourteenth."

As White saw it, "The legislative history of Title VI, administrative regulations interpreting the statute, subsequent congressional and executive action, and the prior decisions of this Court compel this conclusion. None of these sources lends support to the proposition that Congress intended to bar all race conscious efforts to extend the benefits of federally financed programs to minorities who have been historically excluded from the full benefits of American life."

The memo then went on in detail into the legislative history, interpretive regulations, later Congressional and executive action, and decisions of the Court. All, White asserted, "establish that Congress has [not] prohibited state agencies and private institutions from voluntarily endeavoring in a manner consistent with the Constitution, to eliminate racial segregation and to eradicate the effects of racial discrimination."

Title VI, in White's interpretation, "did not create any new standard of equal treatment beyond that contained in the Constitution." The statute thus does not reach "programs and activities for any reason other than the consideration of race or national origin by the recipient institution in a manner inconsistent with the standards incorporated in the Constitution."

There was, the memo affirmed, "no support for the proposition that Congress intended to impose statutory *limitations* upon constitutionally permissible racial preferences designed to extend the benefits of federally financed programs to racial minorities such as blacks that have been historically excluded from the full benefits of American life as a result of racial discrimination." Indeed, all the pertinent materials "strongly support the conclusion that prohibitions upon voluntary action employing racial criteria in a manner consistent with the Constitution for the purposes of eliminating racial discrimination or remedying injuries caused by past racial discrimination were distant from and, indeed, contrary to, the congressional purpose in enacting Title VI."

Title VI thus "surely did not intend to compel neutrality toward the effort to eliminate the legacy left by the Nation's history of racial injustice." On the contrary, "the statute permits the use of racial preferences to aid minorities wherever constitutionally permissible." It follows that "the view that Title VI, independent of the Fourteenth Amendment, bars a remedial racial preference such as that employed by the University of California cannot be plausibly maintained."

The memo's key conclusion was that of "Congress' equation of Title VI's prohibition with the commands of the Constitution." It further concluded "that Congress intended the meaning of the statute's prohibition upon discrimination to evolve with the interpretation of the commands of the Fourteenth Amendment and did not desire to precisely fix the scope of the nondiscrimination principle for all time."

To Justice White, the Stevens "claim that the use of racial criteria is barred by the plain language of the statute must fail in light of the remedial purpose of Title VI and its legislative history which demonstrates that it was the unconstitutional use of race which Congress intended to prohibit." There is no indication "that Congress desired to prohibit . . . affirmative action to the extent that it is permitted by the Constitution," or prohibit "the consideration of race as part of a remedy for societal discrimination."

The last five pages of the White memo summarized the prior Court decisions, particularly *Lau v. Nichols*,[3] where (in White's summary) "the Court held that the failure of the San Francisco school system to provide English language instruction to students of Chinese ancestry who do not speak English, or to provide them with instruction in Chinese, constituted a violation of Title VI."

To White, *Lau* was significant in two respects: (1) it indicated that educational institutions might "depart from a policy of colorblindness and be cognizant of the impact of their actions upon racial minorities"; (2) *"Lau* clearly requires that institutions . . . be accorded considerable latitude in voluntarily undertaking race-conscious action designed to remedy the exclusion of significant numbers of minorities." *Lau* thus indicates that an institution such as Davis is "permitted to voluntarily undertake corrective action based upon a good faith and reasonable belief that the failure of certain racial minorities to satisfy entrance requirements is not a measure of their ultimate performance as doctors but a result of the lingering effects of past societal discrimination."

Of particular interest to specialists in constitutional law is Justice White's recognition "that *Lau*, especially in light of our subsequent decision in *Washington v. Davis*, 426 U.S. 229 (1976), which rejected the contention that governmental action is unconstitutional solely because it has a racially disproportionate impact, must be read as being predicated upon the view that at least under some circumstances Title VI proscribes conduct which may not be prohibited by the Constitution." That was true because *Lau* implied "that impact alone is in some contexts sufficient to establish at least a prima facie violation of Title VI, contrary to my view that Title VI's definition of racial discrimination is absolutely coextensive with the Constitution's."

"Since I am now of the opinion," White concluded on this point, "for the reasons set forth in this memorandum, that Title VI's standard, applicable alike to public and private recipients of federal funds, is no broader than the Constitution's, I have serious doubts concerning the correctness of the premise of that decision."

But this interpretation of *Lau*, according to the White memo, "would not assist Bakke in the least." Even if "Title VI's prohibitions extend beyond the Constitution's," it was not intended to prohibit institutions "from voluntarily employing race-conscious measures to eliminate the effects of past societal discrimination against racial minorities such as Negroes." And *Lau* itself "strongly supports my view that voluntary race-conscious remedial action is permissible under Title VI." Even if, under *Lau*, "discriminatory racial impact is alone enough to demonstrate a Title VI violation, it is difficult to believe that the Title would forbid the Medical School from attempting to correct the racially exclusionary effects of its initial admissions program."

The White memo then briefly discussed other cases which showed "that the Court has also declined to adopt a 'colorblind' interpretation of other statutes containing nondiscrimination provisions similar to that contained in Title VI." Stress was placed on *UJO v. Carey*,[4] which White (who had delivered the opinion there) interpreted "as permitting States to voluntarily take race into account in a way that fairly represents the voting strengths of different racial groups in order to comply with the commands of the statute."

"These prior decisions," the White memo concluded, "are indicative of the Court's unwillingness to construe remedial statutes designed to eliminate discrimination against racial minorities in a manner which would impede efforts to obtain this objective. In the absence of evidence of a legislative judgment to the contrary, there is no justification for departing from such a course."

BEHIND-THE-SCENES MANEUVERING

Aside from the Powell January 5 memorandum and that by Justice White on February 10, the first few months of 1978 were outwardly calm, so far as the *Bakke* decision process was concerned. But there was intensive behind-the-scenes activity, particularly by the Justices who favored a decision striking down the Davis program.

The anti-Davis bloc could now count on four votes for a categorical affirmance—those of the Chief Justice and Justices Stewart, Rehnquist, and Stevens. But they were not united on the basis for the decision. The Chief Justice and Justices Stewart and Rehnquist had indicated, both at the December 9 conference and in the memos circulated by Burger and Rehnquist (supra pp. 67, 71), that they were prepared to invalidate the Davis program on constitutional grounds. But Justice Stevens had been firmly in favor of a Title VI opinion, which would avoid the constitutional issue.

Chief Justice Burger had, however, indicated as early as his October 13 letter to Justice White that he was also willing to affirm on Title VI. Now, in view of Justice Stevens' adamant position on the matter, he moved to secure the adherence of the other anti-Davis Justices to the Stevens approach. In January, the Chief Justice circulated a draft Title VI opinion to Justices Stewart, Rehnquist, and Stevens, as well as to Justice Blackmun. All but Blackmun sent the Chief Justice comments and proposed revisions in his draft.

The Burger draft was intended as a tactical move to secure a Court if possible or, at the least, the four anti-Davis votes behind a Title VI opinion. In the latter aim, the Chief Justice was successful. Justices Stewart and Rehnquist both agreed to join a Title VI opinion (the latter had apparently been persuaded by the December 29 memo, supra p. 106, that there was a private right of action under the statute). This meant that, at this point, there were four firm votes for an opinion affirming under Title VI.

The Chief Justice now devoted his efforts to secure a fifth vote. His attempts in that direction were aimed at Justice Powell, who had originally indicated that he would cast a vote for an unqualified affirmance, though only on constitutional grounds. Burger made three approaches to Powell during the first few months of 1978. In his first visit to the Powell chambers, the Chief Justice said that he could not possibly join the Powell opinion if it included discussion of the Harvard-type program. Justice Powell replied that he was sorry that the Chief Justice felt that way, but that he felt strongly about its inclusion.

A few weeks later, Burger returned and asked Powell if he would join a Title VI opinion affirming the judgment. The Justice again answered that he was sorry, but he strongly believed that the appropriate disposition was the constitutional position he had taken in his draft opinion. Undaunted, the Chief Justice returned some weeks later. This time he asked Powell if he would join the Title VI opinion for the sole purpose of inducing Justice Blackmun to make up his mind. Once more, however, Justice Powell declined.

NOTES

1. Ashwander v. Tennessee Valley Authority, 297 U.S. 288 (1936).
2. DeFunis v. Odegaard, 416 U.S. 312 (1974), supra p. 32.
3. 414 U.S. 563 (1974).
4. 430 U.S. 144 (1977), supra p. 34.

ELEVEN

"Waiting for Harry"

Now began those weeks of waiting that the Justices came to call "waiting for Harry." As we have seen, only Justice Blackmun had not yet indicated where he stood in *Bakke*. The Chief Justice and Justices Stewart, Rehnquist, and Stevens had virtually agreed to an opinion affirming the judgment for Bakke but solely on Title VI grounds. On the other side, Justices Brennan, White, and Marshall were for an unqualified reversal, both on constitutional and statutory grounds. Justice Powell was the "odd man" in this lineup. He agreed with the anti-Davis Justices that the portion of the California judgment that held the special admissions program unlawful and directed that Bakke be admitted to Davis be affirmed, but he also agreed with the Brennan bloc that the portion of the judgment enjoining any consideration of race in the admissions process must be reversed.

Blackmun's vote would therefore decide whether or not all admissions programs would be required to be color-blind. If Blackmun joined the Chief Justice and the other anti-Davis Justices, their categorical invalidation of the special admissions program on Title VI grounds would become the opinion of the Court. If Blackmun abstained, that would make for a four-one-three vote—with the anti-Davis Title VI opinion the plurality opinion and hence the one that would probably set the precedent in future cases.

At this point, the pro-Davis Justices were well aware that they could not obtain a majority for a complete reversal of the California judgment.

Justice Brennan had, as already seen, tried to persuade Justice Powell to join a vote to uphold the Davis program, but Powell had told Brennan that the views stated in his November 22 draft opinion were firmly fixed. But if the Brennan bloc now knew that they could no longer hope to secure a complete victory in the case, Justice Powell's concession, to vote for a partial reversal to allow a Harvard-type program, meant that they might still avoid a total defeat by a decision allowing race as a factor in admissions, even though it struck down the specific "quota" in the Davis program.

For such a result, however, the Brennan bloc needed Justice Blackmun's vote. Each faction would then have four votes, and the crucial opinion would be Justice Powell's. His recognition of "race as a factor" would set the theme for future admissions programs. This would mean a partial victory for the pro-Davis Justices, who could claim in the Brennan opinion joined by them that "the central meaning" of the final decision was that "Government may take race into account" when it sets up an admissions program—i.e., it is not prohibited from "establishing in the future affirmative-action programs that take race into account."[1]

THE BLACKMUN DILEMMA

For the pro-Davis Justices to be able to make such a claim, Justice Blackmun's vote was indispensable. But how were they to go about securing it? One of his law clerks suggested to Justice Brennan that he approach Blackmun personally on the matter. Brennan, however, felt that would be the wrong tactic.

In his earlier days on the Court, Blackmun had been compared to Justice Charles E. Whittaker, whose indecisiveness had been legend on the Warren Court.[2] The overintensive efforts, notably by Justice Felix Frankfurter, to get Whittaker to make up his mind had at times backfired and secured that Justice's resentment instead of his vote.[3] Now Brennan wanted to avoid making the same mistake with Blackmun. It was better, he told his clerk, to sit back and wait to see how Blackmun would vote. Blackmun, he felt, was so sensitive and concerned with appearing independent, now that he was no longer perceived as the junior half of the Minnesota Twins, that any pressure from Brennan could well be counterproductive. (In his early years on the Court, Blackmun had been a virtual Burger disciple and the press had dubbed them the Minnesota Twins, after the baseball team from their hometowns the Twin Cities of Minneapolis and St. Paul).

Brennan's view was confirmed by Blackmun's clerks, who told his own that their Justice was not likely to vote on the case for some time. Indeed, they said, Blackmun would become quite irritable whenever the subject of *Bakke* was raised. In addition, Brennan expected that, if Blackmun was not unduly pressured, he would ultimately come down on the pro-Davis side. Brennan told his clerks that he remembered that Blackmun had once stated publicly (in a speech at Stanford, he thought) that he would have voted to uphold the preferential program if he had reached the merits in the *De-Funis* case.[4]

As time went on, however, Justice Brennan began to have doubts that doing nothing was the way to resolve the Blackmun dilemma—especially as his law clerks again reported stories of Blackmun's increasing irritation whenever his clerks alluded to *Bakke*. Toward the end of February, Brennan discussed the matter several times with the Chief Justice. They considered the steps that could be taken to persuade Blackmun to vote and break the 4–1–3 division. Burger and Brennan decided that *Bakke* should be added to the agenda of a special conference that had been scheduled for Monday, March 6, to discuss three other cases in which decisions were then pending.[5]

Just before the conference one of Justice Powell's law clerks approached a Brennan clerk to discuss the possibility of their two Justices finding some common ground for an opinion they both could join. Brennan's clerk summarized his Justice's views in a manner that indicated that little ground could exist so long as Powell persisted in the constitutional holding contained in his November 22 draft.

The March 6 conference came—and went. The Justices discussed the other cases on its agenda, but the Chief Justice, who led the proceedings, did not call for a discussion of *Bakke*, because he had been told by Justice Blackmun that he was not yet ready to discuss the case; and no one else raised the matter.

As these weeks of "waiting for Harry" dragged on, the others grew increasingly anxious. This was especially true of the pro-Davis three, who needed Justice Blackmun to avoid a complete defeat in the case.

During the week before the March 6 conference, Justice Brennan, as the senior Justice in the majority, was able to assign the Court opinion in *Franks v. Delaware*.[6] In that case, the Court had voted to overrule the longstanding rule that a court could not look beyond the "four corners" of a search warrant in determining whether a search satisfied the Fourth

Amendment. Justice Blackmun spoke to Brennan immediately after the *Franks* conference and said that, despite his recent surgery, his health would not preclude his working effectively on a major case like *Franks*. In effect, Blackmun was asking for the *Franks* assignment.

Blackmun placed Justice Brennan in a difficult position. Thus far in the term, in Brennan's view, Justice Blackmun had mishandled the Court opinions in two cases.[7] Brennan told his law clerks that he feared that a weak opinion by Blackmun in *Franks* could undercut what he considered a significant victory. But, on the other hand, Brennan recognized that, if he irritated Blackmun on the eve of the scheduled *Bakke* conference, he risked losing Blackmun's *Bakke* vote. So in the end Brennan gave in and assigned *Franks* to Blackmun, to the consternation of the Brennan clerks.

After the March 6 conference had concluded without any consideration of *Bakke*, Justice Brennan discussed the situation with his clerks and decided that he had to take the initiative. He went to see the Chief Justice and told him that they had to do something to get Justice Blackmun to vote in *Bakke*. Brennan suggested that the two of them approach Blackmun together. Brennan thought that such an approach would appeal to Burger since there would be a representative of each bloc in the case. This would avoid the danger that Blackmun might, out of pique, vote against the Justice who first approached him on *Bakke*.

The Chief Justice, however, said that the responsibility to approach Justice Blackmun was his alone. Burger did go to see Blackmun and reported back to Justice Brennan that Blackmun said that he was not yet ready to vote and then asked who had put the Chief Justice "up to this." Burger told Brennan that he responded that no one had put him up to it, but that he had responsibilities of his own. When Brennan told his clerks what the Chief Justice had said, the clerks suggested that Burger had in fact replied that Bill Brennan was the moving force behind the meeting. Brennan stated that he was sure that Burger would not have done this.

BAKKE AND BALDWIN

"One of the great ironies of the saga of *Bakke*," according to one Justice, "is that its fate was to become entwined with the question, raised in *Baldwin*, of the constitutionality of Montana's practice of discriminating against out of staters who wished to hunt elk." The Justice was referring to the case of *Baldwin v. Montana Fish & Game Commission*.[8] At issue there was the

Montana law governing elk-hunting licenses, which imposed substantially higher license fees on nonresidents. The challenge to the law was based upon the Constitution's Privileges and Immunities Clause. Under it, "The Citizens of each State shall be entitled to all Privileges and Immunities of Citizens in the several States." This clause protects nonresidents against discrimination by states in favor of their own residents. "It was designed to insure to a citizen of State A who ventures into State B the same privileges which the Citizens of State B enjoy."[9]

The Court had, however, held that there was an exception to the nondiscrimination requirement in cases involving wildlife within state boundaries. The governing concept in them was that the states had "complete ownership over wildlife within their boundaries" and this gave them "the power to preserve this bounty for their citizens alone."[10] In *Baldwin*, it was contended that this doctrine was no longer valid and should not shield the challenged Montana discrimination.

Compared with *Bakke*, *Baldwin* was, of course, what Justice White once termed a "pipsqueak of a case."[11] It was, however, the first direct case on the Privileges and Immunities Clause in many years. This made the Justices devote more attention to it than the case might have otherwise deserved.

Baldwin had been argued during the first week of October 1977. At the postargument conference, most of the Justices agreed with the view that, as stated by Justice Stewart, "recreational destruction of a state's wildlife is not within the clause—the state has something close to proprietary interest in its wildlife." Justice Blackmun, who was to write the *Baldwin* opinion, said that he "had always assumed that a state could charge a nonresident more than a resident if properly justified." As he saw it, even if there was "no cost justification," there was also "no right of the nonresident to hunt."

The conference vote was seven-to-two (Justices Brennan and Marshall dissenting) in favor of the Montana law (though Justice White later switched and joined the Brennan dissent). The case was assigned to Justice Blackmun. His opinion upheld the Montana law and rejected the argument that the concept that the states as owners of the wildlife within their boundaries had power to preserve it for their own residents "has no remaining vitality." Instead, it held that the state's control over wildlife allowed it to impose the higher license fees on nonresidents. "Appellants' interest in sharing this limited resource on more equal terms with Montana residents simply does not fall within the purview of the Privileges and Immunities Clause."[12]

The Blackmun opinion in *Baldwin* obtained five votes soon after it was circulated and its author was eager to have it come down as soon as possible. Justice Brennan, however, who had led the conference discussion for reversal, was having difficulty both with the Blackmun opinion and with the majority decision affirming the judgment upholding the Montana law. Brennan told his law clerks that, since *Baldwin* was his first real encounter with the Privileges and Immunities Clause and was the first significant case before the Court involving that clause in thirty years, he wanted to be very careful.

On February 13, Brennan wrote Blackmun that he would write separately in *Baldwin* although Brennan stated that he was not sure whether it would be a concurrence or a dissent. While working on his opinion, Brennan became convinced that *Baldwin* was linked with the case of *Hicklin v. Orbeck*,[13] which was scheduled for argument on March 21. *Hicklin* also involved a challenge based upon the Privileges and Immunities Clause—this time to an Alaska law requiring the employment of qualified Alaska residents in preference to nonresidents on oil and gas production or pipeline work on lands leased from the state.

On March 9, Brennan sent a "Dear Harry" letter. "I am sorry," it began, "to have kept you waiting in this case, but I continue to find it very difficult." Brennan then informed Blackmun of the connection between *Baldwin* and *Hicklin*. "I now believe that what I have to say in *Baldwin* may well be informed by the way we decide and the approach we take in No. 77–324, *Hicklin* v. *Orbeck*, which [also] presents a Privileges and Immunities Clause challenge." In effect, Brennan was telling Blackmun that he would not be ready on *Baldwin* until he had come to rest on *Hicklin*. "I hope," Brennan's letter concluded, "this further delay does not inconvenience you, but I find it difficult to address the issue in *Baldwin* without looking over my shoulder at *Hicklin*."

BLACKMUN AND BRENNAN

Toward the end of March the Chief Justice and Justice Brennan had further discussions concerning what steps to take to encourage Justice Blackmun to make up his mind on *Bakke*. They decided to raise the matter with him at the conference scheduled for March 31. At that conference *Baldwin* first became overtly involved in the *Bakke* decision process.

During the conference, the Chief Justice was leading a survey of where they all stood on circulated opinions. Without any warning, Blackmun suddenly launched an attack on Brennan for holding up the Court on *Baldwin*, which he noted was the oldest outstanding argued case. Blackmun complained that over the years the press had often accused him of holding up the work of the Court. His voice filled with outrage, Blackmun asserted that he had never done so. He then produced an issue of the *Fordham Law Review* which contained an article on *United States Trust Co. v. New Jersey*.[14] The article referred to the fact that the majority opinion there had been written by Blackmun. A footnote then commented on the delay in issuing the opinion, saying, "This had been expected by veteran Court-watchers who know that Justice Blackmun is one of the slower authors on the Court. By April, five months after argument, he was running several opinions behind his pace of a year earlier and it was concluded that United States Trust was one of the cases occupying his time."[15]

Blackmun declared that this comment indicated that the long delay between the argument and the issuance of the *United States Trust* opinion was his fault. The Justice angrily said that it was not so, and told the conference that he had written the Law Review on the matter and that they had promised a retraction. He then announced that he was going to hold a press conference to refute the "charges." After this tirade, all thoughts of asking for Blackmun's views on *Bakke* that day were put aside.

Justice Brennan was, of course, quite upset by the incident. He returned to his chambers and instructed his law clerk to accelerate work on the *Baldwin* opinion. Over the weekend, however, the Justice decided that it would be wrong to give in to that kind of pressure; so on Monday, Brennan countermanded the Friday order.

The following Wednesday, Blackmun called and asked Brennan to have lunch with him on April 10. Brennan accepted with some trepidation, but at the luncheon, Blackmun was as gentle and reasonable as could be. He assured Brennan that he understood about *Baldwin* and told Brennan not to worry. He said that he was angry not with Brennan, but rather with the Chief Justice who had insulted Blackmun by assigning him only one Court opinion out of the March sitting. Burger had angered him further by approaching Blackmun concerning his *Bakke* vote while Blackmun was exercising, which was, he said, a sacred period for him.

At the next conference, on April 14, the Chief Justice again raised the subject of *Bakke*. Despite what he had said at the April 10 lunch, Blackmun once again attacked Brennan. This time he said that he would not vote in

Bakke until Brennan voted in *Baldwin*. The others were all but incredulous. One asked what the two cases had to do with each other. Justice Rehnquist, showing why he had a reputation as a wit, asked if it was the fact that both cases began with "B." At this, Blackmun softened slightly and announced that he was working on a *Bakke* memo which would not be ready for at least two weeks.

The Brennan law clerks say that the Justice's face was bright red when he returned to his chambers following this conference. At lunch that day, Brennan indicated that he was still shaken. The others there tried to console him by attributing the Blackmun outbursts to the enormous strain he had been under because of his illness and his insistence on continuing to work. Brennan told his clerks that he had not realized the strain that Blackmun had been under. He had not fully appreciated that Blackmun was having great difficulty recovering from his surgery. Brennan worried that perhaps Blackmun's mental state was such that he should not be permitted to cast the decisive vote in a case. While he seemed entirely cool and rational most of the time, these occasional outbursts were troublesome. Brennan later said, however, that he had concluded that the outbursts were aberrations, and he had no doubt that Blackmun's *Bakke* vote was, in no sense, the product of the strain he was experiencing.

It should be noted that Justice Blackmun was really proud of his *Baldwin* opinion as the first on the Privileges and Immunities Clause in more than a quarter century. A year later Justice Brennan circulated a draft opinion of the Court in another case[16] involving a state prohibition against shipping fish caught in the state to other states, which did not refer to *Baldwin*. Blackmun immediately wrote him a plaintive letter: "Of course, you don't know how you wound me by omitting any reference to *Baldwin* v. *Montana Fish and Game Commission*, 436 U.S. 317, 385–387, which probably has nothing whatsoever to do with this case."[17] Brennan hastened to reply: "The oversight leaves me a bit red faced. In the next circulation *Baldwin* will be cited at an appropriate place."[18]

"THE CRUELEST IRONY"

Mention should also be made of an April 13 MEMORANDUM TO THE CONFERENCE circulated by Justice Marshall. It was an eloquent statement by the only black on the Court. As Marshall saw it, "the decision in this case depends on whether you consider the action of the Regents as *admitting* certain students or as *excluding* certain other students. If you view the program as admitting qualified students who, because of this Nation's sorry history of racial discrimination, have academic records that prevent them from effectively competing for medical school, then this is affirmative action to remove the vestiges of slavery and state imposed segregation by 'root and branch.' If you view the program as excluding students, it is a program of 'quotas' which violates the principle that the 'Constitution is color-blind.'"

To Marshall, the latter principle could not properly be applied in 1978. "If only," he wrote, "the principle of color-blindness had been accepted by the majority in *Plessy*[19] in 1896, we would not be faced with this problem in 1978. We must remember, however, that this principle appeared only in the dissent. In the 60 years from *Plessy* to *Brown*,[20] ours was a Nation where, by law, individuals could be given 'special' treatment based on race. For us now to say that the principle of color-blindness prevents the University from giving 'special' consideration to race when this Court, in 1896 licensed the states to continue to consider race, is to make a mockery of the principle of 'equal justice under law.'"

Marshall then tried "to address the question of whether Negroes have 'arrived.'" In his view "Just a few examples illustrate that Negroes most certainly have not." His first example was in the Court itself. "In our own Court, we have had only three Negro law clerks, and not so far have we had a Negro Officer of the Court." The same was even more true on a broader scale. The memo noted that "this week's U.S. News and World Report has a story about 'Who Runs America.' They list some 83 persons—not one Negro, even as a would-be runnerup. And the economic disparity between the races is increasing."

Marshall's conclusion was that "The dream of America as the melting pot has not been realized by Negroes—either the Negro did not get into the pot, or he did not get melted down." Instead, all the statistics "document the vast gulf between White and Black America. That gulf was brought about by centuries of slavery and then by another century in which, with the approval of this Court, states were permitted to treat Negroes 'specially.'"

"This case is here now," Marshall asserted, "because of that sordid history." And, he went on, "despite the lousy record, the poorly reasoned lower court opinion, and the absence as parties of those who will be most affected by the decision (the Negro applicants), we are stuck with this case."

To decide against the Davis program would be to apply the color-blindness principle almost a century too late. "We are," the Marshall memo concluded, "not yet all equals, in large part because of the refusal of the *Plessy* Court to adopt the principle of color-blindness. It would be the cruelest irony for this Court to adopt the dissent in *Plessy* now and hold that the University must use color-blind admissions."

It was not, however, clear that Marshall's eloquent statement of outrage at the treatment of blacks would help the pro-Davis cause. Justice Brennan told one of his clerks that Marshall might have done more harm than good, for he seemed to assume that the constitutional standard really should be colorblindness. The memo appeared to be arguing that a contrary test should be adopted only because the Court initially took a different view in *Plessy v. Ferguson.* As Brennan saw it, Marshall's underlying theory was "Goddamnit, you owe us"; and he feared that that would not be persuasive to Justice Blackmun.

Brennan need not have worried on the matter. In his May 1 memorandum, discussed in the next chapter, Blackmun was to indicate his support for Marshall, writing expressly, "There is much to be said for Thurgood's 'cruelest irony' approach as set forth in his memorandum of April 13." At any rate, Blackmun was now finally to cast his *Bakke* vote and to do so in a manner that placed him solidly in the pro-Davis camp.

NOTES

1. Bakke, 438 U.S. at 325.
2. See Schwartz, *Super Chief: Earl Warren and His Supreme Court* 217 (1983).
3. See Woodward and Armstrong, *The Brethren: Inside the Supreme Court* 176 (1979).
4. DeFunis v. Odegaard, 416 U.S. 312 (1974), supra p. 32.
5. The cases were Bankers Trust Co. v. Mallis, 435 U.S. 381 (1978); Monell v. Department of Social Services, 436 U.S. 658 (1978); and Butz v. Economou, 438 U.S. 478 (1978).
6. 438 U.S. 154 (1978).
7. Central Illinois Public Service Co. v. United States, 435 U.S. 21 (1978); Ballew v. Georgia, 435 U.S. 223 (1978).
8. 436 U.S. 371 (1978).
9. Toomer v. Witsell, 334 U.S. 385, 395 (1948).

10. Baldwin, 436 U.S. at 384.
11. White, MEMORANDUM TO THE CONFERENCE, June 18, 1979. White was referring to Barry v. Barchi, 443 U.S. 55 (1979).
12. 436 U.S. at 386.
13. 437 U.S. 518 (1978).
14. 431 U.S. 1 (1977).
15. McTamaney, United States Trust Company of New York v. New Jersey— The Contract Clause in a Complex Society, 46 *Fordham Law Review* 1, 45, n.243 (1977).
16. Hughes v. Oklahoma, 441 U.S. 322 (1979).
17. Blackmun-Brennan, March 9, 1979.
18. Brennan-Blackmun, March 9, 1979. The final Hughes opinion did, in fact, cite Baldwin. 441 U.S. at 335, n.15.
19. Plessy v. Ferguson, 163 U.S. 537 (1896).
20. Brown v. Board of Education, 347 U.S. 483 (1954).

TWELVE

End of Waiting and Opinions

J USTICE Blackmun had not circulated his promised memorandum by the final conference of the term when the Justices discussed the remaining argued cases. After the conference the Chief Justice called Justice Brennan and told him that he planned to circulate a memo to the effect that no assignments would be made on April cases until all votes were in on all cases argued during the 1977 Term. Brennan said that this proposal was a fine idea, and the memo was circulated. But the long wait for the Blackmun vote was now to end. Justice Blackmun circulated his thirteen-typed-page *Bakke* MEMORANDUM TO THE CONFERENCE on May 1 (Appendix E). On the same day the Brennan dissent in the *Baldwin* case[1] was also circulated.

BLACKMUN'S MEMO

"The Chief," the Blackmun memo began, "not inappropriately, has been pressing me for a vote in this case." The Justice then explained why he had taken so long in *Bakke*. "Since my two months' relegation to the sidelines— from November 11 to early January—although constantly stewing about the *Bakke* case, I purposefully and I think properly, gave priority to the attempt to stay even with all the other work. I feel that I have been successful in this and that, except for *Bakke*, I have held nothing up either for a dissent or for any other reason."

For Blackmun, deciding *Bakke* was anything but easy, since the positions presented had "proved to be so oppositely persuasive for members of the Court." Yet, he had now read "the voluminous and eager writings . . . word by word" and was able to outline his views, after "having given the matter earnest and, as some of my clerical friends would say, 'prayerful' consideration."

There followed Blackmun's discussion of the merits, which was similar in substance to the separate opinion issued by the Justice in the case. The Blackmun treatment of the merits was divided into four parts. The first was headed *General Considerations*. It contained thirteen numbered paragraphs. The first two paragraphs were essentially the same as those in Part I of Blackmun's *Bakke* opinion, stressing the small percentage of minority physicians and attorneys and medical and law students as well as the hope that affirmative action programs would soon become unnecessary. However, the memo stated (in a passage omitted from Blackmun's opinion), "This is not an ideal world. It probably never will be. It is easy to give legislative language a literal construction when one assumes that the factual atmosphere is idealistic. But we live in a real world."

The memo then, like Blackmun's opinion, noted that the selection process in medical schools inevitably resulted in the denial of admission to many qualified applicants. The memo gave an illustration from the Justices' own experience: "We see this very same thing, on a smaller and more intimate scale, when those of us who personally choose our law clerks are confronted annually with a surplus of well-trained, highly qualified young men and women, all of whom could do the work expected of a clerk, and do it acceptably. Yet we must, and do, make the selection and thereby deny to many what they earnestly desire to have. That selection process perhaps affects the applicants' professional careers one way or the other, for better or for worse. I doubt that the crisis of clerk selection is very different from the crisis of graduate school admission, except that it comes at a later point in the applicants' professional experiences."

The issues involved in *Bakke*, the Blackmun memo went on, are "both vital and unusually difficult." They are made even "more difficult when Bakke, an excluded person not charged with discrimination, is the one who is disadvantaged, and when the University itself is not charged with past discrimination."

The memo, like Blackmun's opinion, noted that enlargement of the numbers in graduate schools was not feasible, that the Davis 84.–16 division had no special significance, and that other preferences had long been present in admissions programs. "No one seems to have evinced much concern about such practices. There are grumblings here and there, but no action."

The memo next indicated that admissions programs were basically the responsibility of the educators concerned. "As the Chief said in his typed circulation, the Court consistently has acknowledged that the administration and management of educational institutions is beyond the competence of judges and is within the special competence of educators, provided always that the latter perform within legal and constitutional bounds. Lewis' references to comments by Felix Frankfurter and Bill Brennan are in the same vein."

Thus, Blackmun concluded, "An admissions policy that has an awareness of race as an element seems to me to be the only possible and realistic means of achieving the societal goal I have mentioned above. The question, then, is whether it is legally and constitutionally permissible."

The first part of the Blackmun memo then ended with the observation, "Our individual answers to the issues here will depend, I suspect, in large part upon our respective personal conceptions of the kind of America that was contemplated by Title VI and by the Fourteenth Amendment." The second and third parts of the memo were devoted to Title VI and the Fourteenth Amendment.

The second part of the Blackmun memo was headed *Title VI*. It does not appear in Blackmun's *Bakke* opinion even though the memo's discussion of Title VI begins by asserting, "I agree that we must confront this issue and decide it, and that we cannot, or at least should not, sidestep it. If it proves to be dispositive, that is an end to the matter."

Opponents of the Davis program had stressed a statement by Senator Hubert Humphrey, which they claimed showed that the statute barred "distinction in treatment . . . given to different individuals because of their different race."[2] In the Court itself, the Chief Justice and Justice Stevens had relied on the Humphrey statement. Now Blackmun, in his memo, rejected their approach. "I do not," Blackmun wrote, "read the legislative remarks the way the Chief Justice does. In particular, I do not read Senator Humphrey's remarks that way. Hubert, I believe, was merely expressing again *his* American dream and saying, in a different and, of course, better way, what I have tried to say above about a mature society that looks upon each other as just Americans and not as ethnic or minority groups. Hubert's emphasis was inclusive, not exclusive." Indeed, Blackmun asserted, Senator Humphrey would have decided *Bakke* in favor of Davis. "I suspect, from what I know of the Senator, there could be only one answer for him to the *Bakke* case; indeed, I doubt if he would find it very difficult at all."

Blackmun's own interpretation of the statute was "that Congress, in Title VI, as with the Amendment, was concerned with the unconstitutional use of race criteria, not with the use of race as an appropriate remedial feature." In addition, Blackmun wrote, "For me, it is hard to conclude that Title VI reads more extensively than the Fourteenth Amendment."

Blackmun also stated that his view was "that there is no independent cause of action under Title VI." But, for purposes of the case, "I am willing to *assume* that a private cause of action exists under Title VI and to go on from there."

However, Blackmun stated that the constitutional issue should not be avoided. "I tentatively agree with Lewis that a decision on Title VI alone is not the way to go in this case." And he closed the second part of his memo by asserting that the decision should deal with the racial factor issue. "I . . . agree," Blackmun wrote, "with Byron and Bill Brennan that the Court should decide whether race can ever be a permissible consideration."

The third part of the Blackmun memo was headed, *The Fourteenth Amendment and Equal Protection*. It began (as does the final Blackmun opinion) by stating four governing Fourteenth Amendment principles and emphasizing the Amendment's original purpose. Blackmun then urged, "The very raison d'etre of the Fourteenth Amendment may not be set aside entirely or ignored for a 'new era' when we are dealing with the kind of disadvantage bred by the discrimination of our own past, the 'unrequited toil,' to use Lincoln's words, the Equal Protection Clause was designed to counter. To do otherwise is to ignore history."

Next Blackmun asserted what he saw as the key principle, which permitted racial factors to be considered: "it is the unconstitutional use of race that is prohibited, not the constitutional use."

As in his *Bakke* opinion, Blackmun turned to other cases, notably *Lau*[3] and *UJO*.[4] He noted that "there is the growing body of cases among the lower courts requiring specific racial employment features until the status is achieved that would have prevailed had past discrimination not taken place." He also stated, "I doubt that the sex classification cases are so easily brushed aside just because they are 'relatively manageable' and less complex."

As Blackmun saw it, "The weakness, of course, in the specific Davis program is its susceptibility to labeling as a blatant quota system, which Lewis so effectively attacks." On the other hand, "Lewis would uphold the Harvard-Columbia-Pennsylvania-Stanford program where race or ethnic background is put forward as only one of many factors and where good faith in its administration is professed. I, too, am willing to accept that element of good faith, if for no other reason, I suppose, than that I saw it in operation when I worked a little in past years on admissions in the field."

At the same time, Blackmun stated that the Davis program was within constitutional bounds. He justified this conclusion by a passage not present in his *Bakke* opinion: "The Davis program is a benign one and carries no stigma. Its race-conscious aspect could be far better formulated, but the numbers it employs are reasonably acceptable to the necessary social goal. Its very race-consciousness had no invidious purpose and meets Fourteenth Amendment requirements."

The third part of Blackmun's memo concluded with a discussion of the position taken by Professor Alexander Bickel, a leading academic opponent of the Davis-type program. "Alex Bickel's elegant and shining words," Blackmun wrote, "of course, speak of the idealistic and have great appeal. But I say, once more, that this is not an ideal world, yet."

Blackmun asserted that Bickel's "position is—and I hope I offend no one, for I do not mean to do so—the 'accepted' Jewish approach. It is to be noted that nearly all the responsible Jewish organizations who have filed amicus briefs here are one side of the case. They understandably want 'pure' equality and are willing to take their chances with it, knowing that they have the inherent ability to excel and to live with it successfully. Centuries of persecution and adversity and discrimination have given the Jewish people this great attribute to compete successfully and this remarkable fortitude."

Blackmun concluded with a short *Summary*. It began with a paragraph summarizing the Blackmun position on the case: "In general, then, my position, as of now, is to embark upon at least a cursory examination of Title VI, with a statement of general principles as to statutory and constitutional solutions; to express doubt about the existence of a private right of action under Title VI; to assume, nevertheless, that such a right of action does exist; to equate rights under Title VI with those under the Fourteenth

Amendment; and to hold that the Davis program, despite its superficial vestments, comports with the Fourteenth Amendment. I therefore vote to reverse."

Blackmun ended his memo by expressing appreciation for "the patience of each and all of you." The case, the Justice wrote, "is of such importance that I refused to be drawn to a precipitate conclusion. I wanted the time to think about it and to study the pertinent material. Because weeks are still available before the end of the term, I do not apologize; I merely explain."

POWELL REDRAFT AND "ROADMAP"

In his May 1 memo finally announcing his *Bakke* vote, Justice Blackmun noted, "I have not had the benefit of the Conference discussion of early December, so I do not know precisely how my vote affects the ultimate tally."

In fact, of course, Blackmun's vote ended the *Bakke* logjam and paved the way for the final decision in the case. The vote was now definitely four-one-four, with Justices Brennan, White, Marshall, and Blackmun for reversal on both Title VI and Fourteenth Amendment grounds, and the Chief Justice and Justices Stewart, Rehnquist, and Stevens for affirmance on Title VI grounds. Justice Powell was for affirmance on the ground that the Davis program violated equal protection, but for reversal of the California holding that race could never be considered as a factor in admissions programs.

On May 2, the day after the Blackmun memo, the Chief Justice circulated a MEMORANDUM TO THE CONFERENCE attempting to work out a procedure for decision of the case. "Given the posture of this case," it began, "Bill Brennan and I conferred with a view to considering what may fairly be called a 'joint' assignment. There being four definitive decisions tending one way, four another, Lewis' position can be joined in part by some or all of each 'four groups.'" In these circumstances, the memo stated, "the case is assigned to Lewis who assures a first circulation within one week from today."

A week later, on May 9, Justice Powell circulated a new draft of his opinion, which was headed, "MR JUSTICE POWELL announced the judgment of the Court." Though further drafts were circulated on June 9 and 23, this May 9 version was virtually the same as the final Powell *Bakke* opinion. The draft was accompanied by a MEMORANDUM TO THE

CONFERENCE, which indicated that the Burger-Brennan assignment to Powell was to prepare a "judgment" rather than an opinion of the Court. "In accordance with the assignment from the Chief Justice and Bill Brennan," the Powell memo stated, "I have prepared—and now circulate—a proposed 'judgment' decision in this case."

The judgment portion of the Powell draft was contained in its first page and a half. "As suggested by the Chief and Bill," the memo informed the others, "the format attempts to follow that of *Mitchell* v. *Oregon*, 400 U.S. 112 (Mr. Justice Black)."

The judgment drafted by Powell was based upon the fact that, as the memo noted, "there are four votes to affirm the judgment of the Supreme Court of California in its entirety, and four votes to reverse it." To obtain the judgment, Powell wrote, "I will join the four votes to affirm as to Bakke himself and the invalidity of petitioner's program, but I take a different view—and therefore will reverse—as to the portion of the judgment enjoining petitioner from any consideration of race in its admission program. Accordingly, the judgment of this Court would be: 'Affirmed in part and reversed in part.'"

Enclosed with the Powell memo was a two-page document headed, *Outline of Draft Opinion*. The memo explained this outline as follows: "I attach a rough 'roadmap' of the enclosed opinion, hoping it will be helpful." Since this is its author's summary of the opinion which commentators accept as stating the constitutional views accepted by *Bakke*, it is worthwhile to quote from this "roadmap" in some detail.

The Powell outline begins by summarizing Parts I and II of his opinion, which were not contained in his original November 22 draft, discussed in chapter 7. Part I, Powell writes, is a statement of the facts and case history. Part II deals with Title VI. It assumes the existence of a cause of action and then "considers the meaning of the statute and concludes that it proscribes only those racial classifications that would violate the Equal Protection Clause or the Fifth Amendment."

"The remainder of the opinion," the outline says, "tracks quite closely the memorandum that I circulated on December 1, 1977, as I recall"—i.e., the second circulation of Powell's original draft. It begins with Part III, which "is a short section dealing with the irrelevancy of the semantic wrangle over the terms 'quota' and 'goal.'" Then comes Part IV, "devoted to determination of the appropriate level of scrutiny." As Powell's outline states, this part "is a brief statement of this Court's traditional view of all racial classifications as suspect." It "explores the historical underpinnings of that view, and ... deals with what I view as the doctrinal problems entailed by adoption of any other view." At its end, Part IV "distinguishes prior decisions cited as approving less exacting levels of scrutiny."

In Part V, "the various justifications for petitioner's classification are examined to determine whether they are 'compelling.'" The opinion "concludes that increased minority representation, *per se*, is not a legitimate goal." Powell then "finds that eliminating the effects of past discriminating is a compelling state interest, but that such effects and their incidence have not been identified with sufficient precision in the instant case to permit petitioner to claim that it actually is advancing that goal."

The Powell "roadmap" then states that this part of his opinion "also recognizes improved health care for underserved citizens as a goal of great importance, but concludes that nothing in this record establishes that this program actually advances it." On the other hand, the opinion "finds that because of the existence of countervailing and substantial First Amendment interests, the achievement of educational diversity is a compelling interest for an educational institution to advance." Part V then ends by indicating "that petitioner's program must serve this goal in the least intrusive manner."

As summarized by Powell, Part VI of his opinion "involves 'means' analysis." It "concludes that petitioner's program is not the least intrusive method of serving its avowedly constitutional goal." The opinion then "identifies a widely used program that I view as a less restrictive alternative. It concludes that the California court erred in assuming that even such a program would be invalid and in barring its implementation."

This part of the opinion next "summarizes the conclusion that petitioner's program is invalid, and ... states the judgment that the court below went too far in proscribing all consideration of race as a relevant factor." This leads to the last part of Powell's opinion, Part VII, which, according to the "roadmap," "states the judgment that Bakke is entitled to admission and explains why a remand is not called for."

BRENNAN'S OPINION

On May 10, Justice Brennan sent a "Dear Lewis" letter, "I have read your opinion very carefully and have regretfully come to the conclusion that I should write out my own views." His views, Brennan wrote, "differ so substantially from your own that no common ground seems possible."

Three weeks later, on May 30, Brennan wrote to Justice White that he was working on an opinion which he hoped would be joined by the pro-Davis Justices. "I am shooting for the beginning of next week to get a copy of the constitutional treatment to you, Harry and Thurgood." Brennan informed White that he was "determined to do what I possibly can to have Harry, you and I and, if possible at all, to have Thurgood agree on a joint opinion."

On June 12, Justice Brennan sent a working draft of his opinion to Justices White, Marshall, Blackmun, and Powell. Though there were three recirculations, on June 16, 22, and 26, Brennan's draft was essentially similar to his final opinion, which was joined by Justices White, Marshall, and Blackmun. The first Brennan draft was stronger in its language condemning racial discrimination than the final opinion. This led Justice White to write to Brennan, on June 13, "I am inclined to keep the decibel level as low as possible. We won't accomplish much by beating a white majority over past ills or by describing what has gone by as a system of apartheid." This in turn led Brennan to tone down the language in later drafts.

The key passage of Brennan's opinion[5] was contained in the June 12 draft. This was the statement in the draft's first paragraph on "the central meaning of this Court's judgment: Government may take race into account when it acts not to demean or insult any racial group, but to remedy disadvantages cast on minorities by past racial prejudice."

After he had sent around the draft, Justice Brennan telephoned Justice Powell to ask whether this sentence was accurate as to Powell's opinion as well as Brennan's. Powell replied by a June 23 letter: "If your statement is read literally, I doubt that it does reflect accurately the judgment of the Court. In terms of 'judgment,' my opinion is limited to the holding that a state university validly may consider race to achieve diversity."

Powell did, however, concede, "my opinion recognizes broadly (perhaps one could call it dicta) that consideration of race is appropriate to eliminate the effects of past discrimination when appropriate findings have been made by judicial, legislative or administrative bodies authorized to act." This led Brennan to add the modifying phrase to his "central meaning" statement—"at least when appropriate findings have been made by judicial, legislative, or administrative bodies with competence to act in this area."

Powell stated that, in his opinion, the Brennan "central meaning" statement went too far. In Powell's view, "the *judgment* itself does not go beyond permissible use of race in the context of achieving a diverse student body at a state university. This holding could be stated more broadly in one simple sentence as follows:

'Government validly may take race into account in furthering the compelling state interest of achieving a diverse student body.'"

"Despite the foregoing," Powell wrote, "I have not objected to your characterization of what the Court holds as I have thought you could put whatever 'gloss' on the several opinions you think proper. I believe that one who reads my opinion carefully will conclude that your gloss goes somewhat beyond what I have written and what I think."

Powell ended his letter to Brennan by indicating that he would do nothing further on the matter. "In sum," the letter concluded, "while I might prefer that you describe the judgment differently, I have no thought of making any response on this point beyond what I have already circulated."

Even if Powell's view was correct, Brennan's statement appeared virtually without contradiction from the other Justices. The demurrer in a footnote in Justice Stevens's opinion that "only a majority can speak for the Court or determine what is the 'central meaning' of any judgment of the Court"[6] scarcely changed this. The result has been that Brennan's statement has been taken as the "central meaning" of *Bakke* by most commentators[7] and has molded the post-*Bakke* law on the subject.

OTHER OPINIONS AND ANNOUNCEMENT

The Justices who joined the Brennan opinion also issued their own opinions. Blackmun's draft was circulated June 19, White's on June 21, and Marshall's on June 23. These were essentially the same as their final opinions, though minor modifications were made in further recirculations.

In his May 30 letter to Justice White, Justice Brennan wrote, "the scuttlebutt has it that the 'gang of four' will shortly have their Title VI disposition in circulation." Two weeks later, on June 12, Justice Stevens circulated the first draft of his opinion affirming on Title VI grounds alone.

On the same day, Justices Stewart and Rehnquist wrote joining the Stevens opinion; the Chief Justice sent a similar letter on June 13. Further drafts of the Stevens opinion, containing minor changes, were circulated on June 19 and 22.

One further step was necessary before the *Bakke* decision could come down. This was the preparation of the public statement announcing the Court's judgment. The normal practice when decisions are handed down by the Court is for the Justice who wrote the Court opinion to announce the decision, and Justices who wrote concurring or dissenting opinions to state their views as well. In *Bakke*, however, the Court was so fragmented that it was necessary for the decision announcement to be preceded by a detailed explanation of the judgment in the case.

Justice Powell, apparently on his own initiative, undertook the writing of a statement explaining the *Bakke* judgment. He sent around a draft on June 21. It was headed, *Proposed Statement from Bench*. "On the assumption that I will announce the judgment in this case," the covering memo stated, "I have tried my hand at a statement." The memo then stated Powell's main goal in his statement: "My primary purpose was to assist the representatives of the media present in understanding 'what in the world' the Court has done!"

On June 27, Justice Powell circulated what his covering memo said was "a revised draft of . . . my proposed announcement of the judgment in this case." After noting that the new draft made some changes (none of them was important), the memo concluded, "As I am a 'chief' with no 'indians,' I should be in the rear rank, not up front!"

NOTES

1. Baldwin v. Montana Fish and Game Commission, 436 U.S. 371 (1978).
2. See Bakke, 438 U.S. at 415.
3. Lau v. Nichols, 414 U.S. 563 (1974).
4. UJO v. Carey, 430 U.S. 144 (1977).
5. 438 U.S. at 325.
6. 438 U.S. at 408, n.1.
7. E.g., 2 Rotunda, Novak, and Young, *Treatise on Constitutional Law* 454 (1986); Schwartz, *Constitutional Law: A Textbook* 378 (2d ed. 1979).

THIRTEEN

Decision Day

W<small>EDNESDAY</small>, June 27, 1978. The Supreme Court chamber was un-characteristically uncrowded, for the public was unaware that this was to be anything but the ordinary session. To the acute Court watcher, however, there were definite signs that the day would not be a quiet one. For one thing, Mrs. Brennan, Mrs. Stewart, Mrs. Marshall, and Mrs. Stevens were present—something that rarely happened except on historic occasions. Then Court employees and law clerks drifted into the chamber, for the scuttlebutt in the Marble Palace had it that the *Bakke* decision was to come down that morning.

At 10:01 A.M., exactly one minute late that day, Chief Justice Burger stepped from behind the red velvet curtains and took his place at the center of the bench. The eight other Justices followed and filed behind their high-backed black-leather chairs. The marshal sang out the time-honored intonation: "Oyez, oyez, oyez" and invoking God's protection for "the United States and this honorable Court."

The Chief Justice began the session by asking Justice Stewart to announce a decision in a pensions benefit case.[1] Burger next quickly announced a criminal-law decision[2] himself. Then the Chief Justice leaned forward and stated to the hushed courtroom that Justice Powell would deliver the judgment of the Court in No. 76–811, *Regents of the University of California v. Bakke.*

POWELL'S ANNOUNCEMENT

At this Justice Powell, his mild Virginia drawl never rising above an unemotional monotone, read the announcement of the judgment which he had prepared.[3] "The facts in this case," Powell began, "are too well known to require restatement. Perhaps no case in modern memory has received as much media coverage and scholarly commentary." He then noted that "we will speak today with a notable lack of unanimity." At the same time, "it will be evident from our several opinions that the case—intrinsically difficult—has received our most thoughtful attention over many months."

"So much," Powell concluded the first part of his announcement, "for an introduction." He then said, "As there are six separate opinions, and the judgment itself is a bifurcated one, I will try at the outset to explain the judgment."

Justice Powell started his explanation by pointing out, "The opinion and judgment of the Supreme Court of California presented us with two central questions: the first—and the one widely perceived as the only ultimate question—is whether the medical school's special admissions program discriminated unlawfully against Bakke, either under the Constitution or Title VI of the Civil Rights Act of 1964. I will refer to this as the Bakke admission question."

"The second, and broader question," Powell went on, "is whether it is ever permissible to consider race as a factor relevant to the admission of applicants to a university. I will refer to this question, generally, as whether race may be considered."

The Justice then dealt with the possible answers to the second question. Firstly, "if the answer to the second question is negative—that is, that race may never validly be considered, this answer disposes of both issues. Bakke would be admitted, and the University could not in the future give any consideration to race in its admissions program."

If, on the other hand, "the second question is answered affirmatively—that is, that race may be considered—then it becomes necessary also to address the first question separately: that is whether the special admissions program at Davis is compatible with Title VI and the Constitution." Powell also noted that, if the case "were disposed of under Title VI, there would be no occasion to reach the constitutional issues."

"Now," began the statement's next part, "as to how the questions are decided."

First, Powell summarized the Stevens opinion. "Mr. Justice Stevens, joined by the Chief Justice, and Justices Stewart and Rehnquist, concludes that Title VI does control. As he will state more fully, Mr. Justice Stevens concludes that Bakke was excluded from Davis in violation of Title VI. His plurality opinion therefore concurs in the Court's judgment insofar as it affirms the judgment of the California Court ordering that Bakke be admitted." (Interestingly, the first draft of Powell's statement had referred to this opinion as "the Chief Justice's plurality view." The copy I have used has next to this, in the writing of a Justice, the word, "intentional").

Powell then stated that a majority rejected the Stevens view. "Justices Brennan, White, Marshall, Blackmun and I have a different view as to Title VI. We believe, despite its more detailed provisions, that it goes no further in prohibiting the use of race than the Equal Protection Clause. The five of us therefore reach both of the constitutional questions."

The Justice summarized Brennan's constitutional approach: "On a constitutional analysis, founded on the equal protection clause, Justices Brennan, White, Marshall, and Blackmun in their joint opinion hold not only that race properly may be considered, but that the special admissions program of the Davis Medical School is valid in every respect."

Powell next indicated his own view, saying, "On the first question—whether the special admissions program is invalid—I agree with the result reached by Mr. Justice Stevens' opinion." However, he went on, "I do so on constitutional grounds rather than under Title VI."

This meant, the Justice said, "there are five votes to affirm the judgment invalidating the special program. Under this judgment, Bakke will be admitted to the medical school."

Powell then turned "to the second constitutional issue—whether race may be considered as a factor in an admissions program." With regard to it, Powell stated, "I agree with the result reached by the joint opinion of Mr. Justice Brennan and my Brothers who joined him. Thus, there are five Justices who join in a judgment of reversal on this issue." However, Powell stressed, "the process of constitutional analysis by which I reach this result differs significantly from that of the four Justices who have filed a joint opinion."

The remainder of Powell's announcement from the bench was devoted to what he termed "a brief conclusory statement" summarizing his *Bakke* opinion. This statement is of interest, since it was intended for the courtroom audience and hence summarizes the Powell opinion in a more read-able manner than his "roadmap," discussed in the last chapter.

First of all, said Powell, the Davis special admissions program "is a classification based on race. Our cases establish, beyond question, that a racial classification is inherently suspect, and must be subjected to the most exacting judicial scrutiny."

It is true, the Justice continued, that "our cases have held that some distinctions are justified if necessary to further a compelling state interest." Davis, Powell noted, asserted a compelling interest in "the desire to redress a racial imbalance said to result from general societal discrimination against the minority groups selected for preferential treatment." Powell rejected this claim: "Discrimination by society at large, with no determined effects, is not sufficient to justify petitioner's racial classification."

"In my view," Powell declared, "the only interest that fairly may be viewed as compelling on this record is that of a university in a diverse student body." But, according to the Justice, "there has been no showing in this case that the Davis special program is necessary to achieve educa-tional diversity."

On the other hand, as Powell saw it, "A university's interest in a diverse student body is not limited to ethnic diversity. Rather, its compelling interest in this respect encompasses a far broader array of qualifications and characteristics, of which race is only one."

Powell then noted, "My opinion refers to the Harvard admission pro-gram as an example of how race properly may be taken into account." Under the Harvard admissions procedure, "race is considered in a flexible program designed to achieve diversity, but it is only one factor—weighed competitively—against a number of other factors deemed relevant." Such "a flexible, competitive admissions program in which race may be consid-ered" is used in "many of our finest universities and colleges."

Their experience, in the Powell view, "demonstrates that the Davis-type program—one that arbitrarily forecloses all competition solely on the basis of race or ethnic origin—is not necessary to attain reasonable educational diversity." The necessary conclusion is that the Davis program "therefore violates the Equal Protection Clause in a most fundamental sense."

Yet this was not the only result of the Powell opinion. On the contrary, though the decision meant that Bakke had won admission to Davis, Justice Powell's agreement with the Brennan four that race might be a factor also left the way open for special admissions programs of the Harvard type. Hence, as Powell put it in concluding his announcement from the bench, "the way is open to Davis to adopt the type of admissions program proved to be successful at many of our great universities."

OTHER ANNOUNCEMENTS

It used to be the custom for the Justices to read their opinions on Supreme Court decision days. In recent years, however, the Justices have come to read only summaries of their opinions, such as that by Justice Powell of his *Bakke* opinion. After Powell's statement, Justices Brennan and Stevens read summaries of their plurality opinions. Justices Marshall and Blackmun also made statements giving the gist of their separate opinions. Only Justice White, of the *Bakke* opinion writers, made no oral statement.

Justice Brennan made the most interesting of these statements. In it, even more than in his opinion, he stressed what he claimed was the key *Bakke* holding. Brennan noted that "only five members of the Court address the constitutional question of uniquely paramount importance that this case presents—what race-conscious programs are permissible under the Equal Protection Clause—although it is no secret that the Court took this case as the vehicle for confronting that constitutional issue after avoiding it on mootness grounds in the *DeFunis* case."

"But," Brennan declared, "the fact that only five of the nine Justices address the constitutional question must not obscure the signal importance of today's decision. Five of us, a Court majority, reverse the judgment of the California Supreme Court insofar as it prohibits Davis from establishing race-conscious admissions programs in the future. Thus the central meaning of today's opinion is this: Government may take race into account when it acts not to demean or insult any racial group, but to remedy disadvantages cast on minorities by past racial prejudice, at least when appropriate findings have been made by judicial, legislative or administrative bodies with competence to act in this area."

The Brennan statement of the "central meaning" of *Bakke* was, of course, that asserted at the beginning of the Justice's opinion in the case.[4] As seen in the last chapter, the statement was that contained in Brennan's first draft, as modified to meet the criticism in Justice Powell's June 23 letter (supra p. 139).

In a later portion of his statement, Justice Brennan summarized the review standard that should be applied in such a case. As he saw it, neither the strict-scrutiny nor the rational-basis test furnished the proper standard. Instead, "Our opinion adopts a standard somewhere between." To justify a classification such as that under the Davis program, "an important and articulated purpose for its use must be shown."[5] It also must be shown that the program is not one "that stigmatizes any group or that singles out those least well represented in the political process to bear the brunt of a benign program."[6]

Under such a standard, Brennan concluded that the Davis program was valid. "Our opinion next analyzes the Davis program by that standard and concludes that it passes constitutional muster as a permissible program to remove the disparate racial impact its admissions program might otherwise have, and was adopted on the basis of the reasonable belief that the disparate impact is itself the product of past discrimination, whether the University's or that of society at large."

After Justice Brennan had finished reading his statement from the bench, Justice White, who sat next to him, passed him a handwritten note:

Bill,
You were great, and could I have a copy of your statement?

Byron

The Brennan statement was, however, more than "great." It represented the culmination of the Justice's efforts to secure a victory from an almost certain *Bakke* defeat. Had Brennan not persuaded Justice Powell to join the reversal of the California judgment insofar as it prohibited taking race into account as a factor in admissions decisions, the anti-Davis Justices would have secured a complete victory in the case. But Brennan did not rest with merely defeating that result. Instead, he continually stressed what he called "the central meaning" of the Court's decision—both in the decision process and in his opinion and summarizing statement. As pointed out in the last chapter, Justice Powell did not agree with the Brennan assertion on "central meaning." But he said nothing publicly and this enabled the Brennan interpretation to go virtually unchallenged (except for a relatively mild footnote in Justice Stevens's opinion).[7] We shall see that this has permitted the Brennan view of *Bakke* all but to take over the field. In turn, this has enabled universities to continue their programs that provide for the preferential admission of minority students—provided only that they follow the Harvard, rather than the Davis type format.

His role in the *Bakke* decision process illustrates why Justice Brennan was, next to only the Chief Justice himself, the most influential member of the Warren Court.[8] In the Burger Court, it can be argued that it was Brennan who was primarily responsible for preserving the essential Warren heritage—for ensuring that the Burger years saw, in the phrase of one book, a "counter-revolution that wasn't."[9] In *Bakke*, as in other cases, it was Brennan who turned a quondam conservative vote into what he could claim was a decision supporting his view on special admissions programs.

"PEOPLE WILL BE OVERWHELMED"

Five days before the *Bakke* decision was announced, Chief Justice Burger sent around a June 23 MEMORANDUM TO THE CONFERENCE suggesting changes in the proposed headnote prepared for the case. The most important change suggested was in the draft's statement of the reversal, which read that the judgment below "is reversed insofar as it prohibits petitioner from taking race into account in any way in its future admissions decisions." Burger wrote that this was inaccurate and noted, "I understand from Lewis that he agrees that the three words 'in any way' overstate the holding. He also indicates he would suggest that these three words be stricken and 'as a factor' be substituted."[10]

"Ordinarily," the Burger memo conceded, "we need not worry unduly about headnotes but with the high tension that has been generated, the headnote in this case is crucial and will guide most of what is written and said on the evening and day following announcement."

The Chief Justice ended his memo by noting, "All these final days are under pressure and it is understandable that problems such as this arise." However, he wrote, it was "imperative" that the headnote be accurate. "At best," Burger wryly remarked, "people will be overwhelmed in dealing with this case."

Certainly there were different reactions in the press and public when the *Bakke* decision was announced and the opinions issued. Press headlines ran the gamut from the one extreme in *Time*: "Bakke Wins, Quotas Lose,"[11] to the other in Harlem's *Amsterdam News*: "Bakke—We Lose!"[12] The major newspapers, however, took a more moderate position, which stressed that special admissions programs had gained at least as much as they had lost. The *New York Times*, summarizing the decision, declared, "No one lost."[13] Its news account stressed Brennan's point on the "central meaning" of the decision—that race may be taken into account in government programs.

Without referring to the Brennan statement, the principal *Times* story on
the decision began, "The Supreme Court by a 5-to-4 vote affirmed today
the constitutionality of college admission programs that give special advantage to blacks and other minorities to help remedy past discrimination
against them."[14] This means, said another *Times* article, "that the great
majority of affirmative action programs will continue."[15]

Other leading newspapers, such as the *Washington Post* and *Wall Street
Journal*, took a similar approach to the *Bakke* decision. The latter said that
the Court had approved affirmative action, but rejected rigid quotas. Hence
its story on the case was headed, "The Decision Everyone Won."[16] Certainly, Bakke personally won the case, since the Supreme Court decision
ordered his admission. Because of this the reaction on the Davis campus
was one of disappointment. "It almost brought tears to my eyes when I first
heard it," said a university personnel employee. "[T]here goes all the
progress, everything that's happened in the past 10 years."[17]

On the other hand, Bakke himself indicated uncharacteristic public
pleasure at the outcome. The morning the Supreme Court announced its
decision, he strolled into his office at the NASA research center in Palo
Alto and was greeted by his secretary: "Hi, I heard the news." Bakke
smiled, gave a slight nod, and disappeared into his office. "That was it," she
told the press. "A few people congratulated him. But it was very quiet. He
keeps his personal life to himself."[18]

However, when one of his attorneys called to tell him of the Supreme
Court decision, Bakke showed his delight. "Great," he said. "You guys did
it." Replied the attorney, "No, you did."[19]

Bakke then authorized his attorney, Reynold Colvin, to express his
pleasure at the outcome—the only public statement that he issued about
his case. At 38, a full decade older than most of his future classmates, he
would enter Davis Medical School the following September. Colvin's
statement for Bakke reiterated his basic intention to keep his privacy and
say nothing more. For the rest of his life, however, he would remain the
Bakke plaintiff. As the associate dean at Davis put it, "He will never not be
Allan Bakke"—the man who became a doctor by order of the highest
Court.[20]

NOTES

1. Allied Structural Steel Co. v. Spannaus, 438 U.S. 234 (1978).
2. Swisher v. Brady, 438 U.S. 204 (1978).

3. Since this Powell statement has not been published, it is summarized in detail. The same is true of the Brennan statement summarized later in this chapter.
4. Bakke, 438 U.S. at 325.
5. This was in the Brennan Bakke opinion, 438 U.S. at 361.
6. Compare id. at 369.
7. Id. at 408.
8. Compare Schwartz, *The Unpublished Opinion of the Warren Court* 7 (1985).
9. Blasi, *The Burger Court: The Counter-Revolution that Wasn't* (1983).
10. In the final headnote, "in any way" was changed to "as a factor." 438 U.S. at 267.
11. *Time*, July 10, 1978, p. 5.
12. Eastland and Bennett, *Counting by Race* 173 (1979).
13. See Sindler, *Bakke, DeFunis, and Minority Admissions* 317 (1978).
14. *N.Y. Times*, June 29, 1978, p. A 1.
15. Ibid.
16. See Eastland and Bennett, supra note 12, at 171.
17. "A Reaction of Disappointment on the Davis Campus," *N.Y. Times*, June 29, 1978, p. A 22.
18. *Newsweek*, July 10, 1978, p. 24.
19. *Time*, July 10, 1978, p. 15.
20. *Newsweek*, July 10, 1978, p. 24.

FOURTEEN

Bakke and Bakke Today

A DECADE after it was decided *Bakke* remains the landmark case on the validity of programs which take racial criteria into account. This concluding chapter will discuss the effect of the *Bakke* decision upon affirmative action programs in educational institutions, as well as upon the post-*Bakke* Supreme Court decisions dealing with such programs.

WAS IT ONLY "A FAMOUS VICTORY"?*

Allan Bakke, to be sure, did personally win his battle to be admitted to Davis Medical School. But it was not clear from the Supreme Court decision who had won the war over the constitutionality of preferences based upon racial criteria. As seen in the last chapter, the press and public were sharply divided in their *Bakke* scorecard. Black commentators tended to mirror the *Amsterdam News* headline already quoted: "Bakke—We Lose!" Others stressed that, while Bakke personally had won his case, that scarcely meant the end of affirmative action programs. "Most significantly," wrote the *Wall Street Journal*, "a five-member court majority voted

---

*"But what good came of it at last?"
Quoth little Peterkin.
"Why that I cannot tell," said he;
"But 'twas a famous victory."

R. Southey, "The Battle of Blenheim" (1864).

to overturn the lower court's ruling that race can't ever be a factor in admissions decisions." This meant, the paper went on, that the Supreme Court had given "qualified approval to affirmative action." From this point of view, according to the *Journal* headline, *Bakke* was "The Decision Everyone Won."[1] Or was it the decision that (aside from Bakke himself) nobody actually won?

At the time, most commentators thought that the *Bakke* decision was what one labeled "a Solomonic compromise" that did not really resolve the constitutional issue before the Court. However, examination of what has happened since *Bakke* was decided justifies a more sanguine estimate of its effect. *Bakke* did, in the main, settle the constitutionality of programs involving racial preferences and it did so in a manner that has permitted the widespread continuation of affirmative action programs. That it did so was largely the result of Justice Brennan's efforts during the decision process to change Justice Powell's vote from a flat affirmance to a partial affirmance and partial reversal.

It should not be forgotten that the *Bakke* decision was really two decisions—each decided by a five-to-four vote. The first decision was that the Davis special admissions program was invalid and that Bakke should be admitted to the medical school. Justice Powell joined the Chief Justice and Justices Stevens, Stewart, and Rehnquist to make up the majority supporting this decision. The second decision was that race was a factor which might be considered in an admissions policy without violating the Constitution. Justice Powell joined the other four Justices (Brennan, White, Marshall, and Blackmun) to make up the bare majority behind this decision.

The unifying factor behind both *Bakke* decisions was Justice Powell's vote, which alone gave them the majority required to make them decisions of the Court. Without Powell, there was a four-to-four division in the *Bakke* Court. The consequence of this split was that Justice Powell's opinion— though it was fully endorsed by no other Justice—spoke for the bare majorities on each of the major issues decided by the case.

The result has been that commentators, courts, and admissions officers have treated Justice Powell's opinion as the authoritative opinion in the *Bakke* case. Indeed, according to one survey of the post-*Bakke* situation, "many admissions officers today are according Powell's majority ruling the same deference they would a unanimous ruling."[2] This has made *Bakke* "a famous victory" only for those who oppose affirmative action programs as "reverse discrimination." Though the Davis program was invalidated, the Powell opinion permits admissions officers to operate programs which grant racial preferences—provided that they do not do so as blatantly as was done under the sixteen-seat "quota" provided at Davis.

In the Court itself, the great victor in *Bakke* was Justice Brennan. It was he who persuaded Justice Powell to change his categorical vote for affirmance of the California Supreme Court to a mixed affirmance and reversal. That permitted the decision to approve race as a factor in admissions decisions, which, in turn, has meant the continued validity of affirmative action programs. This has enabled universities and professional schools, particularly medical schools and law schools, to go ahead with their programs designed to secure admission of minority students. In addition, the Supreme Court itself has tended to follow Justice Powell's approach in the post-*Bakke* cases involving the constitutionality of affirmative action programs.

SPECIAL ADMISSIONS STILL SPECIAL

Soon after the *Bakke* decision, the American Council on Education joined with the Association of American Law Schools to set up a committee to report on the Supreme Court decision. The committee issued a report on the implications of *Bakke* for higher education admissions. Its basic conclusion was that the Supreme Court had recognized the authority of institutions of higher education to continue under certain circumstances their affirmative action programs. Referring to Justice Powell, the report stated, "If his opinion were accepted as the touchstone for decisions by the courts in future cases, then the initial message of *Bakke* would be fairly clear: reservation of a specific number of places in each entering class exclusively for students of designated minority groups, whether called a quota or goal, is prohibited while the use of race in a flexible admission policy designed to produce diversity in the student body on various factors is permissible."[3]

In essence, what the *Bakke* Court intended, according to the ACE-AALS report, was to authorize a broad range of discretion by the relevant education authorities. "The opinions in *Bakke* leave broad scope for discretion to be exercised by an institution in constructing an admission policy and by faculty or staff in implementing that policy. Indeed, the basic message of the Court may well have been that the question of preferential admission is one best committed to the judgment of educational and legislative policy makers."[4]

The result has been that *Bakke* has, in practice, served to license, not to prohibit, race-conscious admissions programs. An article on the effect of *Bakke* could consequently be entitled, "Special Admissions Are Still Special: Why Little Has Changed Since Bakke."[5] The author interviewed admissions officials at law schools across the country and concluded, from what they told him, that *Bakke* would not affect the number of minority applicants admitted.[6] He, too, stressed that the Justices had recognized the discretion of universities to structure admissions standards and procedures. "Since law schools were exercising this discretion before *Bakke*, and it does not seem particularly difficult to avoid quotas, no admissions official anticipated that *Bakke* would make a significant difference in the number of minority students enrolled."[7]

As it turned out, the most important language in *Bakke* was that in the Powell opinion on the permissibility of race as a factor in admissions decisions. According to it, "the State has a substantial interest that legitimately may be served by a properly devised admissions program involving the competitive consideration of race and ethnic origin."[8] This recognizes that universities may structure their admissions standards and procedures to consider race as a factor, provided they do not employ Davis-type formal quotas.

As described in the article already quoted, "Powell's decision is being read as delegating to universities the power to balance between the rights of non-minority applicants and the goal of affirmative action, as long as the universities do not exclude non-minority candidates from competing for any seat in an entering class."[9] In effect, this has permitted the continuance of special admissions programs designed to ensure the admission of minority students, even though they may not fully measure up to the academic criteria used to judge the acceptance of white applicants.

What this means can be seen from the effect of *Bakke* upon the admissions process at my own law school—that at New York University. A special committee appointed to analyze the school's admission policy in light of the *Bakke* decision reported that that policy should be guided by the Powell opinion. Under it, an admissions policy in which any places are reserved to members of particular racial groups is invalid. On the contrary, all applicants, regardless of race, must be eligible to compete for every seat. But, while seats may not be reserved for particular races, race may be considered in deciding among applicants, in order to assure diversity in the student body.

The report of the *Bakke* committee, which the New York University Law Faculty adopted, listed the factors which would guide the selection of applicants who did not demonstrate "outstanding academic achievement." Among the factors to be considered is:

"diversity in
(1) age
(2) sex
(3) race
(4) place of residence
(5) socio-economic condition
(6) other unique background factors."

These factors, the report stated, are "designed to assure that the class will be composed of persons who will bring the widest variety of personal characteristics relevant to the law school experience as possible." In particular, the report as adopted by the faculty emphasized that, in the process of creating a diverse student body, "a special effort must continue to be made to produce, at a minimum, a group of minority students of sufficient size to create, in the language of the Harvard admissions policy statement, a 'reasonable environment', i.e., one which will avoid 'a sense of isolation among the [minority] students themselves [which would] make it more difficult for them to develop and achieve their potential.' In our view, this special consideration for minority students [was] implicitly approved by Justice Powell."

Such an approach permits the law school to admit minority applicants in sufficient numbers so that they make up a significant proportion of the student body. To accomplish that result, minority applicants may be given enough of a preference based upon their race to ensure that the school's "goal" of minority enrollment is met. *Bakke*, in other words, is read as vesting admissions officers with very broad discretion to decide how much weight to grant race, as long as Davis-type quotas are not used. Virtually all universities and professional schools have maintained their programs for minority admissions and have operated them to secure roughly the same percentage of minority students each year. What they have eliminated is the Davis-type setting aside of a specific percentage or number of seats which may be filled only by minority applicants.

Is the present admissions approach really different from the *Bakke*-proscribed Davis program? Certainly, as Justice Blackmun put it in his *Bakke* opinion, the line between the invalid Davis program and the Harvard-type program approved by Justice Powell, in which race is one admissions factor, "is a thin and indistinct one. In each, subjective application is at work." One may go further and "say that under a program such as Harvard's one may accomplish covertly what Davis concedes it does openly."10

Yet, even if that is true, the difference between the Davis-type and Harvard-type program has proved crucial in the post-*Bakke* practice. And the discretion recognized in them by Justice Powell's opinion has permitted admissions officers to employ systems of racial preference which have enabled them to attain whatever "goals" they have chosen regarding minority enrollments.

The bottom line then is that *Bakke* has meant anything but the end of special admissions programs. On the contrary, the post-*Bakke* situation is, practically speaking, not very different from what it was before the Supreme Court decision. Minority admissions are still treated as special and universities continue to accord racial preferences to ensure that minority students constitute a significant portion of those enrolled. Has such a result been consistent with the post-*Bakke* caselaw on the subject?

FULLILOVE V. KLUTZNICK

In answering the question just posed, we should bear in mind that there has not been another *Bakke*-type university admissions case since *Bakke* itself was decided—despite the many predictions that *Bakke* would spawn a series of similar challenges to special admissions programs.11 There are two reasons for the dearth of *Bakke*-type cases challenging such programs in educational institutions. In the first place, there has been a financial barrier to such suits. *Bakke*-type litigation is expensive (the cost of the University of California's defense before the United States Supreme Court alone was $160,000)12 and few litigants have been able to assume such a burden.

Even more important has been the difficulty in winning *Bakke*-type suits because of the response by universities to the decision. As just seen, they have eliminated Davis-type quotas but their admissions programs have continued to grant racial preferences to secure a racially diverse student body. These post-*Bakke* programs have been rendered virtually immune, practically speaking, from constitutional attack because of the discretion recognized in admissions officers by Powell's *Bakke* opinion.

According to Justice Powell, it is up to the education authorities to determine how much weight to attribute to a particular factor, such as race, in making their admissions decisions. Nor may a court "assume that a university, professing to employ a racially nondiscriminatory admissions policy, would operate it as a cover for the functional equivalent of a quota system. In short, good faith would be presumed in the absence of a showing to the contrary."[13]

To show "bad faith" would require proof that admissions officers are using their "race as a factor" consideration to mask Davis-type fixed quotas for minorities. It is difficult to see how such a claim can be proven unless the admissions officers themselves acknowledge their own "bad faith"—something that is, to say, the least, most unlikely. As Justice Brennan put it in his October 23, 1977, *Bakke* memorandum, "Unless we want to throw every admissions decision into federal court for a judge somehow to decide whether race was taken too much or too little into account, we should support a school faculty that acts honestly in adopting the type of reasonable affirmative action plan it views as appropriate for its school." Thus it turns out that "The case that many admissions officials feared would end special admissions may instead have shown universities how to insulate themselves from effective legal challenge."[14]

But that does not mean that there have not been cases involving the *Bakke*-type problem of racial preferences outside the field of university admissions. Several of these cases have reached the Supreme Court and will be discussed to determine their relationship to the *Bakke* decision.

The first of the post-*Bakke* cases[15] dealing with racial preference was *Fullilove v. Klutznick*.[16] At issue there was a provision in the Public Works Employment Act, passed by Congress in 1977, which provided that at least ten percent of the grants for public works under the Act be spent for minority business enterprises (MBE), i.e., businesses owned by members of specified minority groups. Plaintiffs were associations of construction contractors who filed suit, alleging that they had sustained economic injury due to the enforcement of the MBE requirement and that the MBE provision violated equal protection.[17]

On its face the MBE provision seems similar to the Davis program condemned in *Bakke*. Under it also, a fixed proportion of the benefits conferred is reserved for members of racial minorities and whites are completely excluded from competing for that proportion. But there were significant differences here. The racially preferential program at issue in *Fullilove* had been set up under an Act of Congress and the legislative history showed that Congress had concluded that private and governmental discrimination had contributed to the negligible percentage of public contracts awarded minority contractors.

In his conference presentation, Chief Justice Burger stressed the fact that the MBE preference was established by Congress. The Court, said the Chief Justice, should "give more latitude to Congress than [to] administrative or state action." Because of this, *Bakke* was not "as pertinent as *Katzenbach v. Morgan*"[18]—the leading case upholding the broad power of Congress to enact laws protecting minorities under the Enforcement Clause of the Fourteenth Amendment. The dominant theme, according to the Chief Justice, should be "deference to Congress."

The Chief Justice also questioned the statutory definition of minority group members because it included Orientals as well as Negroes and Indians. "The inclusion of Orientals," Burger noted "troubles me—what discrimination can be shown against them?" On the other hand, he said, "Indians and blacks are clear. No explicit finding [is] required for me as to them."

The strongest view against the validity of the MBE preference was stated by Justice Stewart. Under "the Constitution as I understand it," he declared, "the Fifth and Fourteenth [Amendments] must mean you can't predicate exclusions on race. It's per se invidious however loftily motivated."

The categorical Stewart view was supported only by Justice Rehnquist. "I feel much as Potter does," he began. Rehnquist also was troubled by the Burger posture of more deference to Congress than to the states in such a case. "It stands the Constitution on its head," he asserted, "to say that Congress has more power than the states. I can't see how we can give more deference to Congress than the state legislatures."

Though Justice Stevens voted with Justices Stewart and Rehnquist against the MBE provision, the others supported its constitutionality. Of particular interest to this discussion of post-*Bakke* law was the view expressed by Justice Powell. "I'd have agreed with Potter twenty years ago," Powell started his conference presentation, "but *Brown*[19] and *Green*,[20] Congress in Title VII [of the Civil Rights Act of 1964], in the Voting

Rights Act—all have led me to assume that . . . a substantial or compelling state interest permits classifications on race."

"The governmental interest here," Powell concluded, "is very substantial." The Justice then went into what he considered a key distinction between this case and *Bakke*. "I wouldn't accept [that] historic discrimination [i.e., that alleged in *Bakke*] is enough. I'd want definitive findings and there is an adequate record here." Powell also stated that he "wouldn't second guess the choice of means."

The vote at the *Fullilove* conference was, as indicated, six-to-three (Justices Stewart, Rehnquist, and Stevens in the minority) to uphold the MBE provision. Chief Justice Burger assigned the opinion to himself. His draft, like his final opinion, focused on the point he had made at the conference— that the MBE program had been set up by Congress and that the Court should defer to the Congressional judgment. This was particularly true, the Chief Justice wrote, because Congress had acted under two of its broadest powers: the spending power and the power to enforce the Fourteenth Amendment.

Neither the Burger draft nor his final opinion contained any discussion of the standard of review in such a case. Indeed, the Chief Justice stated specifically, "This opinion does not adopt, either expressly or implicitly, the formulas of analysis articulated in such cases as *University of California Regents v. Bakke*."[21] This led to an objection by Justices Brennan and Marshall. On June 17, 1980, they wrote to the Chief Justice, "we believe that some standard of review is necessary, and we intend to circulate a concurring opinion that articulates our view of the correct standard and explains how that standard is implicit in the analysis you apply to this case."

The Chief Justice replied in a June 18 MEMORANDUM TO CONFERENCE in which he stated, "it seems to me there is a 'tempest in a saucer' aspect as to terms. I frankly believe that adopting a magic 'word-test' is a serious error and I will neither write nor join in these 'litmus' approaches." Because of this Justice Marshall, joined by Justices Brennan and Blackmun, issued a concurrence stating that the proper standard of review was that articulated in the Brennan *Bakke* opinion and showing that the MBE provision was valid under that standard.

Because of his crucial role in the *Bakke* decision, it is important to note the position of Justice Powell, who also wrote a concurrence in *Fullilove*. The Powell opinion followed the Justice's *Bakke* approach on the review standard. As explained in a Powell June 13, 1980, MEMORANDUM TO THE CONFERENCE, "I have applied . . . the strict scrutiny analysis to the racial classification incorporated in § 103(f) (2)."

How could Justice Powell vote to uphold the MBE provision when he had been the decisive vote to invalidate the Davis program because it had provided for a racial quota? "Like *Bakke*," the Powell memo conceded, "this is a quota system case." To Powell, however, this case was different from *Bakke*, where the Powell opinion stressed that, "In this case . . . there has been no determination by the legislature or a responsible administrative agency that the University engaged in a discriminatory practice requiring remedial efforts."[22]

The Powell memo pointed out that *Fullilove* "differs from *Bakke* in that the congressional record makes clear—at least for me—that Congress made appropriate findings of racial discrimination against minority contractors." Powell also stressed the Congressional power to enforce the Fourteenth Amendment. "Moreover," stated the June 13 memo, "as the opinion of the Chief Justice properly emphasizes, Congress has a unique responsibility under § 5 of the 14th Amendment. Accordingly, I conclude that the set-aside is constitutional."

MORE RECENT CASES

The *Fullilove* decision does not conflict with *Bakke*. The Powell *Bakke* opinion indicated that, if there had been a legislative or administrative finding that the challenged program was necessary to remedy past discrimination by the university, the Davis special admissions program might have been valid.[23] In *Fullilove*, the legislative history demonstrated that Congress had made such a finding. From this point of view, *Fullilove* is consistent with *Bakke* and particularly with the approach followed in the Powell *Bakke* opinion.

The same is true of the more recent cases involving racial preferences under affirmative action. Like *Fullilove*, they involve employment, not university admissions. Most of them were decided under Title VII of the Civil Rights Act, in which Congress prohibited racial discrimination in employment. Hence, they do not bear directly upon the present status of *Bakke*, though they may still be relevant to discussions of that subject.

The one post-*Fullilove* case not decided under Title VII was *Wygant v. Jackson Board of Education*.[24] The issue was whether a school board, consistent with the Equal Protection Clause, might extend preferential protection against layoffs to some teachers because of their race or national origin. The board had entered into a collective bargaining agreement under which layoffs were to be in reverse order of seniority, "except that at no time will there be a greater percentage of minority personnel laid off than the current percentage of minority personnel employed at the time of the layoff." Under this provision, white teachers were laid off, while black teachers with less seniority were retained. Displaced white teachers brought suit claiming that they had been discriminated against because of their race. The Court agreed that equal protection had been violated by the layoffs.

Justice Powell, who delivered the plurality opinion, followed the essentials of his *Bakke* approach. In the first place, the Powell *Wygant* opinion stated, the racial classification at issue, like that in *Bakke* must be subjected to strict scrutiny. It may be upheld only if justified by a compelling state interest and only if narrowly tailored to the achievement of the state's goal. According to Powell, the racial classification in *Wygant* was not justified by a compelling state interest because no evidence existed in the record that the school board had ever discriminated in hiring on the basis of race.

Here Justice Powell followed his *Bakke* view that societal discrimination alone (upon which both Davis Medical School and the board of education in *Wygant* had relied) was not enough to justify a racial classification designed to remedy such discrimination. "Societal discrimination, without more, is too amorphous a basis for imposing a racially classified remedy."[25] Instead, there must have been specific prior discrimination warranting remedial action by the public employer or other agency involved in the case.[26]

Justice O'Connor, the one member of the *Wygant* Court who had not participated in *Bakke*, subscribed to the Powell approach "because it mirrors the standard we have consistently applied in examining racial classifications in other contexts." She noted, citing Justice Powell's *Bakke* opinion, that "a state interest in the promotion of racial diversity has been found sufficiently 'compelling,' at least in the context of higher education, to support the use of racial considerations in furthering that interest."[27] But that would not justify race as the sole determining factor in *Wygant*, any more than it justified race as the sole factor in determining eligibility for the 16 seats set aside under the Davis special admissions program.

To be sure, the more recent cases have involved more than mere application of the *Bakke* approach. In *Firefighters Local Union v. Stotts*,[28] the Court had indicated that a racially preferential program similar to that in *Wygant* was invalid unless it was necessary "to provide make-whole relief to those who have been actual victims of illegal discrimination."[29] This implication that preferential treatment may not be given to nonvictims has been repudiated both in *Wygant* and other cases. No Justice in *Wygant* asserted the view that affirmative action plans are limited to benefiting identifiable victims of past discrimination.

Soon after *Wygant,* in *Local 28, Sheet Metal Workers v. Equal Employment Opportunity Commission*,[30] six Justices specifically agreed that preferential relief may be granted benefiting individuals who are not actual victims of discrimination as a remedy for past discrimination. Among them was Justice Powell who stated expressly that he, too, agreed that preferential relief need not be limited to actual victims of discrimination.[31] This view was wholly consistent with what the Justice had said in *Bakke*. Certainly the use of race as a factor in admissions decisions, which Powell had approved in *Bakke*, gives a preference to minority applicants who had not themselves been actual victims of discrimination.

It is true that, in both the *Sheet Metal* case and a companion case, *Local Number 93 v. Cleveland*,[32] the Court upheld plans which required fixed goals and numbers for hiring and promotion of blacks. At first glance, this may seem inconsistent with the *Bakke* condemnation of the Davis program because it assigned a fixed number of seats to racial minorities. In *Sheet Metal*, however, a long history of continuing discrimination by the union was shown, as well as a record of "foot-dragging resistance" to official efforts to end their discriminatory practices. According to the opinions of both Justices Brennan and Powell, the finding that the union had committed egregious violations clearly established a governmental interest sufficient to justify the imposition of a racially classified remedy.[33] The same result would undoubtedly have been reached in *Bakke* had a similar pattern of egregious discrimination by Davis been proven.

In the *Cleveland* case, the plan upheld had been adopted in a consent decree. The Court treated such a plan as one entered into voluntarily by the parties. Voluntary action by employers and unions seeking to eliminate race discrimination may include race-conscious relief which may not be subject to the *Bakke* or *Wygant* type limitations.

Of course, the Court has not been united in its post-*Bakke* approach to programs providing for racial preferences. But none of its decisions has been inconsistent in important respects with *Bakke* and its interpretation in the field of educational admissions. Like *Bakke* itself, the cases uphold the validity of well-tailored affirmative action programs. That is true even though, as in *Bakke* itself, the Justices have not agreed on the results or even on the appropriate standard of review. Yet, in practice, as Justice O'Connor points out, "the distinction between a 'compelling' and an 'important' governmental purpose may be a negligible one. The Court is in agreement that, whatever the formulation employed, remedying past or present racial discrimination by a state actor is a sufficiently weighty state interest to warrant the remedial use of a carefully constructed affirmative action program."[34]

This, after all, is the most important thing when we consider the effect of the *Bakke* decision today. "Despite the Court's inability to agree on a route, we have reached a common destination in sustaining affirmative action against constitutional attack."[35]

CODA

This chapter has shown that programs granting racial preferences have gained more than they lost from the *Bakke* decision. The Davis program itself may have lost the battle in the Marble Palace, but affirmative action programs have plainly won the constitutional war.

And what of Bakke himself, the plaintiff who gave his name to the landmark case? We left him at the end of the last chapter with an order directing that he be admitted to the Davis Medical School. He was admitted as a member of the class that entered in September 1978. Hostile students demonstrated during his first day at the school. Four years later, however, at the ceremony when the medical graduates obtained their internship assignments, Bakke received the loudest applause.[36] He graduated in June 1982 and then began an internship at the Mayo Clinic in Rochester, Minnesota. He worked there as an anesthesiology resident until the summer of 1986. He had received his license to practice in 1983.

"More than anything else in the world, *I want to study medicine*," Bakke had declared in his application to Davis. Now he had attained his goal—albeit by order of the highest Court. Without any doubt, then—whoever else may have won or lost in the case—Allan Bakke was the undoubted victor from the Supreme Court decision.

NOTES

1. See Eastland and Bennett, Counting by Race 171–172 (1979).
2. Seligman, "Special Admissions Are Still Special," *Student Lawyer* 24, 45 (December 1978).
3. American Council on Education—Association of American Law Schools, The Bakke Decision: Implications for Higher Education Admissions 17 (1978).
4. Id. at 20.
5. Seligman, supra note 2.
6. See similarly Simmons, *Affirmative Action: Conflict and Change in Higher Education after* Bakke 89–90 (1982).
7. Seligman, supra note 2, at 25.
8. Bakke, 438 U.S. at 320.
9. Supra note 7.
10. Bakke, 438 U.S. at 406.
11. Seligman, supra note 2, at 26.
12. Id. at 47.
13. 438 U.S. at 319–320.
14. Seligman, supra note 2, at 47.
15. United Steelworkers v. Weber, 443 U.S. 193 (1979), was not a *Bakke*-type case, since it dealt with private, not governmental, action.
16. 448 U.S. 448 (1980).
17. Technically, the claim was that it violated the equal protection component of the Due Process Clause of the Fifth Amendment.
18. 384 U.S. 641 (1966).
19. Brown v. Board of Education, 347 U.S. 483 (1954).
20. Green v. County School Board, 391 U.S. 430 (1968).
21. 448 U.S. at 492.
22. 438 U.S. at 305.
23. Ibid.
24. 106 S. Ct. 1842 (1986).
25. Id. at 1848.
26. Though the Court now recognizes that findings are not required, so long as there has been actual discrimination by the public employer. Id. at 1855.
27. Id. at 1853.
28. 467 U.S. 561 (1984).
29. Id. at 580.
30. 106 S. Ct. 3019 (1986).
31. Id. at 3054.
32. 106 S. Ct. 3063 (1886).
33. Id. at 3053, 3054.
34. Wygant, id. at 1853.
35. Id. at 1861, Marshall, J., dissenting.
36. *New York Times*, June 4, 1982, P. A 14.

Warren E. Burger, Memorandum of October 21, 1977

Supreme Court of the United States
Washington, D. C. 20543

CHAMBERS OF
THE CHIEF JUSTICE
October 21, 1977

CONFIDENTIAL

MEMORANDUM TO THE CONFERENCE

Re: No. 76-811   Regents of the University of California
v. Allan Bakke

     I have made a tentative and preliminary analysis of
what this case appears to be at the present stage, based
on the assumption that a way can be found to affirm the
decision of the California Supreme Court without putting
the states, their universities, or any educational
institutions in a straitjacket on the matter of broader
based admissions programs.

     Establishing fixed ground rules for educators is not
the business of courts except when, as in desegregation
cases, we are confronted with a pattern of affirmative de
jure conduct, based exclusively on race. We have far more
competence to say what cannot be done than what ought to
be done.

     I have always tried to keep in mind the great
expression of Brandeis:

> "To stay experimentation in things social
> and economic is a grave responsibility. Denial
> of the right to experiment may be fraught with
> serious consequences to the Nation. It is one
> of the happy incidents of the federal system
> that a single courageous State may, if its
> citizens choose, serve as a laboratory; and try
> novel social and economic experiments without
> risk to the rest of the country. This Court
> has the power to prevent an experiment. ***
> But in the exercise of this high power, we must
> be ever on our guard, lest we erect our
> prejudices into legal principles." New State
> Ice Co. v. Liebmann, 285 U.S. 262, 311
> (dissenting).

     The Regents adopted their program to accomplish a
number of commendable, long-range objectives, but as

-2-

presently structured, the program is one of the more extreme methods of securing those objectives. The program excluded Bakke from the medical school on the basis of race and this is not disputed. I am open to being shown how, consistent with the prior decisions of the Court, we can escape the significance of this fact.

Having come thus far, I am confronted with the tactical consideration of how best to structure and shape a result so as to confine its impact and yet make it clear that the Court intends to leave states free to serve as "laboratories" for experimenting with less rigidly exclusionary methods of pursuing desirable social goals. My inclination at this point is to emphasize the particularly troubling aspects of the Regents' Program and the difficult statutory and constitutional problems they raise, but to go only a little beyond that point in addressing the question of what alternatives might be devised.

The basic facts are not subject to dispute.

(1)   Bakke was not allowed to compete for any of the 16 seats reserved for the Regents' Program solely because of his race.

(2)   Bakke's individual qualifications were such that he would have been admitted if all 100 seats had been open and free from any arbitrary exclusion based on race.

(3)   The university evaluated minority applicants as a separate group and did not compare their individual qualities with those of other applicants.

STANDARD OF REVIEW

The first question for the Court is what level of scrutiny should be applied in this case. Although I have long been uneasy with the "slogans" that have evolved in equal protection analysis, I think that the Court must give the very closest look possible -- essentially "strict scrutiny" -- to any state action based on race. No member of this Court, so far as I recall, has ever had any question but that racial classifications are suspect under all circumstances. Having said this, I can find no principled basis for holding that this program is exempt from close scrutiny because it only excludes

-3-

members of the "majority." We cannot assume that
individuals who appear to be part of a "majority" have
consented to racial discrimination against themselves.
Obviously, Bakke does not consent to the discrimination
against him. Furthermore, a racial classification that
appears "benign" to some members of a minority may not
seem "benign" to other members of the same minority.   See
United Jewish Organizations of Williamsburg v. Carey, 430
U.S. 144, 173-4 (Brennan, J., concurring).

Given the "no person" language of Title VI and the
"any person" language of the Fourteenth Amendment, I
become confused by the glib attribution of either a benign
or invidious purpose to an exclusionary classification
solely on the basis of whether it appears to a reviewing
court that minorities are favored thereby. Furthermore,
the analysis proceeds on the dubious assumption that
minorities are readily indentifiable "blocs" which in some
way function as units and are generally harmed or
benefited in roughly the same degree by the same external
forces such as social programs like the one at issue
here. That is a superficial and problematic
characterization of intent that does not satisfy me as the
"trigger" for one level or another of equal protection
scrutiny.

The second question is whether the university's sound
and desirable objectives provide sufficient justification
for the rigid, plainly racial basis of the Regents'
Program. I do not think they do. The university desires
to remedy the general effects of broad historic social
discrimination, not discrimination by the university or by
the state but by society at large, in and outside
California. However, it is understandable that the
Regents want to ensure that a diversity of viewpoints and
experiences are reflected in its student body and
ultimately in the medical profession, so as to produce
doctors who can and will serve areas and patients who
currently lack adequate medical care, and to erode racial
stereotypes. Parenthetically, the program seems deficient
in not binding the admittees by contract to carry out the
commitment to serve the blighted, neglected areas. A
contracted, five-year commitment is a familiar mechanism
in other areas.

-4-

ALTERNATIVES

There are many ways that the University can pursue these goals short of completely excluding whites from competing for a certain number of places in its entering class. On this record, I must reject the Regents' assertion that there are no realistic alternatives to their program. They can't <u>know</u> because they have not tried any alternatives.

The various admission standards and procedures that might be designed to account fully for the individual capabilities of each minority applicant and fairly compare each one with other applicants have not yet been explored. The record in this case indicates dissatisfaction on the part of university administrators with present methods of evaluating applicants for professional education. The Regents intimate that there is no universal agreement as to the proper objectives of medical schools, other than the truism that the mission of medical school is to produce the best possible doctors for service to the ailing and injured among us.

The task of setting standards for admission to medical school, I repeat, is beyond judicial competence. I think that the Court should encourage efforts and experimental programs to redefine admissions criteria in view of the possible changing attitudes as to the mission of medical schools, keeping in mind only the limited constraint imposed by a narrow affirmance here -- that race <u>alone</u> can never be a permissible basis for excluding an applicant. <u>Brown I</u> settled that and I cannot believe anyone wants to retreat.

I am convinced that remedial educational programs can be devised to give "disadvantaged" applicants an opportunity to compete successfully for admission to medical schools. In <u>Milliken II</u>, the Court endorsed special training for disadvantaged children whose "habits of speech, conduct, and attitudes" reflect "cultural isolation" from the mainstream of society. <u>Milliken</u> v. <u>Bradley</u>, 76-447, 45 L.W. 4873, 4879. Similar measures ought to be explored and might be applied in the context of higher education. As of now, I am not convinced that the Court should forbid efforts to establish programs primarily for those who have sustained deprivations

-5-

which closely correlate with race but might affect anyone
isolated from the cultural mainstream. I am not ready to
say now that in evaluating "disadvantage" race may not be
given some consideration.

DISPOSITION

     As of now I would say only that this rigidly cast
admissions program is impermissible on this record because
it does precisely what has long been condemned by this
Court -- it excludes applicants on the basis of race. On
this record there is nothing to suggest any inquiry into
alternatives was made. I simply cannot believe the
Regents' frankly race-based program is the least offensive
or least intrusive method of promoting an admittedly
important state interest. Subject to what the
supplemental briefs tell us, the Regents' program surely
appears to be in plain conflict with the explicit language
of Title VI. Since the Fourteenth Amendment and Title VI
are cast in similar terms except that Title VI is more
specific and is a summary mechanism for federal regulation
of its grants of money, I have some difficulty reading
their respective prohibitions on racial discrimination
differently.

     If, after receiving the requested briefs, we conclude
that Bakke is covered under Title VI, it seems to me, as
of now, that our long practice and policy has been to base
our decision on the statutory ground. But I defer further
consideration or firm conclusions on this score until we
have all had time to study the requested supplemental
submissions.

     In exploring the idea of a very narrow affirmance,
making clear that other avenues are open, I do not ignore
Byron's concern with the question of whether there is a
principled basis for distinguishing other racially
sensitive programs from the practice of rigidly reserving
"seats" for minorities. I do not think that we can or
should address that problem in the abstract. In this case
we do not have to pass on the constitutionality of the
possible alternative admissions programs. Acknowledging
the plain and obvious proposition that there are other
alternatives does not require us to bless them in advance.

-6-

For now I would leave open whether and to what extent
indirect consideration of race is compatible with
constitutional or statutory proscriptions. I find that
articulating this concept is far from easy but I am
optimistic that a way can be found.

Perhaps that can be deferred until the question
arises in the context of an admissions program which
involves a less explicit racial quotient. Or possibly
someone may point the way to doing so in this case.
Confining ourselves to a narrow affirmance along these
lines would seem both prudent and generally consistent
with our traditional method of developing principled
approaches to complex social issues through a case by case
process rather than by wholesale, uninformed pronouncement.

With all deference to the distinguished array of
counsel who have been plunged into a very difficult case
on a record any good lawyer would shun, I see no reason
why we should let them (aided by the mildly hysterical
media) rush us to judgment. The notion of putting this
sensitive, difficult question to rest in one "hard" case
is about as sound a trying to put all First Amendment
issues to rest in one case. Brown I bears date May 17,
1954 and case by case evolution has followed up to our
recent Milliken II last June. I see no signs of abatement
in the refinement process there.

If it is to take years to work out a rational
solution of the current problem, so be it. That is what
we are paid for.

                        Regards,

                        WEB

William H. Rehnquist, Memorandum of November 10–11, 1977

Supreme Court of the United States
Washington, D. C. 20543

CHAMBERS OF
JUSTICE WILLIAM H. REHNQUIST

November 11, 1977

MEMORANDUM TO THE CONFERENCE

Re: No. 76-811 Regents of the University of California
v. Allen Bakke

This memo was intended to accompany the stream of
consciousness memo which I circulated earlier today. As
Byron said in his circulation just before our first Conference
on the case, it is not the "usual practice", but I think I
have derived some benefit from his and other's subsequent
written circulations. I also think that some written comments
before Conference on a case this complicated and multifaceted could save a lot of time in what is bound to be a long
Conference discussion anyway.

Sincerely,

Supreme Court of the United States
Washington, D. C. 20543

CHAMBERS OF
JUSTICE WILLIAM H. REHNQUIST

November 10, 1977

MEMORANDUM TO THE CONFERENCE

Re: No. 76-811 Regents of the University of California
v. Allan Bakke

The University's admissions policy in this case seems to
me to make its "affirmative action" program as difficult to
sustain constitutionally as one conceivably could be. Two
factual elements in particular stand out, and the Regents
make no bones about them. First, the limitation of the special
admissions programs to blacks, Hispanics, native Americans,
and other minorities is not simply a shorthand method of
finding people who may have been "culturally deprived" or
"disadvantaged" in such a way that, although they might be
very good medical students or doctors, they would not do well
on standardized tests. Rather, the University's ultimate
goal is to place additional members of these ethnic minorities
in the medical school.

- 2 -

I take it as a postulate that difference in treatment of individuals based on their race or ethnic origin is at the bull's eye of the target at which the Fourteenth Amendment's Equal Protection Clause was aimed. I don't think the Court has ever held foursquare with the first Mr. Justice Harlan's view that the Constitution was "color blind", and therefore forbade every conceivable differentiation in treatment on the basis of race. But certainly the cases are too numerous to require citation that differentiation between individuals on this basis is "suspect", subject to "strict scrutiny" or whatever equivalent phrase one chooses to use.

Because the Regents' policy is to deliberately prefer minorities for sixteen of the seats in the medical school, I don't think that cases such as Washington v. Davis, 426 U.S. 229 (1976) or Jefferson v. Hackney, 406 U.S. 535 (1972), where the Court held that mere disparate impact as between minority groups and majority groups is not sufficient, in the absence of a showing of intent, to sustain a finding of unconstitutional discrimination, cannot serve to sustain the policy.

- 3 -

The second factual aspect of the program is that the actual individualized determination made by the University of who is admitted and who is excluded is, with respect to these sixteen seats, made to depend on racial or ethnic classifications. This fact, for me at any rate, makes the case substantially different from Byron's U.J.O., 430 U.S. 144 (1977), several parts of which I joined last Term. There it was undisputed that the legislators, in making their decision, had taken race into account in redistricting for the New York legislature; the Court nevertheless upheld the redistricting statute, pointing out that no individual was deprived of the right to have his vote counted, and that "there was no fencing out of the white population from participation in the political processes of the country, and the plan did not minimize or unfairly cancel out white voting strength." Id., at 165.

I would think that most, if not all, legislators consider racial or ethnic factors in voting on bills that come before them. Legislators from inner city areas with a large part

- 4 -

of their constituency made up of minority groups are going to
vote differently than legislators from affluent suburban areas
with a different sort of constituency. So long as the resulting
statute does not make race or ethnic status the determining
factor in whether an individual receives a benefit or is denied
one, I don't think the Fourteenth Amendment speaks to these
sort of deliberations. For example, if the state had determined
that it would obtain more minority students in the state
medical schools were it to open such a school in some part
of Los Angeles County which was heavily populated with one or
more of the minority groups which it sought, I would think
there would be no equal protection objection so long as
individual applications were processed on a basis that did not
make race determinative. The difficulty with the state's
program here is that it has not followed this course (perhaps
because it felt it simply would not accomplish the objective
which it desired).

Nor is the state program here able to bring itself within
the holding of Swann v. Charlotte-Mechlenburg Board of Education,

- 5 -

402 U.S. 1, without a considerable expansion of both the holding
and reasoning of that case. In the context of litigation about
a school district which had been <u>de jure</u> segregated, the Court
said that school administrators were free on their own (without
court supervision) to take race into account in drawing boundary
lines. Assuming that this statement be taken literally and
therefore be made applicable to any school district, whether
or not it had at one time been <u>de jure</u> segregated, it remains
the same sort of doctrine as was enunciated in U.J.O.: The
school board may on its own strive for racial balance. But
surely the Court would not have agreed that a student could
have been denied a place in any school in the system by
reason of race, even though he might be assigned to a school
which he would not voluntarily choose to attend.

Even more obviously, the Regents' program cannot be
brought under the holdings of <u>Swann</u> and other school desegregation cases, where a governmental body which has previously been
guilty of discriminating on the basis of race is judicially

- 6 -

required to remedy that discrimination in order to make whole

its victims, and in the course of implementing such a remedy

may be required to take race into consideration. Neither

does Bill Brennan's Franks v. Bowman Transportation Co., 424

U.S. 747 (1976) afford petitioner much comfort on this score.

There, not only were the plaintiffs being compensated for

specific discriminatory practices, but the Caucasian workers

who were being disadvantaged by the race-explicit remedial

measures were the identifiable, albeit innocent, beneficiaries

of the specific acts of discrimination being remedied. Neither

of these conditions obtain here.

In short, while it certainly cannot be said that we start

with a clean slate, I find little in our previous cases upon

which I would feel comfortable in resting if I were to uphold

the Davis admissions program.

That, of course, does not end the matter. Two other

inquiries remain to be pursued. Need the Davis scheme pass only

a rational basis equal protection test (which it clearly does --

obtaining doctors to serve in ghetto areas is certainly a

permissible state concern and the Davis system, though not

- 7 -

perfectly tailored to that end, is close enough)? And, if

more rigorous scrutiny is mandated, are the proffered

justifications sufficiently "compelling" to sustain the program?

In view of what the Court has said in past cases based on

race, I think one can avoid strict scrutiny only if it is

said that whites who are in the majority may not assert a claim

for denial of equal protection by reason of a classification

based on race. But I find that notion ultimately quite

unsatisfying.

Neither the language nor the history of the Fourteenth

Amendment provides much support for the view that the Amendment

protects only members of a minority class. Even assuming the

immediate purpose of the Framers of the Amendment was at least

in part to strike down the so-called "black codes" of the South,

the language they chose is a good deal more general than would

be required for such a limited purpose. Moreover, that they

in fact intended to go beyond simply eliminating "black codes"

finds some support in the historical background of the Amendment

Thurgood's opinion in <u>Santa Fe</u> v. <u>McDonald</u>, 427 U.S. 273,

- 8 -

analyzed in Part III the legislative history of 42 U.S.C.

§ 1981, the language of which was certainly more favorable

to a construction excluding whites from its protection than

the language of the Fourteenth Amendment. Canvassing legislative

history occurring virtually simultaneously with the drafting

of the Fourteenth Amendment, that opinion concluded that

whites as well as others were entitled to the protection of

§ 1981. I joined Byron's dissent from this portion of the

opinion, not because I disagreed with the analysis of the

legislative history, but because I was persuaded that § 1981

was not directed to private discrimination against either whites

or blacks.

Moreover, I see nothing in our prior cases to suggest

different Fourteenth Amendment analysis should be applied to

Caucasians as opposed to members of minority groups. Proponents

of this view invariably refer to the language originating in

the footnote in the Carolene Products case, 304 U.S. 144,

153 n. 4, speaking of "discrete and insular minorities." The

Court then used the phrase (and I would think its subsequent

use has been in the same vein) to derive a legal formula for

- 9 -

identifying odious and irrelevant classifications which
although not based on race, were based on a characteristic
sufficiently like race to warrant protection under the Fourteenth
Amendment's Equal Protection Clause. I do not think it has
been held or even suggested that this doctrine lends support
to the limitation of claims of racial discrimination to the
non-Caucasian races.

There is more than one logical weakness to the justification
offered in support of the view that the Fourteenth Amendment
protects only minorities. Proponents of this view generally
seem to rely heavily on the majority-minority analysis advanced
in some of the briefs: in essence, as I understand it, the
Fourteenth Amendment does not prohibit a legislature controlled
by one race or ethnic group from discriminating against members
of that group.

My first problem with this argument is that I think it
confuses the substance of the prohibition with the reason
for placing the prohibition in the Constitution. As I
indicated above, I think that the language (and the related

- 10 -

legislative history discussed in <u>Santa Fe</u>) suggest that the

<u>thing</u> <u>prohibited</u> is discrimination on the basis of race, any

race. The reason for this prohibition is not because minority

ethnic and racial groups are the most frequent victims of such

discrimination, although in fact they are; the reason for

the prohibition is that classification of individuals on the

basis of race is, except in the rarest of cases, not a permissible

basis of governmental action.

The reason for placing this prohibition in the Constitution,

on the other hand, is undoubtedly because minority racial

and ethnic groups are much more likely to suffer from racial

discrimination than are members of majority racial or ethnic

groups. It was in order to make the principle that race is an

invalid basis for differentiation among individuals secure

against the vicissitudes of legislative pulling and hauling

that it was put in the Constitution. The benefit to minorities

resulting from placing it in the Constitution is that it

prohibits the enactment of laws in violation of it which

majority-dominated legislatures might otherwise be quite willing

to enact. But because its placement in the Constitution

confers a benefit on minorities which "majorities" do not need

as much does not mean that on those occasions when a Caucasian

- 11 -

dominated legislature chooses to discriminate against a
Caucasian, the principle contained in the Equal Protection
Clause does not likewise apply to that discrimination.

    This view of the Fourteenth Amendment has other problems
as well. Even passing the questions of whether

the faculty of a professional school is generally responsive
to majoritarian influence and whether the view of the
democratic process on which this theory is predicated is
defensible, I think it hard to dispute the Chief's observation
that this view assumes, contrary to reason and experience, that
all Caucasians are always a monolithic unit when they go to the
polls or vote in legislatures or city councils. This view of
the Fourteenth Amendment also leads to the disquieting result,
pointed out in some of the briefs, that a law which would be
unconstitutional in California would be unconstitutional in the
District of Columbia or in the Commonwealth of Puerto Rico and
vice versa.

- 12 -

Thus for me this is a case requiring "strict scrutiny" If by strict scrutiny we mean that sort of justification which will avail to sustain a racial classification such as this, the phrase "compelling state interest" really asks the question rather than answers it, unless we are to revert simply to what Holmes called our own "can't helps."

As an initial observation, I am inclined to agree with the Chief that it would be very difficult to view as constitutionally sufficient most of the proffered non-race goals, such as more doctors in the ghetto. Not that these interests are illegitimate or unimportant, but by definition all are based on notions of administrative convenience and I think our cases indicate that under the rubric of "strict scrutiny" it generally takes something more to justify a classification based on race. At least in this case, as the Chief suggests, there are other, much less troubling methods of accomplishing these goals.

- 13 -

Other proffered goals, although phrased in non-racial terms,
are, at heart, very clearly predicated at least in part on the
idea that racial characteristics are, in and of themselves,
socially significant and permissible bases for governmental
action. For example, this would seem true of the racial
diversity in the student body rationale (at least to the
extent it is not bottomed simply on a rationale of administrative
convenience). Apart from the Fourteenth Amendment, it may be
both important and desirable to have more members of racial
minorities in the student body because such people, simply
by the fact of their minority status, have a different,
valuable perspective. But I would think that the Fourteenth
Amendment holds that for governmental purposes nobody "has"
anything simply by virtue of their race. Members of minority
groups are not less valuable human beings simply because of
their minority status and, it would seem to me, are not more
valuable either. Many educators obviously feel that this
rule of the Fourteenth Amendment is wrong, but it is impossible
to make an exception just on that basis.

- 14 -

By this point there remains only the notion that past
societal discrimination justifies these affirmative action
programs. This is not an unappealing rationale. But I
ultimately think it also unacceptable.

As indicated above, where a school district or an
employer is found to have discriminated against blacks in the
past, the school district or employer may be required to take race
into consideration in implementing a remedy. But these
principles have thus far been limited in cases from this
Court to remedying wrongs at the behest of identifiable victims
of particular discriminatory practices. Just as the states
were not allowed to defend their enforcement of restrictive
covenants in Shelley v. Kraemer, 334 U.S. 1 (1948), by saying
they would equally enforce restrictive covenants against whites,
or to say that they would furnish Gaines a legal education at
some law school other than the University of Missouri in
Missouri ex rel. Gaines v. Canada, 305 U.S. 337 (1938), it
should not be enough here for the state to say that the
applicants admitted under the minority program were victims
of generalized past discrimination. The reason, I submit,
is that advanced in Shelley and Gaines -- that the right not

- 15 -

to be discriminated against is personal to the individual,
and in this case Bakke's right to equal protection of the laws
cannot be denied him simply because at some other place or at
some other time minority group members have been discriminated
against.

Here the state program goes well beyond the examples in
the school desegregation cases and Title VII cases referred
to above, and treats racial groups en bloc rather than individually.
The state proposes to remedy past discrimination against blacks
as a group by present discrimination in favor of individual
blacks and against individual whites. Nothing in our cases
that has been cited to us in the briefs or argument holds that
this sort of practice is consistent with the Equal Protection
Clause.

One still might argue, of course, that simply because the
judiciary is limited to enforcing individual rights (and
therefore cannot compel the use of racial classification as
a remedial measure in the absence of specific discriminatory
practices against the persons seeking relief), there is no
reason that the legislative or executive branches should be
so limited. While I have no quarrel with that as a general

- 16 -

proposition, I am extremely skeptical of it in the context of racial classifications. These proposed remedial schemes are based on assumptions that are, in my opinion, impermissible predicates for governmental action in light of the Fourteenth Amendment. The state is assuming that every minority applicant who worked his way through school has been discriminated against. While it is clear that every person who has suffered racial discrimination on account of being a member of a minority is, by definition, a member of a minority, I am unwilling to agree that every member of a minority has been discriminated against, in the sense that under the Fourteenth Amendment it is permissible for the state to provide a remedy. The fit between the two groups (members of minority groups and persons who have been discriminated against on account of membership in a minority group) is far from exact and thus an insufficient basis for use of racial classifications. In short, just because it is easier to identify blacks than people who have suffered discrimination on account of race, the state should not be excused from making a more individualized determination, ultimately looking past race for disabilities which are both relevant and permissible bases of classification under the Fourteenth Amendment. I admit that unlike the normal administrative convenience justification offered in support

- 17 -

of a legislative scheme, this one has some appeal because
not only does race have some empirical correlation to discrimination, it is, as a definitional matter, closely related to the
very attribute we are trying to identify; in fact, it is a
necessary component of that attribute. But when we define
that attribute with any precision, which all branches of
government must do when considering the propriety of classifications based on race, it is clear that it is not race itself
about when we may be legitimately concerned, but the fact of
past discrimination. It then seems apparent to me that even
this justification cannot really support the Davis program in
a constitutional sense.

Indeed, I think there is some resemblance in the argument
of petitioners and the <u>amici</u> who support it to the Court of
Appeals' opinion in <u>Buckley</u> v. <u>Valeo</u>, which we largely rejected
when we decided that case. The Court of Appeals there, it
seemed to me, appeared to say that in order to achieve the
"compelling state interest" of allowing everybody to be heard
to some extent, Congress did not abridge the First Amendment
by preventing some people from talking as much as they wanted.
This seemed to me like something out of George Orwell, or like
Rousseau's idea that people would be forced to be free, and I
have something of the same feeling, though perhaps to a lesser
extent, about the idea that discrimination based on race

- 18 -

can be justified because the opposite type of discrimination
has been and probably still is practiced in other places.

In short, I don't think the Davis plan is valid under
the Equal Protection Clause of the Fourteenth Amendment. I have
no doubt that a program which sought out culturally deprived,
disadvantaged, or similarly situated people who were thought
to have ability to be good doctors or good medical students,
even though they did not test well, would be valid. I would
also have no doubt about the validity of university efforts
to recruit heavily among minority students, so long as race
were not used as a sole factor in determining admission.

A question which is not presented by this case, and which
I do not thnk we have to decide, is whether even though race
may not be used as the sole factor, it may be used as one of a
number of factors. Though in my view of the case I would
certainly reserve the question, I think it would probably be
difficult under the foregoing line of reasoning to allow express
consideration of race as a substantial factor at all. I think
the best way to test this proposition is to go back to Anderson

· - 19 -

v. <u>Martin</u>, 375 U.S. 399 (1964), where the Court unanimously
struck down Louisiana's requirement that the race of each
candidate appear below his name on the ballot. The Court stated
that in areas where blacks were a majority, this would help
a black candidate, in areas where whites were in a majority
it would help the white candidate, but in no event was it permissible
under the Equal Protection Clause. What if, in addition to
:ace, Louisiana had required the listing of six additional
factors which were at least arguably relevant to a voter's
decision as to which candidate should be elected? Would the
law then have been upheld?

Since we are awaiting briefs on Title VI, and the sort
of research that has been done in Thurgood's and John's chambers
has not been done in mine, I withhold judgment on that question.

Lewis F. Powell, Jr., Memorandum of November 22, 1977

Supreme Court of the United States
Washington, D. C. 20543

CHAMBERS OF
JUSTICE LEWIS F. POWELL, JR.

November 22, 1977

76-811 Regents v. Bakke

MEMORANDUM TO THE CONFERENCE:

In accord with the suggestion of the Chief Justice
that this is an appropriate case for the pre-conference
circulation of memoranda, I join those of you who have done
this and now circulate the accompanying memorandum.

It addresses only the constitutional issue.
Although my review of the Title VI briefs has been rather
hurried, those briefs and the memoranda previously
circulated leave little doubt that there was no legislative
intent to have Title VI depart from the dictates of the
Fourteenth Amendment. The principles by which the validity
of the action are to be judged are the same. Thus, it may
be that the narrower mode of decision would be to avoid
reaching out for the statutory ground. A decision under
Title VI would require resolution of several significant
questions not argued or addressed below, e.g., whether
there is an implied private right of action under Title VI,
whether such a right would entail private remedies, and
whether it would require exhaustion of administrative
remedies.

In short, there is no reason to avoid the
constitutional issue. This was the basis of the holding in
the California supreme court, was the issue that prompted
us to grant certiorari, and was - until we requested Title
VI briefing - the only substantive issue addressed by the
parties.

L. F. P.

L.F.P., Jr.

ss

To: The Chief Justice
    Mr. Justice Brennan
    Mr. Justice Stewart
    Mr. Justice White
    Mr. Justice Marshall
    Mr. Justice Blackmun
    Mr. Justice Rehnquist
    Mr. Justice Stevens

From: Mr. Justice Powell

Circulated: ___**NOV** 2 4 1977___

1st DRAFT   Recirculated: _____

SUPREME COURT OF THE UNITED STATES

No. 76–811

Regents of the University of California, Petitioner, *v.* Allan Bakke.	On Writ of Certiorari to the Supreme Court of California.

[November —, 1977]

Memorandum to the Conference from MR. JUSTICE POWELL.

I

Petitioner does not deny that decisions based on race or ethnic origin by faculties and administrations of state universities are judicially reviewable. See, *e. g., Missouri ex rel. Gaines* v. *Canada*, 305 U. S. 337 (1938); *Sipuel* v. *Board of Regents*, 332 U. S. 631 (1948); *Sweatt* v. *Painter*, 339 U. S. 629 (1950); *McLaurin* v. *Oklahoma State Regents*, 339 U. S. 637 (1950). For his part, respondent does not argue that all racial or ethnic classifications are *per se* invalid. That, too, would appear to be an untenable position. See, *e. g., Hirabayashi* v. *United States*, 320 U. S. 81 (1943); *Korematsu* v. *United States*, 323 U. S. 214 (1944); *Lee* v. *Washington*, 390 U. S. 333, 334 (1968) (Black, Harlan, and STEWART, JJ., concurring); *United Jewish Orgs.* v. *Carey*, — U. S. —, 97 S. Ct. 996 (1977).

The parties do disagree as to the level of scrutiny to be applied to the special admissions program. This raises a threshold question that may be central to a resolution of the equal protection challenge asserted by respondent. Petitioner argues that the court below erred in applying strict scrutiny, as this inexact term has been applied in our cases.

76–811—MEMO

2   UNIVERSITY OF CALIFORNIA REGENTS v. BAKKE

That level of review, petitioner asserts, should be reserved for classifications disadvantaging "discrete and insular minorities." See *United States* v. *Carolene Products Co.*, 304 U. S. 144, 152 n. 4 (1938). Respondent, on the other hand, contends that the California court correctly rejected the notion that the degree of judicial scrutiny accorded a particular racial or ethnic classification hinges upon membership in a discrete and insular minority and duly recognized that the "rights established [by the Fourteenth Amendment] are personal rights." *Shelley* v. *Kraemer*, 334 U. S. 1, 22 (1948).

En route to this crucial battle over the proper scope of judicial review,[1] the parties fight a sharp preliminary action over the proper characterization of the special admissions program. Petitioner prefers to see it as establishing a "goal" of minority representation in the medical school. Respondent, echoing the courts below, labels it a racial quota.[2]

---

[1] That issue has generated a considerable amount of scholarly controversy. See, e. g., Ely, The Constitutionality of Reverse Racial Discrimination, 41 U. Chi. L. Rev. 723 (1974); Greenawalt, Judicial Scrutiny of "Benign" Racial Preferences in Law School Admissions, 75 Colum. L. Rev. 559 (1975); Kaplan, Equal Justice in an Unequal World: Equality for the Negro, 61 Nw. L. Rev. 363 (1966); Karst & Horowitz, Affirmative Action and Equal Protection, 60 Va. L. Rev. 955 (1974); O'Neil, Racial Preference and Higher Education: The Larger Context, 60 Va. L. Rev. 925 (1974); Posner, The DeFunis Case and the Constitutionality of Preferential Treatment of Racial Minorities, 1974 Sup. Ct. Rev. 1; Redish, Preferential Law School Admissions and the Equal Protection Clause: An Analysis of the Competing Arguments, 22 U. C. L. A. L. Rev. 343 (1974); Sandalow, Racial Preferences in Higher Education: Political Responsibility and the Judicial Role, 42 U. Chi. L. Rev. 653 (1975); Sedler, Racial Preference, Reality and the Constitution: Bakke v. Regents of the University of California, 17 Santa Clara L. Rev. 329 (1977).

[2] Petitioner defines "quota" as a requirement which must be met but can never be exceeded, regardless of the quality of the minority applicants. Petitioner declares that there is no "floor"; completely unqualified students will not be admitted simply to meet a "quota." Neither is there a "ceiling" on the total number of minority students admitted, since an unlimited number could be admitted through the general admissions process. On

76–811—MEMO

UNIVERSITY OF CALIFORNIA REGENTS *v.* BAKKE   3

This semantic distinction is beside the point: the special admissions program is undeniably a classification based on race and ethnic background.   To the extent that there existed a pool of at least minimally qualified minority applicants to fill the 16 special admissions seats. white applicants could compete only for 84 seats in the entering class. rather than the 100 open to minority applicants.   Whether this limitation is described as a quota or a goal, it is a line drawn on the basis of race.[3]

II

The guarantees of the Fourteenth Amendment extend to persons.   Its language is explicit: "No state shall . . . deny to any person within its jurisdiction the equal protection of the laws."   It is thus settled beyond question that the "rights created by the first section of the Fourteenth Amendment are. by its terms. guaranteed to the individual.   They are personal rights."   *Shelley* v. *Kraemer*, 334 U. S. 1, 22 (1948).   It also is clear that the guarantee of equal protection cannot mean one thing when applied to one individual and something else when applied to a person of another color.   If both are not entitled to the same protection, then it is not equal.

Nevertheless, petitioner argues that the court below erred

---

this basis, the special admissions program does not meet petitioner's definition of a quota.

The court below found—and petitioner does not deny—that white applicants could not compete for the 16 places reserved solely for the special admissions program. 18 Cal. 3d, at 44.   Both courts below characterized this as a "quota" system.

[3] Moreover, the University's special admissions program involves a purposeful use of racial criteria.   This is not a situation in which the classification on its face is racially neutral. but has a disproportionate racial impact.   In that situation. plaintiff must establish an intent to discriminate. *Village of Arlington Heights* v. *Metropolitan Housing Devel Corp.,* 429 U. S. 252, 264–265 (1977); *Washington* v. *Davis.* 426 U. S. 229, 242 (1976); see *Yick Wo* v. *Hopkins.* 118 U. S. 356 (1886).   Here. the classification is not neutral on its face; the intention to restrict competition by whites is evident and not denied.

4   UNIVERSITY OF CALIFORNIA REGENTS *v.* BAKKE

in applying strict scrutiny to the special admissions programs
because white males, such as respondent, are not a "discrete
and insular minority" requiring extraordinary protection from
the majoritarian political process. *United States* v. *Carolene
Products Co.*, 304 U. S., at 152–153, n. 4. This rationale,
however, has never governed our decisions invalidating racial
or ethnic distinctions. See, *e. g.*, *Brown* v. *Board of Education*, 347 U. S. 483 (1954). Nor has this Court held that
discreteness and insularity constitute necessary preconditions
to strict scrutiny of otherwise sensitive classifications.[4] See,
e. g., *Skinner* v. *Oklahoma*, 316 U. S. 535, 541 (1942); *Carring-
ton* v. *Rash*, 380 U. S. 89, 94–97 (1965). Indeed, classifications
based on gender elicit a form of heightened scrutiny, *e. g.*,
Frontiero v. *Richardson*, 411 U. S. 677, 691–692 (1965)
(POWELL, J., concurring), yet there can be no contention that
women are a "minority" group. These characteristics may be
among the relevant criteria in deciding whether or not to add
new types of classifications to the list of "suspect" categories.
See, *e. g.*, *San Antonio Indep. School Dist.* v. *Rodriguez*, 411
U. S. 1, 28 (1973) (wealth); *Graham* v. *Richardson*, 403 U. S.
365, 372 (1971) (aliens); *Oregon* v. *Mitchell*, 400 U. S. 112,
295 n. 14 (1970) (STEWART, J., concurring in part and dissenting in part) (persons between ages 18 and 21). Racial and
ethnic classifications, however, are odious without regard to
these additional characteristics. We declared as much in the
first cases to recognize racial distinctions as suspect:

"Distinctions between citizens solely because of their

---

[4] Until 1970, there is no reference in our decisions to the element of
"discreteness and insularity." *Oregon* v. *Mitchell*, 400 U. S. 112, 295 n. 14
(1970) (STEWART, J., concurring in part and dissenting in part). It has
been relied upon in a holding of the Court only in one class of cases, those
involving aliens. *E. g.*, *Graham* v. *Richardson*, 403 U. S. 365, 372 (1971).
Prior citations to "footnote 4" generally concerned the "preferred" position of First Amendment freedoms. Compare *Everson* v. *Board of Education*, 330 U. S. 1, 62 n. 61 (1947) (Rutledge, J., dissenting), with *Kovacs*
v. *Cooper*, 336 U. S. 77, 90–91 (1949) (Frankfurter, J., concurring).

76–811—MEMO

UNIVERSITY OF CALIFORNIA REGENTS *v.* BAKKE   5

ancestry are by their very nature odious to a free people whose institutions are founded upon the doctrine of equality." *Hirabayashi, supra,* at 100.

". . . [A]ll legal restrictions which curtail the rights of a single racial group are immediately suspect. That is not to say that all such restrictions are unconstitutional. It is to say that courts must subject them to the most rigid scrutiny." *Korematsu, supra,* at 216.

The Court has never questioned the validity of those pronouncements. Racial and ethnic distinctions of any sort are inherently suspect and thus call for the most critical judicial examination.

This perception of racial and ethnic distinctions is rooted in our Nation's constitutional and demographic history. This Court's initial view of the Fourteenth Amendment was that its "one pervading purpose" was "the freedom of the slave race, the security and firm establishment of that freedom, and the protection of the newly-made freeman and citizen from the oppressions of those who had formerly exercised dominion over him." *Slaughter-House Cases,* 16 Wall. 36, 71 (1873). The Equal Protection Clause, however, was "[v]irtually strangled in its infancy by post-civil-war judicial reactionism."[5] It was relegated to decades of relative desuetude while the Due Process Clause of the Fourteenth Amendment, after a short germinal period, flourished as a cornerstone in the Court's defense of property and liberty of contract. See, *e. g., Mugler v. Kansas,* 123 U. S. 623, 661 (1887); *Allgeyer v. Louisiana,* 165 U. S. 578 (1897); *Lochner v. New York,* 198 U. S. 45 (1905). In that cause, the Fourteenth Amendment's "one pervading purpose" was displaced. See, *e. g., Plessy v. Ferguson,* 163 U. S. 537 (1896). It was only as the era of substantive due process came to a close, see, *e. g., Nebbia v. New*

---

[5] Tussman & Ten Broek, The Equal Protection of the Laws, 37 Calif. L. Rev. 341, 381 (1949).

76–811—MEMO

6   UNIVERSITY OF CALIFORNIA REGENTS v. BAKKE

York, 291 U. S. 502 (1934); *West Coast Hotel* v. *Parrish,* 300
U. S. 379 (1937), that the Equal Protection Clause began to
attain a genuine measure of vitality. see. *e. g., Carolene Products, supra; Skinner* v. *Oklahoma, supra; Korematsu, supra.*

By this time it was no longer possible to peg the guarantees
of the Fourteenth Amendment to the struggle for equality of
one racial minority. During the dormancy of the Equal Protection Clause. the United States had become a nation of
minorities.[6] Each had to struggle [7]—and to some extent struggles still [8]—to overcome the prejudices not of a monolithic
majority, but of a "majority" composed of various minority
groups of whom it was said—perhaps unfairly in many cases—
that a shared characteristic was a willingness to disadvantage
other groups.[9] As the Nation filled with the stock of many
lands, the reach of the Clause was gradually extended to all
groups seeking protection from official discrimination. See
Strauder, supra, at 308 (Celtic Irishmen) (dictum); *Yick
Wo* v. *Hopkins,* 118 U. S. 356 (1886) (Chinese); *Truax* v.
Raich, 239 U. S. 33. 41 (1915) (Austrian resident aliens);
Korematsu, supra (Japanese); *Hernandez* v. *Texas,* 347 U. S.
475 (1954) (Mexican-Americans). The guarantees of equal
protection. said the Court in *Yick Wo,* "are universal in their
application. to all persons within the territorial jurisdiction,

[6] M. Jones. American Immigration 177–246 (1960).

[7] J. Higham, Strangers in the Land (1955); G. Abbott, The Immigrant
and the Community (1917); P. Roberts, The New Immigration 66–73,
86–91, 248–261 (1912); E. Fenton. Immigrants and Unions: A Case Study
561–562 (1975).

[8] "Members of various religious and ethnic groups, primarily but not
exclusively of eastern, and middle and southern European ancestry. such
as Jews, Catholics. Italians, Greeks and Slavic groups [continue] to be
excluded from executive. middle-management and other job levels because
of discrimination based upon their religion and/or national origin." 41
CFR § 60–50 1 (b).

[9] *E. g..* P. Roberts, The New Immigration 75 (1912); G. Abbott, The
Immigrant and the Community 270–271 (1917). See also n. 7, *supra.*

without regard to any differences of race. of color, or of nationality; and the equal protection of the laws is a pledge of the protection of equal laws." 118 U. S., at 369.

Although many of the Framers of the Fourteenth Amendment conceived of its primary function as one of bridging the vast distance between members of the former slave race and the white "majority." *Slaughter House Cases, supra,* the Amendment itself was framed in universal terms, without reference to color. ethnic origin, or condition of prior servitude.   As this Court recently remarked, in interpreting the 1866 Civil Rights Act to claims of racial discrimination against white persons, "the 39th Congress was intent upon establishing in federal law a broader principle than would have been necessary to meet the particular and immediate plight of the newly freed Negro slaves." *McDonald* v. *Santa Fe Trail Transp. Co.,* 427 U. S. 273. 296 (1976). And that legislation was specifically broadened in 1870 to ensure that "all persons," not merely "citizens," would enjoy equal rights under the law. See *Runyon* v. *McCrary,* 427 U. S. 160. 192-202 (1976) (WHITE. J.. dissenting).   Indeed. it is not unlikely that among the Framers were many who would have applauded a reading of the Equal Protection Clause which states a principle of universal application and is responsive to the racial. ethnic and cultural diversity of the Nation. See. *e. g.,* Cong. Globe. 39th Cong., 1st Sess.. 1056 (1866) (remarks of Rep. Niblack); *id.,* 2891-2892 (remarks of Sen. Corness); *id.,* 40th Cong.. 2d Sess.. 883 (1868) (remarks of Sen. Howe) (Fourteenth Amendment "protect[s] classes from class legislation").   See also Bickel, The Original Understanding and the Segregation Decision. 69 Harv. L. Rev. 1. 60-63 (1955).

Over the past 30 years, this Court has been embarked upon the crucial mission of interpreting the Equal Protection Clause so as to guarantee "the protection of equal laws." *Yick Wo, supra,* at 369, in a Nation confronting a legacy of slavery and racial discrimination.   See, *e. g., Shelley* v. *Kraemer,* 334 U. S.

76–811—MEMO

8   UNIVERSITY OF CALIFORNIA REGENTS *v.* BAKKE

1 (1948); *Brown* v. *Board of Education*, 347 U. S. 483 (1954); *Gomillion* v. *Lightfoot*, 364 U. S. 339 (1960); *Hills* v. *Gautreaux*, 425 U. S. 284 (1976).   The landmark decisions in this area, because they arose in response to the continued exclusion of Negroes from the mainstream of American society, ~~exclusion of Negroes from much of the mainstream of American society,~~ could be characterized as involving discrimination by the "majority" white race against the Negro minority. But they need not be read as depending upon that characterization for their results.   It suffices to say that "[o]ver the years, this Court consistently repudiated '(d)istinctions between citizens solely because of their ancestry' as being 'odious to a free people whose institutions are founded upon the doctrine of equality.'" *Loving* v. *Virginia*, 388 U. S., at 11 (1967). quoting *Hirabayashi, supra*, 320 U. S., at 100.

Petitioner urges us to adopt for the first time a more restrictive view of the Equal Protection Clause and hold that discrimination against members of the white "majority" can never be suspect.   The clock of our liberties, however, cannot be turned back to 1868.   *Brown* v. *Board of Education, supra*, at 492; accord. *Loving* v. *Virginia, supra*, at 9.   It is far too late to argue that the guarantee of equal protection to *all* persons permits the recognition of special wards entitled to some degree of protection greater than that accorded others. "The Fourteenth Amendment is not directed solely against discrimination due to a 'two-class theory'—that is, based upon differences between 'white' and Negro." *Hernandez, supra*, at 478.

Once the artificial line of a "two-class theory" of the Fourteenth Amendment is put aside. the difficulties entailed in varying the level of judicial review according to a perceived "preferential" status of a particular racial or ethnic minority are likely to be intractable.   The concepts of "majority" and "minority" necessarily reflect temporary judgments and political arrangements.   As observed above. the white "majority" itself is composed of various minority groups. each of which can lay claim to a history of prior discrimination at the hands of the

UNIVERSITY OF CALIFORNIA REGENTS *v.* BAKKE   9

state and private individuals. Not all of these groups can receive favorable treatment. and corresponding judicial tolerance of distinctions drawn in terms of race and nationality. for then the only "majority" left would be a new minority of White Anglo-Saxon Protestants. There is no principled basis for deciding which groups will merit "heightened judicial solicitude" and which will not. Courts would be asked to evaluate the extent of the prejudice and consequent harm suffered by various minority groups. Those whose societal injury is found to exceed some presumed level of tolerability would then be entitled to preferential classifications at the expense of individuals belonging to other groups. Those classifications would be free from exacting judicial scrutiny. As these preferences began to have their desired effect. and the consequences of past discrimination were undone. new judicial rankings would be necessary. The kind of variable sociological and political analysis necessary to produce such rankings simply does not lie within the judicial competence—even if it were socially desirable. *DeFunis* v. *Odegaard,* 416 U. S. 312, 337-340 (1974) (Douglas. J.. dissenting).

There are serious problems of justice connected with the idea of preference itself. First. it may not always be clear that a so-called preference is in fact benign. Courts may be asked to validate burdens imposed upon individual members of particular groups in order to advance the group's general interest. See *United Jewish Organizations, supra,* at 1013–1014 (BRENNAN. J.. concurring in part). Nothing in the Constitution supports the notion that individuals may be asked to suffer otherwise impermissible burdens for the greater good of their ethnic groups. Second. preferential programs may only reinforce common stereotypes holding that certain groups are unable to achieve success without special protection based on a factor having no relationship to actual individual worth. See *DeFunis* v. *Odegaard,* 416 U. S.. at 343 (Douglas. J.. dissenting). Third. there is no warrant in the Constitution

76-811—MEMO

10   UNIVERSITY OF CALIFORNIA REGENTS *v.* BAKKE

for forcing innocent persons in respondent's position to bear
the burdens of redressing grievances not of their making.

Moreover, by hitching the meaning of the Equal Protection
Clause to these transitory considerations, we would be holding,
as a constitutional principle, that judicial scrutiny of classifications touching on racial and ethnic background may vary
with the ebb and flow of political forces. Disparate constitutional treatment of such classifications well may serve to
exacerbate racial and ethnic antagonisms rather than alleviate
them. *United Jewish Org.* v. *Carey,* — U. S. —. 97 S. Ct.
996. 1014 (1977) (BRENNAN. J.. concurring). Also. the muta-
bility of a constitutional principle based upon shifting political
and social judgments undermines the chances for consistent
application of the Constitution from one generation to the
next, a critical feature of its coherent interpretation. *Pollock*
v. *Farmers Loan & Trust Co.,* 157 U. S. 429. 650–651 (1895)
(WHITE. J.. dissenting). In expounding the Constitution. the
Court's role is to discern "principles sufficiently absolute to
give them roots throughout the community and continuity
over significant periods of time, and the pragmatic political
judgments of a particular time and place." A. Cox. The Role
of the Supreme Court in American Government 114 (1976).

If it is the individual who is entitled to judicial protection
against classifications touching upon his racial or ethnic background because such distinctions impinge upon personal rights,
rather than the individual only because of his membership in
a particular group. then constitutional standards may be applied consistently. Political judgments regarding the necessity
for the particular classification may be weighed in the constitutional balance. *Korematsu, supra,* but the standard of justification will remain constant. This is as it should be. since
those political judgments are the product of rough compromises struck by contending groups within the democratic
process.[10] When they touch upon an individual's race or

---

[10] R. Dahl. A Preface to Democratic Theory (1956): Posner. The
DeFunis Case and the Constitutionality of Preferential Treatment of

76–811—MEMO

UNIVERSITY OF CALIFORNIA REGENTS *v.* BAKKE   11

ethnic background, he is entitled to a judicial determination that the burden he is asked to bear on that basis is precisely tailored to serve a substantial governmental interest. The Constitution guarantees that right to every person regardless of his background. *Shelley* v. *Kraemer*, 334 U. S. 1. 22 (1948); *Missouri ex rel. Gaines* v. *Canada*, 305 U. S. 337. 351 (1938).

B

Petitioner contends that on several occasions this Court has approved preferential classifications based on race or ethnic background. without applying strict scrutiny. Most of the cases upon which petitioner relies are drawn from three areas: school desegregation. employment discrimination. and sex discrimination. Each of the cases cited presented a situation radically different from the facts of this case.

The school desegregation cases are simply inapposite. In each. a court had formulated or approved remedies for adjudicated findings of constitutional violation. *E. g., Swann* v. *Charlotte-Mecklenburg Board of Education*, 402 U. S. 1 (1971); *Green v. County School Board*, 391 U. S. 430 (1968). Racial classifications were designed as remedies for the vindication of constitutional rights.[11] Here. there was no judicial

---

Minorities, 1974 Sup. Ct. Rev. 1, 27; cf. Stewart, The Reformation of American Administrative Law, 88 Harv. L. Rev. 1683–1685, and nn. 64–67 (1975) and sources cited therein.

[11] Petitioner cites three lower court decisions allegedly deviating from this general rule in school desegregation cases: *Offermann* v. *Nitkowski*. 378 F. 2d 22 (CA2 1967); *Wanner* v. *County School Board*. 357 F. 2d 452 (CA4 1966); *Springfield School Committee* v. *Barksdale*. 348 F. 2d 261 (CA1 1965). Of these, *Wanner* involved a school system held to have been *de jure* segregated and placed under injunctive orders prohibiting further segregation; racial districting was deemed necessary. 357 F. 2d, at 454. Cf. *United Jewish Organizations of Williamsburgh* v. *Carey*. —— U. S. ——, 97 S. Ct. 996 (1977). In *Barksdale* and *Offermann*, courts did approve voluntary districting designed to eliminate *de facto* segregation. In neither, however, was there any showing that the school board planned extensive pupil transportation that might threaten liberty or privacy interests. See *Keyes* v. *School District No. t.* 413 U. S. 189, 240–250

76–811—MEMO

12   UNIVERSITY OF CALIFORNIA REGENTS *v.* BAKKE

determination of constitutional violation as a predicate for the formulation of a remedial classification. Hence, to analogize petitioner's special admission program to a remedy in a desegregation case and suggest that it should therefore be judicially "approved" is to transform a remedy, fashioned to correct a wrong, into a right in and of itself. See *Pasadena City Board of Education* v. *Spangler*, 427 U. S. 424 (1976).

The employment discrimination cases also do not advance petitioner's cause. For example, in *Franks* v. *Bowman Transportation Co.*, 424 U. S. 747 (1975), we approved a retroactive award of seniority to a class of Negro truck drivers who had been the victims of past discrimination. While this relief imposed some burdens on other employees, it was held necessary "'to make [the victims] whole for injuries suffered on account of unlawful employment discrimination.'" *Id.*, at 771, quoting *Albemarle Paper Co.* v. *Moody*, 422 U. S. 405, 418 (1975). The courts of appeals have fashioned various types of racial preferences as remedies for constitutional or statutory violations resulting in specifically identified, race-based injuries to members of the classes held entitled to the preference. *E. g.*, *Bridgeport Guardians, Inc.* v. *Civil Service Commission*, 482 F. 2d 1333 (CA2 1973); *Carter* v. *Gallagher*, 452 F. 2d 315, modified on rehearing en banc, 452 F. 2d 327 (CA8 1972). Such preferences also have been upheld where an impartial legislative or administrative body charged with the responsibility made determinations of past discrimination and fashioned remedies deemed appropriate to rectify the discrimination. *E. g.*, *Contractors Association of Eastern Pennsylvania* v. *Secretary of Labor*, 442 F. 2d 159 (CA3), cert. denied, 404 U. S. 954 (1971); [12] *Associated General Contractors of Mas-*

(1973) (POWELL, J., concurring in part and dissenting in part). Nor were white students deprived of an equal opportunity for education.

[12] Every decision upholding the requirement of preferential hiring under the authority of Executive Order 11246 has emphasized the existence of previous discrimination by the parties involved as a predicate for the imposition of a preferential remedy. *Contractors Association, supra;*

76-811—MEMO

UNIVERSITY OF CALIFORNIA REGENTS *v.* BAKKE   13

sachusetts, Inc. v. *Altschuler,* 490 F. 2d 9 (CA1 1973). cert. denied, 416 U. S. 957 (1974); cf. *Katzenbach* v. *Morgan,* 384 U. S. 641 (1966). Where the preferential classification is not tailored as a remedy for a proven constitutional or statutory violation. proper analysis requires the application of strict scrutiny.[13]

Nor is a different view supported by the fact that classifications touching upon sex. which are designed to compensate women for identified discrimination, are not subjected to this level of scrutiny. *E. g., Califano* v. *Webster,* — U. S. —. 97 S. Ct. 1192. 1194 (1977). Neither are classifications that disadvantage women. see, *e. g., Craig* v. *Boren,* 427 U. S. 190, 211 n.* (1976) (POWELL, J.. concurring).

Apart from other arguments that have been advanced (*e. g.,*

Southern Illinois Builders Assn. v. *Ogilvie.* 471 F. 2d 680 (CA7 1972): *Joyce* v. *McCrane.* 320 F. Supp. 1284 (N. J. 1970); *Weiner* v. *Cuyahoga Community College District,* 19 Ohio 2d 35, 249 N. E. 2d 907, cert. denied, 396 U. S. 1004 (1970). See also *Rosetti Contr. Co.* v. *Brennan,* 408 F. 2d 1039, 1041 (CA7 1975); *Associated General Contractors of Massachusetts, Inc.* v. *Altschuler.* 490 F. 2d 9 (CA1 1973), cert. denied, 416 U. S. 957 (1974); *Northeast Const. Co.* v. *Romney,* 157 U. S. App. D. C. 381, 485 F. 2d 752, 754, 761 (1973).

[13] This view would not affect duly authorized administrative actions, such as consent decrees under Title VII or approval of reapportionment plans under § 5 of the Voting Rights Act of 1965. 42 U. S. C. § 1973c. In such cases, there has been detailed legislative consideration of the various indicia of previous constitutional or statutory violations, *e. g., South Carolina* v. *Katzenbach.* 383 U. S. 301, 308–310 (1966) (§ 5), and particular administrative bodies have been charged with monitoring various activities in order to detect such violations and oversee appropriate remedies.

Furthermore, we are not here presented with an occasion to review legislation by Congress pursuant to its powers under § 2 of the Thirteenth Amendment and § 5 of the Fourteenth Amendment to remedy the effects of prior discrimination. *Katzenbach* v. *Morgan.* 384 U. S. 641 (1966); *Jones* v. *Alfred H. Mayer Co.,* 392 U. S. 409 (1968). We have previously recognized the special competence of the legislature to make findings with respect to the effects of identified past discrimination and its discretionary authority to take appropriate remedial measures.

14   UNIVERSITY OF CALIFORNIA REGENTS *v.* BAKKE

women are the *majority* sex group). gender-based distinctions
are less likely to create the analytical and practical problems
present in preferential programs premised on racial or ethnic
criteria. With respect to gender there are only two possible
classifications. The incidence of the burdens imposed by preferential classifications is clear. There are no rival groups who
can claim that they. too. are entitled to preferential treatment.
Classwide questions as to the group suffering previous injury
and groups which fairly can be burdened are relatively simple
for reviewing courts. See. *e. g., Califano* v. *Goldfarb,* 430
U. S. 199. 212–217 (1977); *Weinberger* v. *Weisenfeld,* 420 U. S.
636. 645 (1975). The resolution of these same questions in
the context of racial and ethnic preferences presents far more
complex and intractable problems than gender-based classifications. In any event. we have consistently declined to view
gender-based classification as suspect or as comparable to racial
classifications for the purpose of equal protection analysis.

Petitioner also cites *Lau* v. *Nichols,* 414 U. S. 563 (1974).
in support of the proposition that discrimination favoring
racial or ethnic minorities has received judicial approval without the exacting inquiry ordinarily accorded "suspect" classifications. In *Lau,* we held that the failure of the San
Francisco school system to provide remedial English instruction for some 1,800 students of oriental ancestry who spoke no
English amounted to a violation of Title VI of the Civil Rights
Act of 1964. 42 U. S. C. § 2000d. and the regulations promulgated thereunder. Those regulations required remedial
instruction where inability to understand English excludes
children of foreign ancestry from participation in educational
programs. *Id.,* at 568. Because we found that the students
in *Lau* were denied a meaningful opportunity to participate in
the educational program," *ibid.,* we remanded for the fashioning
of a remedial order.

Lau provides little support for petitioner's argument. The
decision rested solely on the statute, which had been construed

by the responsible administrative agency to reach methods of school administration "which have the effect of subjecting individuals to discrimination." 414 U. S.. at 568. We stated: "Under these state-imposed standards there is no equality of treatment merely by providing students with the same facilities, textbooks, teachers and curriculum; for students who do not understand English are effectively foreclosed from any meaningful education." *Id.*, at 566. Moreover, the "preference" approved did not result in the denial of the relevant benefit—"meaningful participation in the educational program"—to anyone else. No other student was deprived by that preference of the ability to participate in San Francisco's school system.

In a similar vein,[14] petitioner contends that our recent decision in *United Jewish Organizations of Williamsburgh* v. *Carey,* —— U. S .——, 97 S. Ct. 996 (1977), indicates a willingness to approve racial classifications designed to benefit certain minorities, without denominating the classifications as "suspect." The State of New York had redrawn its reapportionment plan to meet objections of the Department of Justice under § 5 of the Voting Rights Act of 1965, 42 U. S. C. § 1973c. Specifically, voting districts were redrawn to enhance the electoral power of certain "nonwhite" voters found to have been the victim of unlawful "dilution" under the original reapportionment plan. Although the revised reapportionment plan to some extent was drawn along ethnic lines, there was no

---

[14] Petitioner also cites our decision in *Morton* v. *Mancari*, 417 U. S. 535 (1974), for the proposition that the State may prefer members of traditionally disadvantaged groups. In *Mancari*, we approved a hiring preference for qualified Indians in the Bureau of Indian Affairs of the Department of the Interior (BIA). We observed in that case, however, that the legal status of BIA is *sui generis*. *Id.*, at 554. Indeed, we found that the preference was not racial at all, but "an employment criterion reasonably designed to further the cause of Indian self-government and to make the BIA more responsive to groups [,] . . . whose lives are governed by the BIA in a unique fashion." *Ibid.*

76-811—MEMO

16   UNIVERSITY OF CALIFORNIA REGENTS *v.* BAKKE

showing that the plan resulted in the unlawful dilution of any individual's vote or in the underrepresentation of any racial or ethnic group in the legislature as a whole. 97 S. Ct.. at 1008–1009; *id.,* at 1016–1017 (STEWART. J.. concurring). *United Jewish Organizations,* like *Lau,* is viewed properly as a case in which the remedy for an administrative finding of discrimination encompassed measures to improve the previously disadvantaged group's ability to participate. without excluding individuals belonging to any other group from enjoyment of the relevant opportunity—meaningful participation in the electoral process.

In this case. unlike *Lau* and *United Jewish Organizations,* there has been no determination by the legislature or a responsible administrative agency that the University maintained a discriminatory condition requiring remedial efforts. Moreover. the operation of petitioner's special admissions program is quite different from the program in those cases.   It prefers the designated minority groups at the expense of other individuals who are totally foreclosed from competition for the 16 special admissions seats in every medical school class. Because of that foreclosure. some individuals are excluded from enjoyment of a state provided benefit—admission to the medical school—they would otherwise receive.   When a classification denies an individual opportunities or benefits enjoyed by others solely because of his race or ethnic background. it must be regarded as suspect. *E. g., McLaurin* v. *Oklahoma State Regents,* 339 U. S. 637, 641–642 (1950).

III

We have held that in "order to justify the use of a suspect classification. a State must show that its purpose or interest is both constitutionally permissible and substantial. and that its use of the classification is 'necessary . . . to the accomplishment' of its purpose or the safeguarding of its interest." *In re Griffiths,* 413 U. S. 717, 722–723 (1973) (footnotes omitted):

76–811—MEMO

UNIVERSITY OF CALIFORNIA REGENTS *v.* BAKKE   17

Loving v. *Virginia*, 388 U. S. 1, 11 (1967); *McLaughlin* v. *Florida*, 379 U. S. 184, 196 (1964). The special admissions program purports to serve the purposes of: (i) "reducing the historic deficit of traditionally disfavored minorities in medical schools and the medical profession," Brief for Petitioner, at 32; (ii) countering the effects of societal discrimination; [15] (iii) obtaining the educational benefits that flow from an ethnically diverse student body; and (iv) increasing the number of physicians who will practice in communities currently underserved. We must decide which, if any, of these purposes is substantial enough to support the use of a suspect classification.

A

If petitioner's purpose is to assure within its student body some specified percentage of a particular group merely because of its race or ethnic origin, such a preferential purpose must be rejected not as insubstantial but as constitutionally impermissible. Preferring members of any one group for no reason other than race or ethnic origin is discrimination for its own sake. This the Constitution forbids. *E. g., McLaughlin* v. *Florida, supra; Brown* v. *Board of Education, supra,* 483, 495.

---

[15] A number of distinct sub-goals have been advanced as falling with the rubric of "compensation for past discrimination." For example, it is said that preferences for Negro applicants may compensate for harm done them personally, or serve to place them at economic levels they might have attained but for discrimination against their forebears. Greenawalt, *supra,* n. 1, at 581–586. Another view of the "compensation" goal is that it serves as a form of reparation by the "majority" to a victimized group as a whole. B. Bittker, The Case for Black Reparations (1973). That justification for ethnic preference has been subjected to much criticism. *E. g., Greenawalt, supra,* at 581; Posner, *supra,* n. 1, at 16–17, and n. 33. Finally, it has been argued that ethnic preferences "compensate" the group by providing examples of success whom other members of the group will emulate, thereby advancing the group's interest and society's interest in encouraging new generations to overcome the barriers and frustrations of the past. Redish, *supra,* n. 1, at 391. For purposes of analysis, these sub-goals need not be considered separately.

18   UNIVERSITY OF CALIFORNIA REGENTS v. BAKKE

B

The State certainly has a legitimate and substantial interest in ameliorating, or eliminating where feasible, the disabling effects of past discrimination.   The line of school desegregation cases, commencing with *Brown*, attests to the importance of this state goal and the commitment of the judiciary to affirm all lawful means towards its attainment.   In the school cases, the States were required by court order to redress the wrongs worked by specific and identifiable racial discrimination.   That goal was far more focused than the remedying of the effects of "societal discrimination," a concept of injury that may be ageless in its reach into the past.

We have never approved a classification that aids persons perceived as members of relatively victimized groups at the expense of other innocent individuals in the absence of adjudicated, legislative, or administrative findings of constitutional or statutory violations.   See, *e. g., United Jewish Organizations*, — U. S. —, 97 St. Ct., at 1005; *South Carolina* v. *Katzenbach*, 383 U. S. 308 (1966).   After such findings have been made, the governmental interest in preferring members of the injured groups at the expense of others is substantial, since the legal rights of the victims must be vindicated.   In such a case, the extent of the injury and the consequent remedy will have been judicially or legislatively defined.   Also, the remedial action usually remains subject to continuing oversight to assure that it will work the least harm possible to other innocent persons competing for the benefit.   Without such findings of constitutional or statutory violations, it cannot be said that the government has any greater interest in helping one individual than in refraining from harming another.

A public university is not in a position to make such findings. Its mission is education, not the formulation of legislative policy or the adjudication of particular claims of illegality. For the reasons stated in Part III of this opinion, isolated segments of our vast governmental structures are ill equipped

76-811—MEMO

UNIVERSITY OF CALIFORNIA REGENTS *v.* BAKKE   19

to make such decisions. at least in the absence of legislative mandates and legislatively determined criteria.   Cf. *Hampton* v. *Mow Sun Wong*, 426 U. S. 88 (1976).   Compare n. 13, *supra.* Thus, the purpose of helping certain persons whom the faculty of the Davis Medical School perceived as victims of "societal discrimination" does not support the consequent casting of burdens upon persons like respondent, who bear no responsibility for whatever harm the beneficiaries of the special admissions program are thought to have suffered.   To hold otherwise would be to convert a remedy heretofore reserved for violations of legal rights into a privilege that institutions throughout the Nation can grant at their pleasure.   That is a step we have never approved.   Cf. *Pasadena City Board of Education* v. *Spangler*, 427 U. S. 424 (1976).

C

Petitioner identifies. as another purpose of its program. improving the delivery of health care services to communities currently underserved.[16]   Even assuming that a State's interest in facilitating the health care of its citizens is sufficiently compelling to support the use of a suspect classification. there is virtually no evidence in the record indicating that petitioner's special admissions program is either needed or geared to promote that goal.   The court below addressed this failure of proof:

> "The University concedes it cannot assure that minority doctors who entered under the program. all of whom express an "interest" in participating in a disadvantaged community. will actually do so.   It may be correct to assume that some of them will carry out this intention. and that it is more likely they will practice in minority communities than the average white doctor.   (See Sandalow. *Racial Preferences in Higher Education: Political*

---

[16] The only evidence in the record with respect to such underservice is a newspaper article.   R. 473.

76–811—MEMO

20   UNIVERSITY OF CALIFORNIA REGENTS *v.* BAKKE

Responsibility and the Judicial Role (1975) 42 U. Chi. L. Rev. 653. 688). Nevertheless. there are more precise and reliable ways to identify applicants who are genuinely interested in the medical problems of minorities than by race. An applicant of whatever race who has demonstrated his concern for disadvantaged minorities in the past and who declares that practice in such a community is his primary professional goal would be more likely to contribute to alleviation of the medical shortage than one who is chosen entirely on the basis of race and disadvantage. In short. there is [sic] no empirical data to demonstrate that any one race is more selflessly socially oriented or by contrast that another is more selfishly acquisitive." 18 Cal. 3d. at 56.

Petitioner simply has not carried its burden of demonstrating that it must prefer members of a particular ethnic group over other individuals in order to promote better health care delivery to deprived citizens. Indeed. petitioner has not shown that its preferential classification is likely to have any significant effect on the problem.

D

The fourth goal asserted by petitioner is the attainment of a diverse student body. This clearly is a constitutionally permissible goal for an institution of higher education. Academic freedom. though not a constitutional right in itself. long has been viewed as a special concern of the First Amendment. The freedom of a university to make its own judgments as to education includes the selection of its student body. Mr. Justice Frankfurter summarized the "four essential freedoms" that comprise academic freedom:

" '. . . . It is the business of a university to provide that atmosphere which is most conducive to speculation. experiment and creation. It is an atmosphere in which there

prevail 'the four essential freedoms' of a university—to
determine for itself on academic grounds who may teach,
what may be taught, how it shall be taught, and who may
be admitted to study.'"   *Sweezy* v. *New Hampshire,* 354
U. S. 234, 263 (1957) (Frankfurter, J., concurring).

Our national commitment to the safeguarding of these
freedoms within university communities was emphasized in
Keyishian v. *Board of Regents,* 385 U. S. 589, 603 (1967):

> "Our Nation is deeply committed to safeguarding aca-
> demic freedom which is of transcendent value to all of us
> and not merely to the teachers concerned.   That freedom
> is therefore a special concern of the First Amendment. . . .
> The Nation's future depnds upon leaders trained through
> wide exposure to that robust exchange of ideas which
> discovers truth 'out of a multitude of tongues, rather
> than through any kind of authoritative selection.'
> *United States* v. *Associated Press,* 52 F. Supp. 362, 372."

The atmosphere of "speculation, experiment and creation"—so
essential to the quality of higher education—is widely believed
to be promoted by a student body diverse in many respects.
As we noted in *Keyishian,* it is not too much to say that the
"nation's future depends upon leaders trained through wide
exposure" to the ideas and mores of students as diverse as this
Nation of many peoples.

It may be argued that there is greater force to these views
at the undergraduate level than in a medical school where the
training is centered primarily on professional competency.
But even at the graduate level, our tradition and experience
lend support to the view that the contribution of diversity is
substantial.   Physicians serve a heterogenous population.
An otherwise qualified medical student with a particular
background—whether it be ethnic, geographic, culturally advantaged or disadvantaged—may bring to a professional school
of medicine experiences, outlooks and ideas that enrich the

76-811—MEMO

22   UNIVERSITY OF CALIFORNIA REGENTS *v.* BAKKE

training of its student body and better equip its graduates to
render with understanding their vital service to humanity.

Ethnic diversity. however. is only one element in a range of
factors a university properly may consider in attaining the goal
of a heterogeneous student body.   Although a university must
have wide discretion in making the sensitive judgments as to
who should be admitted. constitutional limitations protecting
individual rights may not be disregarded.   Specifically. respondent urges—and the courts below have held—that petitioner's
dual admissions program is a racial classification that imper-
missibly infringes his rights under the Fourteenth Amendment.
As the interest of diversity served by the program is substantial.
the question remains whether the program's racial classification
is necessary to promote this interest.   *In re Griffiths, supra,*
413 U. S., at 721–722.   We turn now to that question.

IV

We may assume that the reservation of a specified number
of seats in each class for individuals from the preferred ethnic
groups would contribute to the attainment of ethnic diversity
in the student body.   But petitioner's argument that this is
the only effective means of serving the interest of diversity is
seriously flawed.   In a most fundamental sense the argument
misconceives the nature of the state interest.   It is not an
interest in simple ethnic diversity. in which a specified percentage of the student body is in effect guaranteed to be
members of selected ethnic groups. with the remaining percentage' an undifferentiated aggregation of students.   The
diversity that furthers a substantial state interest encompasses
a far broader base of qualifications and characteristics of
which racial or ethnic origin is but a single element.   Petitioner's special admissions program. focused solely on ethnic
diversity. would hinder rather than further attainment of
genuine diversity.

Nor would the state interest in genuine diversity be served
by expanding petitioner's two-track system into a multitrack

UNIVERSITY OF CALIFORNIA REGENTS *v.* BAKKE   23

program with a prescribed number of seats set aside for each identifiable category of applicants. Indeed, it is inconceivable that a university would thus pursue the logic of petitioner's two-track program to the illogical end of insulating each category of applicants with certain desired qualifications from competition with all other applicants.

Other universities have not found it necessary to adopt any such system, whether two or multitracked. An illuminating example of an admissions system designed to achieve meaningful diversity in the broad sense of this term is found in the Harvard College program:

> "In recent years Harvard College has expanded the concept of diversity to include students from disadvantaged economic, racial and ethnic groups. Harvard College now recruits not only Californians or Louisianans but also blacks and Chicanos and other minority students.
>
> .   .   .   .   .   .
>
> "In practice, this new definition of diversity has meant that race has been a factor in some admission decisions. When the Committee on Admissions reviews the large middle group of applicants who are 'admissible' and deemed capable of doing good work in their courses, the race of an applicant may tip the balance in his favor just as geographic origin or a life spent on a farm may tip the balance in other candidates' cases. A farm boy from Idaho can bring something to Harvard College that a Bostonian cannot offer. Similarly, a black student can usually bring something that a white person cannot offer."

(Appendix, Amicus Brief filed on behalf of Harvard, Columbia, Pennsylvania, and Stanford at 2).   See Appendix hereto.

But the Harvard College program specifically eschews quotas:

> "In Harvard college admissions the Committee has not set target-quotas for the number of blacks, or of musicians, football players, physicists or Californians to be admitted

76–811—MEMO

24   UNIVERSITY OF CALIFORNIA REGENTS *v.* BAKKE

in a given years. . . . But that awareness [of the necessity of including more than a token number of black
students] does not mean that the Committee sets the
minimum number of blacks or of people from west of the
Mississippi who are to be admitted. It means only that
in choosing among thousands of applicants who are not
only 'admissible' academically but have other strong
qualities, the Committee, with a number of criteria in
mind, pays some attention to distribution among many
types and categories of students." (Appendix Harvard,
et al., Amicus Brief at 3).

In such an admissions program, race or ethnic background
may be deemed a "plus" in a particular applicant's file, but it
does not insulate the individual from fair comparison with all
other candidates for the available seats. The file of a particular black applicant may be examined for its potential
contribution to diversity without the factor of race being
decisive when compared, for example, with that of an applicant
identified as an Italian-American if the latter is thought to
exhibit qualities more likely to promote beneficial educational
pluralism. Such qualities could include unique personal talents
or service experience, leadership potential, maturity, demonstrated compassion, a history of overcoming disadvantage,
ability to communicate with the poor, or other qualifications
deemed at the time to be relevant. In short, an admissions
program operated in this way is flexible enough to consider all
pertinent elements of diversity and to place them on the same
footing for consideration, although not necessarily receiving
the same weight.[17] Indeed, the weight attributed to a particular quality may vary from year to year depending upon the
"mix" both of the student body and the applicants for the

_____

[17] For an illuminating discussion of such a flexible admissions system,
see Manning, The Pursuit of Fairness in Admissions to Higher Education,
in Carnegie Council on Policy Studies in Higher Education, Selective
Admissions in Higher Education 19, 57–59 (1977).

76–811—MEMO

UNIVERSITY OF CALIFORNIA REGENTS *v.* BAKKE   25

incoming class. The applicant who loses out on the last available seat to an applicant receiving a "plus" on the basis of ethnic background will not have been foreclosed from consideration simply because he was not the right color or had the wrong surname. It would mean only that his combined qualifications, which may have included similar nonobjective factors, did not outweigh those of the other applicant. His qualifications would have been weighed fairly and competitively, and he would have no legitimate basis to complain of unequal treatment.

It has been suggested that the Harvard-type program is simply a subtle and more sophisticated—but no less effective—means of according racial preference than the Davis program. A facial intent to discriminate, however, is evident in petitioner's preference program and not denied in this case. No such facial infirmity exists in an admissions program where race or ethnic background is simply one element—to be weighed fairly against other elements—in the selection process. A court would not assume that a university, professing to employ a facially nondiscriminatory admissions policy, would operate it as a cover for the functional equivalent of a quota system. In short, good faith would be presumed in the absence of a showing to the contrary in the manner permitted by our cases. See, *e. g., Arlington Heights* v. *Metropolitan Housing Development Corp.,* 429 U. S. 252 (1977); *Washington* v. *Davis,* 426 U. S. 229 (1976); *Swain* v. *Alabama,* 380 U. S. 202 (1965).

V

In summary, it is evident that the Davis special admission program involves the use of an explicit racial classification never before countenanced by this Court. It tells applicants who are not Negro, Asian, or "Chicano" that they are totally excluded from a specific percentage of the seats in an entering class. No matter how strong their qualifications, quantitative and extracurricular, including their own potential for contribu-

76–811—MEMO

26   UNIVERSITY OF CALIFORNIA REGENTS *v.* BAKKE

tion to educational diversity, they are never afforded the chance to compete with applicants from the preferred groups for special admission seats. At the same time, the preferred applicants have the opportunity to compete for every seat in the class.

The fatal flaw in petitioner's preferential program is its disregard of individual rights as guaranteed by the Fourteenth Amendment. *Shelley* v. *Kraemer*, 334 U. S. 1, 22 (1948). Such rights are not absolute. But when a State's distribution of benefits or imposition of burdens hinges on the color of a person's skin or on his ancestry, he is entitled to a demonstration that the challenged classification is necessary to promote a substantial state interest. Petitioner has failed to carry this burden.

William J. Brennan, Jr., Memorandum of November 23, 1977

circulated 11/23

Supreme Court of the United States
Washington, D. C. 20543

CHAMBERS OF
JUSTICE WM. J. BRENNAN, JR.

November 23, 1977

MEMORANDUM TO THE CONFERENCE

RE: No. 76-811, Regents of the University of
        California v. Bakke

I fully share the hope that circulation of views in advance of conference will be helpful in deciding this significant case. In the following, I set out my own views without necessarily attempting to answer different approaches taken in other memoranda. Since the Title VI briefs are in, I've added a section to state the reasons, largely in agreement with the Solicitor General, why I've concluded that Title VI affords no escape from deciding the constitutional issue. Specifically, I agree with the SG that decision of this case can no more easily be made on the "delphic" wording of Title VI than on the language of the Fourteenth Amendment. My discussion of the constitutional problem therefore precedes my Title VI discussion.

If Davis' program is unconstitutional, I am clear that this is not because the law requires the automatic

Regents v.. Bakke
Page 2

invalidation of all decisionmaking which, like Davis'
admissions decisions, takes race into account. We long
ago crossed that bridge in cases that approved
race-sensitive policies and remedies, and thus firmly
settled the principle that not every remedial use of race
is constitutionally forbidden. Last Term's United Jewish
Organization v. Carey, 430 U.S. 144, definitely imbedded
that principle in concrete, and Bakke's claim for
admission is of no more constitutional significance than
the Hasidim's claimed right, in UJO, to vote as a single
bloc.

Moreover, to read the Fourteenth Amendment to state an
abstract principle of color-blindness is itself to be
blind to history. The brief for the NAACP Legal Defense &
Education Fund, Inc., at 10-53, convincingly demonstrates
that the Fourteenth Amendment was thought necessary to
enable Congress to adopt measures giving special treatment
to "freedmen," and that Congress acted before and after
the adoption of the amendment to secure for blacks real,
not just abstract equality. I therefore think it clear
that states are free to pursue the goal of racial
pluralism in their institutions in order to afford
minorities full participation in the broader society. As

Regents v. Bakke
Page 3

Felix commented in concurring in a case sustaining a state
program also not constitutionally compelled: "To use the
Fourteenth Amendment as a sword against such State power
would stultify that Amendment." Railway Mail Association
v. Corsi, 326 U.S. 88, 98.

And certainly any invalidity of Davis' program is not
the result of the illegitimacy or weaknesses of the
program's objectives. More justifications are found in
the Bakke record (elaborated upon in the many briefs) to
support this race-sensitive policy than were provided in
UJO. Of these, one in particular is of pressing
importance. (I put to one side the subsidiary, though
also very important, benefits of integration of the
medical school and the medical profession, such as student
enrichment and better distribution of medical services in
the community.) It is undisputed that prior to the
adoption of race-sensitive programs, the numbers in which
minorities were admitted to medical schools were so
niggling as to severely embarass the nation's
determination that minorities should fully participate at
all levels of society. Moreover, the percentage of black
physicians remained a constant 2.2% during the period
1950-1970, with three-fourths of these physicians trained

Regents v. Bakke
Page 4

in two black schools. Odegaard, Minorities in Medicine
18-23 (1977). Confronted with this situation, I think
that medical educators, who stand at the gateway to the
profession, are entitled to embark upon affirmative action
programs in order to achieve the participation of
minorities in the profession as an end in itself. I
therefore turn to the considerations which bear upon
whether the means which Davis selected were
constitutional.

   I don't have to debate the question whether the
Fourteenth Amendment protects whites as well as blacks.
Surely it does. The difficult question is deciding what
triggers the protection. If I thought for a moment that
Davis' failure to admit Bakke represented a governmental
slur of whites -- for example, a statement from Davis that
Bakke was being denied admission because "whites are too
dumb to be good doctors," or because "Bakke is Mick
Irish, or Jew, or Hungarian, or Englishman" -- then I
would not hesitate to apply the strictest of scrutiny.
But we all know that Davis' action represents absolutely
nothing of this. Despite the interesting abstract
discussions in the briefs concerning whether whites are
capable of discriminating against whites (WASPS against

Regents v. Bakke
Page 5

Irish, or Poles, or Italians, etc. etc.), or whether
whites are a monolithic bloc, etc., I think I'm right that
all nine of us agree that Davis in this case did not use
race with ill will toward Bakke or anyone.

Instead the Davis program uses race, inter alia, in
furtherance of an immediate goal to increase the number of
minority doctors; but the long-range goal is to reduce the
degree to which California and American society are
overall racially conscious societies. This to me is
crucial to our approach to the constitutional issue.
Davis would provide more blacks as classmates for whites
not from desire that the medical class reflect the
community's racial make-up, but because as educators its
faculty believes that professional association between
blacks and whites will decrease the degree to which whites
think of blacks, not as people, but as a race, and thus
the degree to which blacks think of themselves as
inferior. Davis also wants the program to provide "role
models" for future black doctors, not just that black boys
and girls should find adult models only among blacks, but
because our dismal history of racial discrimination has
made black children, as Brown emphasized, so conscious of
their own race, that whites' success, at least as of now,

Regents v. Bakke
Page 6

has no real meaning for black children.

In essence, the element that is missing from this case
(and would be fatal to the Davis program if present) has
had several labels during my 21 years here: stigma,
insult, badge of inferiority, invidiousness, -- to name
some. Brown v. Board of Education and its innumerable
progeny are primarily about stigma and insult. Brown
prohibited segregated schools because, in Earl Warren's
words, to separate Negro children "generates a feeling of
inferiority as to their status in the community and may
affect their hearts and minds in a way unlikely ever to be
undone." 347 U.S., at 494. All subsequent race cases
similarly struck down government policies that either
openly or covertly "despoil colored citizens." Gomillion
v. Lightfoot, 364 U.S. 339, 347. This same concern is now
predominant in our sex discrimination cases. I refer
particularly to Harry's rejection in Stanton v. Stanton,
421 U.S. 7, of "old notions" that demean women by denying
them any place in the "world of ideas," 421 U.S., at 15,
and John's rejection of "traditional ways of thinking"
that assume all members of the female sex to be
dependents. Califano v. Goldfarb, 430 U.S., at 222-223.

Regents v. Bakke
Page 7

The constitutional principle I think to be supported
by our cases can be summarized as follows: government may
not on account of race, insult or demean a human being by
stereotyping his or her capacities, integrity, or worth as
an individual. In other words, the Fourteenth Amendment
does not tolerate government action that causes any to
suffer from the prejudice or contempt of others on account
of his race. UJO is a paradigm example of what the
Fourteenth Amendment does not condemn. There can be no
question that the racial line used there disadvantaged the
Hasidim. Yet you will remember that in the opinions
Byron, Potter and I wrote, each of us viewed as crucial
the fact that the use of race was not insulting or
invidious and therefore not improper. Byron wrote, for
example, that the "plan represented no racial slur or
stigma with respect to whites or any other race." 430
U.S., at 165. Potter emphasized that the obvious benign
nature of the plan "forecloses any finding that New York
acted with the invidious purpose of discriminating against
white voters." Id., at 180. And I rejected "the
possibility that the decisionmaker intended a racial
insult or injury" to whites. Id., at 178. The
redistricting therefore was upheld as a legitimate

Regents v. Bakke
Page 8

remedial step, notwithstanding its impact on the Hasidim.

To the same effect is John's explanation of why the
statute involved in Goldfarb was not discriminatory: it
"(did) not imply that (whites) are inferior to (Negroes),
(did) not condemn whites on the basis of the misconduct of
an unrepresented few, and (did) not add to the burdens of
an already disadvantaged discrete minority." 430 U.S., at
218. And it seems to me that a similar principle must
explain the difference between an indivious law and a
genuinely benign or remedial one that we have always
approved without applying the strict scrutiny test. E.g.,
UJO; Franks v. Bowman Transportation Co., 424 U.S. 747;
Swann v. Charlotte-Mecklenburg Board of Education, 402
U.S. 1; United States v. Montgomery County Board of
Education, 395 U.S. 225. This has been true even when, as
in this case, the racial line is voluntarily adopted
without court order. See UJO; McDaniel v. Barresi, 402
U.S. 39.

Our older Fourteenth Amendment opinions concentrate
upon classifications disadvantaging "discrete and insular"
groups but they also can be seen to represent the
principle enunciated above. Such classifications have
always been automatically, in the terms introduced by Hugo

Regents v. Bakke
Page 9

Black, "suspect" -- because the history and political
weakness of the group convinced the Court that the
classifications were intended to insult them and do them
harm. Whites do not share this history and political
powerlessness. Of course, I know that whites, too, can
suffer from bad faith, and invidiousness, and of course I
know that our laws protect them when they do. Santa Fe v.
McDonald, 427 U.S. 273, which I joined, was just such a
case. And, in fact, I may have been more troubled than
some of my colleagues that the Hasidim in UJO might have
been the victims of discrimination, anti-semitic and
invidious by design. But I feel, and I doubt any of my
colleagues disagree, that Davis' admissions policies as
applied to Bakke are not of that nature. It is true that
Bakke, like thousands of other applicants who fail of
admission, was not admitted to medical school. But he was
never stereotyped as an incompetent, or pinned with a
badge of inferiority because he is white. Therefore, we
would simply ignore the history of our country and of the
Fourteenth Amendment, as well as the University of
California's true purposes in adopting the Davis program,
if we were to conclude that the child in Brown in 1954 and
Alan Bakke in 1977 appear before this Court on the same
footing.

Regents v. Bakke
Page 10

Moreover, under any standard of Fourteenth Amendment review other than one requiring absolute color-blindness, the Davis program passes muster.

All would agree that the alternatives suggested by the California Supreme Court are fanciful. The only serious alternative which has been suggested by anyone is that a system be devised which accurately predicts the abilities of minority applicants to be good doctors so that minority and nonminority applicants may be chosen from a single pool solely on the basis of "merit." I assume such a system would achieve significant integration, and I have no quarrel with this suggestion as an abstract matter. Surely, administrators are entitled, and indeed compelled, to seek admissions criteria which fairly reflect the qualifications of the minority applicants vis-a-vis nonminority applicants. See Albermarle Paper Co. v. Moody, 422 U.S. 404.

But as yet the medical profession is only on the threshhold of developing admission's standards that can fairly be applied to all races.

It is only since 1968 that medical educators began giving serious attention to the problem of under-representation of minorities in the profession, and, of

Regents v. Bakke
Page 11

the 112 medical schools in the U.S., 90% of the 89 which
responded to a questionnaire did not begin significantly
to involve themselves in "equal educational opportunity
efforts" until 1968 or later. Odegaard, supra, at 11-12.
Consequently, the experience with minority admissions is
quite limited. There is general agreement that minorities
were not admitted in significant numbers until
race-sensitive admissions criteria were used, and that
those admitted generally have done adequately or well, if
not as well as whites. Odegaard, supra, at 34-42.

There are empirical studies indicating that formal,
cognitive predictors of academic success understate
minority applicants' ability to perform well vis-a-vis
white applicants, e.g., Sedlacek & Brooks, Predictors of
Academic Success for University Students in Special
Programs, Research Report #4-12, Cultural Study Center, U.
of Md., and, significantly, that while race is positively
correlated with differences in GPA and MCAT scores,
economic disadvantage is not. Thus, economically
disadvantaged whites do not score less well than
economically advantaged whites, while economically
advantaged blacks score less well than do disadvantaged
whites. Waldman, Economic & Racial Disadvantage as

Regents v. Bakke
Page 12

Reflected in Traditional Medical Selection Factors: A
Study of 1976 Applicants to U.S. Medical Schools, AAMC
(1977). There are strong indications, moreover, that
certain non-cognitive factors are useful in predicting the
success of minority applicants, but there is no single set
of factors, cognitive or non-cognitive which is capable of
fair prediction regardless of race. See Odegaard, supra,
at 103-108.

I do not rely on these studies, but I do think that
they illustrate that which medical educators have been
telling us, namely, that the factors surrounding
prediction of success are far too complicated and
experience with their use is far too limited for educators
to devise a single rating which fairly evaluates minority
and nonminority students on the basis of a common
denominator. Thus, while there has been dissatisfaction
with reliance on GPA's and MCAT's as a basis for selection
both for minority and nonminority students, at this point
educators have not been able to devise ameliorative
programs other than a race-conscious admissions system
such as Davis employs. See Odegaard, supra, at 102-114.
Within the last several years, however, studies funded by
various foundations have been begun to explore some of the

Regents v. Bakke
Page 13

problems associated with predictive testing and admissions
criteria in order to make the admissions process fairer to
both minorities and nonminorities. See id. I would not
abort these experiments and hamstring the efforts of
educators to develop sound admissions programs. I, for
one, am not inclined to second-guess the apparently
unanimous conclusion of the amici representing the
nation's medical and law schools, the teachers at those
schools, and knowledgeable professional associations (like
the AMA and ABA), that without programs like Davis'
qualified minorities would essentially disappear from
their institutions. Their view is that an affirmance here
will deny them any use of race as a factor in admissions
with the result that they will be unable to fulfill what
they take to be their responsibilities to the nation.
Such a result would truly be a national tragedy, and I
cannot acccpt that legal doctrine points in that direction.

My concurrence in UJO was an attempt to explain my
view of the proper judicial role in cases like this. I
believe that a court must assure itself that the decision
maker relying on race intends no insult or slur to whites
-- that the reliance is in fact a benign attempt to remedy
discrimination in our society. Califano v. Webster, 430

Regents v. Bakke
Page 14

U.S. 313, settled the propriety of this when Congress
deliberately legislated an advantage for women to redress
past societal discrimination. I should think the
propriety of the approach follows a fortiori in the case
of reliance on race to redress past racial
discrimination. But, of course, it would always be
relevant to make certain that particular whites are not
unfairly singled out to their unique disadvantage. Once
this is done, however, any further inquiry, in my view,
should be limited to whether the affirmative action policy
actually adopted is a reasonable and considered one in
light of the alternatives available and the opportunities
that it leaves open for whites.

    I fully appreciate that an affirmative action program
such as that employed by Davis may generate some
undesirable side effects that are at odds with Fourteenth
Amendment values. Such programs may well have the
immediate short-term effect of promoting thinking in
racial terms. However, I remain convinced, as those
responsible for the Davis program undoubtedly were, that
such short-term race consciousness is a necessary and
constitutionally acceptable price to pay if we are to have
a society indifferent to race, in which blacks and whites

Regents v. Bakke
Page 15

have equal access to both the medical profession and
medical services, in the long run.

Turning to Davis' program, I cannot say that the
decision to set aside 16 places out of 100 for <u>qualified</u>
<u>minority</u> students (the emphasis is very important for
Davis would not fill the number of places set aside unless
there were 16 minority applicants it considered clearly
qualified for medical education) is an unreasonable one,
especially in California where far more than 16% of the
population is minority. I agree with Byron that we are
just deluding ourselves if we think that there is a
meaningful, judicially enforceable distinction between
setting aside a reasonable number of places for <u>qualified</u>
<u>minorities</u> and a process that accomplishes the same end by
taking race into account as one of several admissions
factors. If admissions officers understand that they may
increase the number of minorities in school they obviously
will manage to make the various subjective judgments
necessary to accomplish their goal, whether or not that
goal is explicitly stated in terms of a set number.
Admissions decisions in their very nature (as I think the
Davis "benchmark" scoring system illustrates) are highly
subjective. They certainly aren't administrative

Regents v. Bakke
Page 16

decisions that lend themselves to a reviewable record.
How much weight a faculty admissions committee decides to
allow the factor of race will almost certainly depend on
how many minority applicants should be admitted -- which,
in Davis' case, is 16%. Unless we want to throw every
admissions decision into federal court for a judge somehow
to decide whether race was taken too much or too little
into account, we should support a school faculty that acts
honestly in adopting the type of reasonable affirmative
action plan it views as appropriate for its school. We
have no business substituting our speculative judgment
about the probable consequences of educational policies
for the judgment of professional educators.

When educators with virtually one voice tell us that
only programs like Davis' offer any significant promise of
achieving that goal, and that if they are declared
unconstitutional then only a handful of minority students
will make medical or other professional schools in the
foreseeable future, we turn a deaf ear at our peril.

Regents v. Bakke
Page 17

Title VI

I readily accept the conclusion of John's law clerk
that Title VI, like the Fourteenth Amendment, protects
whites as well as Negroes. But this begins rather than
ends the inquiry. The questions here are what government
policies Title VI protects against and particularly
whether Congress meant to forbid a university from taking
affirmative steps, which do not stigmatize either whites
or blacks, to afford educational opportunities -- that
previously were, as a practical matter, closed -- to
persons traditionally the victims of invidious
discrimination on account of their race. The statements
of Senator Kuchel and others quoted by John's and
Thurgood's clerks certainly confirm my impression that
very few people were thinking in terms of affirmative
action back in 1964, but, nevertheless, on the occasions
the subject came up, the clear assumption was that
reasonable affirmative actions programs were not barred by
Title VI--so long of course as the programs were
constitutional. I frankly would have been surprised if
the legislative history had shown otherwise. The obvious

Regents **v.** Bakke
Page 19
[Page 18 missing from author's copy.]

HEW regulation authorizing affirmative action under Title
VI, suggests, if it does not compel, the conclusion that
this administrative interpretation comports with the
Congressional understanding of Title VI. These factors,
in my view, support the further conclusion that Title VI
essentially incorporates Fourteenth Amendment standards
and treats affirmative action as does the Amendment.

W.J.B., Jr.

Harry A. Blackmun, Memorandum of May 1, 1978

Supreme Court of the United States
Washington, D. C. 20543

CHAMBERS OF
JUSTICE HARRY A. BLACKMUN

May 1, 1978

MEMORANDUM TO THE CONFERENCE

> Re: No. 76-811 - Regents of the University of
> California v. Bakke

The Chief, not inappropriately, has been pressing me
for a vote in this case.

Since my two months' relegation to the sidelines -- from
November 11 to early January -- although constantly stewing about
the Bakke case, I purposefully and I think properly, gave priority
to the attempt to stay even with all the other work. I feel that I have
been successful in this and that, except for Bakke, I have held nothing
up either for a dissent or for any other reason.

Absorbing Bakke was not made easier by the voluminous and
eager writings. I have read each and all of these word by word, as well
as the many briefs, for I have felt obliged to review what has proved
to be so oppositely persuasive for members of the Court. Having done
all this, and having given the matter earnest and, as some of my
clerical friends would say, "prayerful" consideration, I outline the
following:

- 2 -

General Considerations

1. At least until the early 1970's, only a very small percentage, perhaps less than 2%, of all physicians and attorneys and
medical students and law students in the United States were members
of what we have come to think of as minority groups. In addition,
three-fourths of our black physicians were trained at two medical
schools. If ways are not found to remedy this situation, the Country
can never achieve its professed goal of a society that is not race
conscious.

2. I yield to no one in my earnest hope that the time soon
will come when an "affirmative action" program is unnecessary and
only a relic of the past. I would hope that we could reach this stage
within a decade, but history strongly suggests that that hope is a
forlorn one. Even the University here anticipates a longer period.
At some time, however, we must reach a stage of maturity, beyond
any transitional inequality, where action along this line is no longer
necessary. Then persons may be regarded as persons, and past discrimination will be an ugly feature of history that has been overcome.

3. This is not an ideal world. It probably never will be. It
is easy to give legislative language a literal construction when one
assumes that the factual atmosphere is idealistic. But we live in a
real world.

- 3 -

4. There is as yet no absolute right to higher education in the United States.

5. The number of qualified, indeed highly qualified, applicants for places in existing medical schools in the United States far exceeds the number of places available. Thus, wholly apart from racial and ethnic considerations, the selection process inevitably results in the denial of admission to many qualified applicants, indeed, to more qualified applicants than to those who are granted admission. This, of course, is a denial to the deserving.

6. We see this very same thing, on a smaller and more intimate scale, when those of us who personally choose our law clerks are confronted annually with a surplus of well-trained, highly qualified young men and women, all of whom could do the work expected of a clerk, and do it acceptably. Yet we must, and do, make the selection and thereby deny to many what they earnestly desire to have. That selection process perhaps affects the applicants' professional careers one way or the other, for better or for worse. I doubt that the crisis of clerk selection is very different from the crisis of graduate school admission, except that it comes at a later point in the applicants' professional experiences.

- 4 -

7. All this, in my view, makes the issues involved in the Bakke case both vital and unusually difficult. The issues are made seemingly more difficult when Bakke, an excluded person not charged with discrimination, is the one who is disadvantaged, and when the University itself is not charged with past discrimination.

8. One theoretical solution, of course, to the need for more minority members in higher education would be to enlarge the number of places in the graduate schools. Then all who desired and were qualified could enter, and talk of discrimination would vanish. Unfortunately, this is not feasible or realistic. The vast resources that would be required apparently are not available, and perhaps the need for just more professional graduates, in the strict numerical sense, has not at all been demonstrated.

9. There is no particular significance in the 84-16 division at Davis. The same considerations necessarily apply if the Special Program were to focus on only 12 or 8 or 4 places or, indeed, on but 1.

10. It is somewhat ironic to have us so convulsed and deeply disturbed over a program where race is an element of consciousness, and yet to be aware of the fact that institutions of higher learning for many years have given conceded preferences up

- 5 -

to a point to the skilled athlete, to the children of alumni, to the affluent who may bestow their largess on the institution, and to those having connections with celebrities and the famous. No one seems to have evinced much concern about such practices. There are grumblings here and there, but no action.

11. Programs of admission to institutions of higher learning are basically a responsibility for academicians and for administrators and the specialists they employ. The Judiciary, in contrast, is ill equipped and poorly trained for this. As the Chief said in his typed circulation, the Court consistently has acknowledged that the administration and management of educational institutions is beyond the competence of judges and is within the special competence of educators, provided always that the latter perform within legal and constitutional bounds. Lewis' references to comments by Felix Frankfurter and Bill Brennan are in the same vein. For me, interference by the Judiciary must be the rare exception and not the rule.

12. An admissions policy that has an awareness of race as an element seems to me to be the only possible and realistic means of achieving the societal goal I have mentioned above. The question, then, is whether it is legally and constitutionally permissible.

- 6 -

13. Our individual answers to the issues here will depend, I suspect, in large part upon our respective personal conceptions of the kind of America that was contemplated by Title VI and by the Fourteenth Amendment.

Title VI

1. I agree that we must confront this issue and decide it, and that we cannot, or at least should not, sidestep it. If it proves to be dispositive, that is an end to the matter.

2. I do not read the-legislative remarks the way the Chief Justice does. In particular, I do not read Senator Humphrey's remarks that way. Hubert, I believe, was merely expressing again his American dream and saying, in a different and, of course, better way, what I have tried to say above about a mature society that looks upon each other as just Americans and not as ethnic or minority groups. Hubert's emphasis was inclusive, not exclusive. I suspect, from what I know of the Senator, there could be only one answer for him to the Bakke case; indeed, I doubt if he would find it very difficult at all. I suspect much the same could be said of Judge Robinson.

3. The administrative regulations, as they read today, approve affirmative action programs and are entitled to some deference.

- 7 -

4. I feel that Congress, in Title VI, as with the Amendment, was concerned with the unconstitutional use of race criteria, not with the use of race as an appropriate remedial feature.

5. I tentatively agree with Lewis that a decision on Title VI alone is not the way to go in this case. For me, it is hard to conclude that Title VI reads more extensively than the Fourteenth Amendment.

6. On balance, and although the issue is not an easy one, I would probably conclude that there is no independent cause of action under Title VI.

7. Nevertheless, along with Byron, I am willing to <u>assume</u> that a private cause of action exists under Title VI and to go on from there. The assumption, for what it is worth, avoids; as Lewis points out, the sticky questions (a) whether there is an implied right of action under Title VI, (b) whether such entails private remedies, and (c) whether there was any administrative remedy yet to be exhausted.

8. Once that assumption is made, it seems to me that the issue under Title VI generally coalesces with the issue under the Fourteenth Amendment.

9. The particular form of that part of the decree entered by the Superior Court, and allowed to remain by the Supreme Court of California, does not prevent us from passing on the constitutional

- 8 -

question. I think a decision is compelled. I therefore agree with

Byron and Bill Brennan that the Court should decide whether race can

ever be a permissible consideration.

The Fourteenth Amendment and Equal Protection

1. I can accept the propositions that (a) Fourteenth Amend-

ment rights are personal, (b) racial and ethnic distinctions where

they are stereotypes are inherently suspect and call for exacting

judicial scrutiny, (c) academic freedom is a special concern of the

First Amendment, and (d) the Fourteenth Amendment has expanded

beyond its confines of 1868 and now, as Lewis states, has reached

the point where it espouses "a broader principle."

2. This expantion of the Fourteenth Amendment, however,

does not mean, for me, that it has broken away from its original

intended purposes. Those original aims persist. And that, in a

distinct sense, is what affirmative action, in the light of proper

facts, is all about. To be sure, it conflicts with idealistic equality

in the sense that Bill Rehnquist proposes, but if there is tension____

here it is original Fourteenth Amendment tension and part of the

Amendment's very nature until equality is achieved. In this sense,

equal protection may be used as a shield.

- 9 -

3. The very raison d'etre of the Fourteenth Amendment may not be set aside entirely or ignored for a "new era" when we are dealing with the kind of disadvantage bred by the discrimination of our own past, the "unrequited toil," to use Lincoln's words, the Equal Protection Clause was designed to counter. To do otherwise is to ignore history.

4. As Byron says, although speaking directly of Title VI, it is the unconstitutional use of race that is prohibited, not the constitutional use.

5. The decided cases may not be set aside. They are, of course, not precisely on point, but neither are they off point. Racial factors have been given consideration in the school desegregation cases, in the employment cases, in Lau v. Nichols, and in United Jewish Organizations. True, some of these may be distinguished on the ground that victimization was directly present. But who is to say that victimization here is not present although, of course, it is of a lesser and different degree... We all remember how the disadvantaged group in United Jewish Organizations complained at what was being done. And surely in Lau v. Nichols we-looked to ethnicity. In addition, there is the growing body of cases-among the lower courts _ requiring specific racial employment features until the status is

256 *Appendix E*

- 10 -

achieved that would have prevailed had past discrimination not taken place. I have in mind specifically the Minneapolis employment-of-firemen case in which, I believe, we denied certiorari a few years ago.

6. I doubt that the sex classification cases are so easily brushed aside just because they are "relatively manageable" and less complex.

7. The weakness, of course, in the specific Davis program is its susceptibility to labeling as a blatant quota system, which Lewis so effectively attacks. Lewis would uphold the Harvard-Columbia-Pennsylvania-Stanford program where race or ethnic background is put forward as only one of many factors and where good faith in its administration is professed. I, too, am willing to accept that element of good faith, if for no other reason, I suppose, than that I saw it in operation when I worked a little in past years on admissions in the field. Nevertheless, the line between the Harvard program and the Davis program is a thin one. In each, subjective application is at work. At worst, one could say that under the Harvard program one may accomplish covertly what Davis does openly. I must agree with Lewis that Harvard's middle-road program seems to be much the better. But despite its two-track aspect, I think the Davis program

- 11 -

is within constitutional bounds, though perhaps barely so.   It is free of stigma.   I am not willing to infer a constitutional violation. We did not do so in <u>United Jewish Organizations</u> and I would not do so here.

8.   For what it is worth, governmental preference has not been a stranger to our legal life.   We see it in veterans' preferences. We see it in the aid-to-the-handicapped programs.   We see it in the progressive income tax.   We see it in the Indian programs.   We may excuse some of these on the ground that they have specific constitutional protection and, as with the case of Indians, that they are governmental wards.   Nevertheless, these preferences may not be ignored. And in the admissions field, as I have indicated above, educational institutions have always used geography, athletic ability, anticipated financial largess, alumni preference, and many other factors.

9.   The Davis program is a benign one and carries no stigma. Its race-conscious aspect could be far better formulated, but the numbers it employs are reasonably acceptable to the necessary social goal.   Its very race-consciousness has no invidious purpose and meets Fourteenth Amendment requirements.

10.   Alex Bickel's elegant and shining words; of course, speak of the idealistic and have great appeal.   But I say, once more, that this is not an ideal world, yet.   And, of course, his position is --

- 12 -

and I hope I offend no one, for I do not mean to do so -- the "accepted" Jewish approach. It is to be noted that nearly all the responsible Jewish organizations who have filed amicus briefs here are one side of the case. They understandably want "pure" equality and are willing to take their chances with it, knowing that they have the inherent ability to excel and to live with it successfully. Centuries of persecution and adversity and discrimination have given the Jewish people this great attribute to compete successfully and this remarkable fortitude.

11. We all are aware, of course, of Bill Douglas' writing and dissent in DeFunis v. Odegaard, 416 U.S., at 320. At the same time, we all remember Bill's hesitance and voting vacillation in that case.

12. There is much to be said for Thurgood's "cruelest irony" approach as set forth in his memorandum of April 13.

Summary

In general, then, my position, as of now, is to embark upon at least a cursory examination of Title VI, with a statement of general principles as to statutory and constitutional solutions; to express doubt— about the existence of a private right of action under Title VI; to assume, nevertheless, that such a right of action does exist; to equate rights

- 13 -

under Title VI with those under the Fourteenth Amendment; and to hold that the Davis program, despite its superficial vestments, comports with the Fourteenth Amendment. I therefore vote to reverse.

I have not had the benefit of the Conference discussion of early December, so I do not know precisely how my vote affects the ultimate tally. All I know is what I read and infer from the several writings.

I appreciate the patience of each and all of you. For me, this case is of such importance that I refused to be drawn to a precipitate conclusion. I wanted the time to think about it and to study the pertinent material. Because weeks are still available before the end of the term, I do not apologize; I merely explain.

H.A.B.

Select Bibliography

Allan Bakke versus Regents of the University of California. Slocum, ed. Dobbs Ferry: Oceana, 1978.

American Council on Education—Association of American Law Schools, *The Bakke Decision: Implications for Higher Education Decisions*. McCormack ed. Washington, 1978.

"Bakke Symposium: Civil Rights Perspectives." 14 *Harv. Civil Rights Rev.* (Spring 1979).

"Bakke v. Board of Regents: A Symposium." 17 *Santa Clara L. Rev.* 271 (1977).

Blasi, Vincent, ed. *The Burger Court: The Counter-Revolution That Wasn't*. New Haven: Yale University Press, 1983.

Calabresi, G. "Bakke as Pseudo-Tragedy." 28 *Catholic U.L. Rev.* 427 (1979).

Eastland, Terry, and William J. Bennett. *Counting by Race*. New York: Basic Books, 1979.

Lindsey, Robert, "White/Caucasian and Rejected." *N.Y. Times Magazine*, April 3, 1977, p. 42.

Mason, Alpheus T., *Harlan Fiske Stone: Pillar of the Law*. New York: Viking, 1956.

O'Neill, Timothy J. *Bakke and the Politics of Equality*. Middletown: Wesleyan 1985.

Osborne, John, "White House, Carter's Brief," New Republic, March 15, 1977.

"Regents of the University of California v. Bakke: A Symposium." 67 *Calif. L. Rev.* 1 (1979).

Rotunda, Ronald D., John E. Nowak, and J. Nelson Young. *Treatise on Constitutional Law*. St. Paul: West Publishing Co., 1986.

Schwartz, Bernard, *Super Chief: Earl Warren and His Supreme Court—A Judicial Biography*. New York: New York University Press, 1983.

Schwartz, Bernard, *Swann's Way: The School Busing Case and the Supreme Court*. New York: Oxford University Press, 1986.

Schwartz, Bernard. *The Unpublished Opinions of the Warren Court.* New York: Oxford University Press, 1985.

Schwartz, Herman, ed. *The Burger Years: Rights and Wrongs in the Supreme Court 1969–1986.* New York: Viking, 1987.

Simmons, Ron, *Affirmative Action: Conflict and Change in Higher Education after* Bakke. Cambridge: Schenkman Publishing Co., 1982.

Sindler, Allan P. *Bakke, DeFunis, and Minority Admissions.* New York: Longman, 1978.

Spitzer, M.L. "Multicriteria Choice Processes: An Application of Public Choice Theory to *Bakke*, the FCC, and the Courts." 88 *Yale L.J.* 717 (1979).

Tribe, L.H. "Perspectives on *Bakke*: Equal Protection, Procedural Fairness, or Structural Justice." 92 *Harv. L. Rev.* 864 (1979).

Wilkinson, J. Harvie, *From* Brown *to* Bakke—*The Supreme Court and School Integration.* New York: Oxford University Press, 1979.

Woodward, Bob, and Scott Armstrong. *The Brethren: Inside the Supreme Court.* New York: Simon and Schuster, 1979.

Index

DATE DUE		
DEC 1 5 2000 4379	ILL 8/15	
ILL 5/07	ILL 7/19	
JUN 2 1 2007		
PP 3/6/08		
JUL 3 1 2009		
AUG 2 4 2009		
ILL 3/11		
AUG 2 8 2012		
ILL 3/14		
MAR 2 0 2015		